LIFE,
LEATHER
AND THE PURSUIT OF
HAPPINESS

LIFE, LEATHER

NELSON BORHEK PRESS MINNEAPOLIS, MINNESOTA

AND THE PURSUIT OF
HAPPINESS

STEVE LENIUS

LEATHER LIFE COLUMNIST,
***LAVENDER* MAGAZINE**

ISBN: 978-0-9843002-2-8
Library of Congress Control Number: 2010921861

Nelson Borhek Press
Minneapolis, Minnesota
www.nelsonborhek.com

Printed in the United States of America

For Bill,
who read (and strengthened) many of these columns
moments after they were written.

Word cloud: a weighted depiction of the 150 most-used words in the entire text of *Life, Leather and the Pursuit of Happiness*

Table of Contents

Part I: The Leather

Chapter 1: **What Is This Thing Called Leather?**
Apparel, accessories, appetites and activities

Part II: The Life

Chapter 2: **Past Life**
Leather history

Chapter 3: **Family Life**
Family, community, tribe or nation? Yes, yes, yes and yes.

Chapter 4: **Married Life**
and other forms of relationships

Chapter 5: **Social Life**

Chapter 6: **Variety is the Spice of Life**
Leather subcommunities

Chapter 7: **Night Life**

Chapter 8: **Club Life**

Chapter 9: **Sash Life**
Leather contests, titles and titleholders

Chapter 10: **Proud Life**

Appendix: **The Practical Leatherman's Guide to Leather**

LIFE,
LEATHER
AND THE PURSUIT OF
HAPPINESS

About this book's cover

Front cover: The inset photo was taken in Minneapolis, Minnesota, on June 29, 2008. It shows the Minnesota leather community's giant leather pride flag (measuring close to 75 feet in length) being carried up Hennepin Avenue as part of the Ashley Rukes GLBT Pride Parade. The photo was taken by the author, who was part of the Minnesota Leather Pride contingent carrying the flag in the parade. (Also visible in the photo are rainbow-flag banners on the lampposts and a United States flag immediately in front of the leather pride flag. That makes this photo a reflection of the "Three Kinds of Pride" discussed on page 196.)

Back cover: The author was photographed by Andrew Bertke.

The leather background wrapping around the book was photographed by Larry Callahan, assisted by Angel Rodriguez.

Your Humble Columnist:
An Introduction
"Oh, you're a writer. What do you write?"

Cocktail party conversation never has been one of my strengths. It's not that I don't enjoy meeting new people; it's just that, when I'm introduced to someone and the conversation starts to flow, I'm never sure how much self-disclosure is appropriate.

Perhaps the person making the introduction has told the other person I'm a writer. Or perhaps the conversational path has wound its way to the question of how each of us occupies our days, and I've said that in addition to my career in advertising I'm also a writer.

Their response: "Oh, you're a writer. What do you write?" I'm actually a columnist. "For what magazine?" For *Lavender.* "And what's the column about?" I'm the leather columnist.

It is at this point that things can get interesting.

When most people hear the word "leather," they think of 1) leather-wear fashion stores at shopping malls, or 2) craft projects for kids at summer camps. Some people may think of 3) apparel worn by motor-cycle enthusiasts. So, when I tell people I'm a leather columnist, they think that means I'm 1) covering a retail sector for a business magazine, 2) dispensing handy tips on how to keep the kids busy, or 3) writing articles about biker gear that are sandwiched between biker-babe photos in cycle magazines.

If the conversation moves on and I tell them the column is called

"Leather Life," they think I'm writing a column about leather-care products. (Well, I did write one column about leather-care products—see page 296.)

In fifteen years of writing my column, I can count on one hand the number of times someone has had an inkling of exactly what it is I'm writing about: "Oh, like whips and chains?" Yeah, like whips and chains, sort of. I'm not really writing about the whips and chains—I'm writing about the people using the whips and chains, or having the whips and chains used on them. And I'm writing about the community that these people have created.

But it can be difficult to communicate all this in the middle of a cocktail party.

It could be worse, though. If "leather" is a somewhat ambiguous descriptor for what I'm writing about, "BDSM" is even more opaque. The only way someone will know what the letters B, D, S and M signify is if they're into it themselves or know someone who is.

BDSM is a four-letter abbreviation that stands for six words: BD (bondage and discipline), DS (domination and submission), and SM (sadism and masochism, often smooshed together as sadomasochism). SM used to be S&M, an abbreviation that nowadays is considered by many in the leather/BDSM/fetish community as less politically correct because of its steamy, salacious, tabloid-fodder image.

Still, if I told people I wrote a column about S&M, they would be more likely to understand (at least partially) what I write about. The S&M shorthand is still more readily recognized by the general public as referring to kinky sexual things that they themselves would never do, but which they nevertheless find fascinating.

So "leather" is ambiguous and "BDSM" isn't an acronym most people recognize or understand. But "fetish" is a word people often recognize right away. Thanks to society's preoccupation for the last hundred years with all things psychiatric and psychological, many people today think of fetishes as psychological or psychiatric disorders. If I told people I wrote a column about fetishes, they would think I was writing for a psychiatric journal—or else that I should be the subject of a case study in one.

Therefore, after considering all the options, I generally don't say I write a column about the leather/BDSM/fetish community—too much information. I simply describe myself as a leather columnist, and let the conversation flow on from there.

So, what do I write? Here's the answer unedited for cocktail-party purposes: For many years I have written the Leather Life column for *Lavender* Magazine. The magazine's primary readers are members of the GLBT (gay, lesbian, bisexual, transgender) and allied communities in Minneapolis and St. Paul, Minnesota, and surrounding areas of the Upper Midwest.

When I started writing the column in 1995 I was addressing an audience of gay leathermen and leather lesbians, and my shorthand for my audience was "the leather community." Within a few years, however, I had expanded the scope of the column to address "the leather/BDSM/fetish community," a group that includes gay men, lesbians, bisexuals, heterosexuals, and transgendered people, all of whom are into many and varied forms of alternative sexual expression.

In the world of leather literature, my column has been somewhat unusual in that it has not appeared in a strictly leather-oriented publication, but rather in a general-interest GLBT publication. That has meant the columns had to be written to appeal not only to people who were already in the leather/BDSM/fetish community, but also to people who were not necessarily a part of that community. It also meant that people who might not have identified as gay, lesbian, bisexual or transgender, but who might identify as kinky, had a reason to pick up a copy of *Lavender*, which is a good way to create allies and build bridges between communities.

How Your Humble Columnist became Your Humble Columnist

For many years *Drummer* Magazine was the archetypal gay men's leather magazine, and it certainly had an influence on me. I don't remember exactly when I saw my first issue of *Drummer*, or how old I was at the time, but as near as I can determine I was in my early twenties. I must have seen the magazine mentioned in a book somewhere, and thought at the time it sounded like something that would be a turn-on—although I wasn't quite sure why, because there was something scary about it as well. "You want to do *what* to me? Gosh, wouldn't that hurt?"

I really didn't know anyone who was into leather until Scott joined my (small) circle of friends. Scott was not yet thirty and didn't expect to make it that far. This wasn't about AIDS; Scott was very diabetic and was of a mind that he'd prefer to live carefree rather than let his disease limit him, and if he died young, he died young. He was an elementary school teacher, but he sometimes talked about wanting to quit teaching and get a job in a greenhouse, where it didn't really matter how he dressed, and therefore he could wear his leather all day if he wanted to. (Today I would say: Leather in a greenhouse? Are you kidding? On the other hand, if he was into sweat . . . .)

I saw Scott in full leather only a few times, but he wore it very well. I was dimly aware that I liked that look, but I also was dimly aware that I would never be able to pull it off. I would never, ever be that butch.

My story now jumps ahead many years to 1993 when a friend invited me to spend a weekend as a houseguest of friends of his in Madison, Wisconsin. We arrived Friday night and were treated to a beautiful piano recital in the living room by one of our hosts who was a concert pianist.

On Saturday morning my host was standing in a hallway going through a closet and wondering what to wear to Rod's, one of the local bars, that night. He took a harness out of the closet, looked at it, and then announced that no, he guessed he wasn't going to wear it after all. I was surprised to hear these words come out of my mouth: "Well, if you aren't going to wear it, can I?"

He graciously let me borrow it, and I wore it to Rod's that evening. I wasn't prepared for the effect produced by that harness. I had never gotten admiring looks like that in a bar, ever. Was it real? What did the other bar patrons see about that harness, or about me, that brought forth looks like that? And where had this been all my life?*

It took me awhile to find another harness like that one, but I finally tracked one down. By then I had accumulated a closetful of leather and had started hanging out at The Men's Room, which was the back room of The Gay 90s (a pioneering gay bar complex in Minneapolis,

---

*I used this story to illustrate a point I was making in a column called "Circuit Boys and Rented Leathers." That column is included in this book, so you will see this story again, in a different context, on page 135.

still in business as of this writing) and which at the time was the only leatherspace in the Minneapolis/St. Paul area. Several people had taken me under their wing and were introducing me to other people. I was learning how the community worked.

In the fall of 1993 I attended my first Mr. Minnesota Leather contest and saw Raymond LeBrun selected as Mr. Minnesota Leather 1994. (Raymond later moved to Seattle and became Washington State Mr. Leather 1995 before succumbing to AIDS.) By this time I also was friends with Mark Warner (not the senator from Virginia), Mr. Minnesota Drummer 1993. Several months later it was time for the Mr. Minnesota Drummer 1994 contest, and both Raymond and Mark encouraged me to enter. I protested that I hadn't even been involved with leather for a year—I should just watch the contest and see what I could learn from it, and maybe enter a contest in a year or two. "Don't wait," said Mark, "enter this contest now. You will be very competitive."

I entered, I competed, I won. I couldn't believe it. After all those years of wishing I could be with those guys in *Drummer,* and/or be like those guys in *Drummer,* I was Mr. Minnesota Drummer 1994.

I should have gone on to compete in that year's regional semifinals competition, the Great Lakes Mr. Drummer contest. But because there were no other Drummer contests that year in the Great Lakes region, there was no semifinal competition, and I was appointed Great Lakes Mr. Drummer 1994. That meant I would be competing in the 1994 International Mr. Drummer Contest in San Francisco.

I went to San Francisco, I competed, and I didn't win. I didn't even do very well. My fantasy was a "message" fantasy, to which the audience reacted favorably but which was not what that year's judges were looking for. To some extent it was a year of "the biggest prop wins"—see chapter 9 for more on that. Also, I had been working out at the gym, but my physique still was not as buff as some of the other contestants. And I was the palest guy on the stage, because my skin doesn't tan—it sunburns.

The day after the contest, however, the results were presented to the contestants and sponsors, and while I didn't do very well overall, I took first place in the speech category. My father is a minister, which makes me a preacher's kid, and the apple evidently didn't fall too far from the tree. I heard there were some grumblings—I did so poorly overall; how did my speech rate so well? But a wise gentleman took me aside and told me there was a lesson to be learned here. There are many men who can strip for the camera and look hot, and bless them for that. But, said this wise gentleman, there doesn't seem to be a surplus of guys who can string together a coherent sentence, or who can state an argument and develop it. That, said this wise gentleman, was my gift to the community, if I chose to give it. That was the talent I had to offer. I also could take my clothes off for the camera and look hot (or try to), but I'd certainly have more competition. And looks sometimes have a shorter shelf life than intellect.

Several months after returning home from San Francisco I was asked to write a leather column for a new publication named *Lavender Lifestyles* (the name eventually was shortened to *Lavender*). I thought about it less than one second before I heard myself say I'd do it.

From Columns to Book

After fifteen years, Your Humble Columnist has finally become Your Humble Author.

It's a rather daunting task to wade through a large accumulation of columns and other writings and try to assemble some of them into a book that flows in some kind of logical order. In putting the book together I have tried to pick the columns and other writings that have the most universal appeal, and I have grouped columns into chapters around certain themes. Taking my cue from the name of the column, "Leather Life," I decided to divide the book into two sections. One shorter section is about the *leather*, i.e. the things that have drawn the community together. The second and more substantial section is about the *life* of the community and its members as I have observed them over the last fifteen years.

At the beginning of each column or article I have listed the date of its original publication as a way of putting the material into historical perspective. I have updated the material where necessary by using footnotes, and I also have occasionally supplied updates, transitions and commentary (in italic type) at the start and end of chapters or between columns.

In an effort to make this book more accessible to readers unfamiliar with certain words or expressions used by members of the GLBT or leather/BDSM/fetish communities, I also have used footnotes to define some of these words or expressions the first time they appear. In addition, footnotes have been used for bibliographic information. At the back of the book you'll find all the definitions in the footnotes (and a few additional terms) collected in a glossary and the bibliographic information from the footnotes collected in a bibliography. Also at the back of the book is an index.

This book is not a comprehensive survey of every facet of the leather community. In all the years I've been writing I haven't covered every conceivable facet of the community, and thank goodness the community is large enough and diverse enough that I haven't.

There are a few things I wish were in this book that aren't. I wish I could include more about bootblacks, the people who keep our boots polished and looking great, because I think bootblacks are among the unsung heroes of our community. Over the years I have tried to be as supportive of their cause as I can and have tried to mention them in the column whenever possible. But when I went back over my columns, everything I had written about bootblacks was too time-bound and of-the-moment for the columns to fit into this collection.

The situation with leather clubs is similar. In this book I was able to include a few columns dealing with leather clubs, but much of what I had written described club events that were either going to happen (so mark your calendars) or that had happened (and, for the record, here's what you missed if you weren't there, and maybe now you'll want to be at their next event). Again, much of what I had written about leather clubs over the years was too timebound for inclusion in the present volume.

This book also includes no interviews, even though over the years I've interviewed many fascinating people for the column. My intention is to collect and publish these interviews as my next book.

Leather is an integral part of my life today, but it's not the only part, and some of those other parts have found their way into various columns. To me leather fits in with some of the spiritual paths I have followed over the years: twelve-step recovery, *A Course in Miracles,* The Body Electric School, and various other eclectic philosophies, theologies and cosmologies. I realize these spiritual approaches won't work for everyone, so take what you like and leave the rest.

So what is this book? It's not porn—I have tried to write porn, but so far I haven't been able to get the hang of it. And this is not a how-to book—there are many other people writing those, and thank goodness there are. No, the substance of this book is observation, reportage, journalism, some analysis, some commentary, some essays. The focus of this book, like the focus of the columns and other writings collected in it, is the leather/BDSM/fetish community and the life, history and culture of that community. It's about what it's like to live a life in which leather and the leather community are significant parts. It's about shared values and ethics.

Some say (and I agree) that if members of the drag* community are the GLBT community's royalty, members of the gay leather community are its knights. Others would agree with writer and activist John Preston who, toward the end of his life, no longer wore his leathers because he thought the leather community had degenerated into the gay community's Kiwanis or Rotary Club.

The point is, we're all socialized the same. As humans we all have the same basic needs and wants; some of us simply have more colorful ways of expressing them. At the heart of it, leatherfolk are not that different from non-leather folk, and I hope some of that commonality comes through in this book. Thanks for reading.

---

*Drag: In the GLBT community, males impersonating females are known as "drag queens" and females impersonating males are "drag kings." Note the royal connotation of both terms.

Part I:
The Leather

Word cloud: *Life, Leather and the Pursuit of Happiness,* Part I

Chapter 1

What Is This Thing Called Leather?

Apparel, accessories, appetites and activities

Recipe for a Leather Vest

Published in *Lavender* #143 (November 17, 2000)

"Daddy, where does leather come from?" If you've ever asked that question, read on. Most people know that animal skins become leather by a process called "tanning." But how is leather tanned? What's the difference between the animal skin before the tanning process and the leather after it has been tanned? And, since leather can be made to be any color of the rainbow, why is the process of making it called "tanning"?

Leather is often irreverently and simplistically referred to as "dead cow." The reality is much more complicated—leather can be made from many different kinds of animal skins. In my collection I have cowhide (durable), pigskin (breathable), lamb (very soft), and even kangaroo (tough as iron). Notice I said I have cow*hide* but pig*skin*. Hides are from large animals like cows, horses, buffalo and zebras. Skins are from smaller animals like pigs or lambs.

If leather were truly just "dead cow," it wouldn't last very long; an animal's skin starts to decompose within hours of the animal's death. Leathermaking is a way of stopping that decomposition, preserving the skin and turning it into something useful and durable. Skin is made mostly of water, fat and various proteins, including a fibrous protein called collagen. Leather is skin with much of the water and all of the stuff that decays (fat, non-fibrous proteins, blood vessels, muscle, etc.) removed and with the bonds between the collagen fibers strengthened.

People have been making leather for over 7,000 years. Early leather-makers dried hides in the sun to remove much of the water, pounded in animal fats or brain matter to soften the hides, and then preserved them by salting or smoking. Vegetable tanning, which is still practiced today, was developed by the Egyptians and Hebrews around 400 BC. The process involves soaking hides in solutions of tannin (tannic acid) extracted from plants. (The tannin is what cements the collagen fibers together. Tannin is why the process is called "tanning.") Chemical tanning, particularly the use of chromium salts, was introduced toward the end of the nineteenth century.

Here's a modern recipe for a leather vest. This is probably not something you'll want to try yourself. It will, however, give you some appreciation for the skill, craft and complex processes that were involved in making the leather you're wearing.

Take one fresh animal skin (probably cow). Wash and clean thoroughly.

Remove hair and epidermis (the thin outer layer of skin) by doing the following: First, soak the skin for several days in a solution of lime and water to soften the hair and epidermis. Then scrape the hair and epidermis away with a large knife.

Turn the skin over and scrape away any remaining flesh and fatty tissue on the underside of the skin. This will leave the thick central layer of skin, known as the dermis or corium, which is what leather is made from.

Soak the skin in deliming solution to remove excess lime, soak in enzymes if desired to remove still more perishable proteins, then soak in a chromium sulfate solution to stabilize and strengthen the collagen fibers in the skin.

The dermis of an average cowhide is about 4½ millimeters thick. If thinner leather is desired (and it usually is), split the skin in half using a special machine with a band-type knife. If you don't have one of those machines, you can just scrape the underside of the skin until you've whittled it down to the proper thickness (that's the way they did it in the old days).

Once the hide has been split, the outer layer will become "top grain" leather, which is generally superior to the inside "split grain" layer. Look closely at the leather—if you see tiny hair holes, you are looking at top grain leather. A lack of hair holes indicates the leather is split grain.*

Next step: Soak the skin in a dye of the desired color (probably black) mixed with oils and fats to soften the leather. The easy way to do this is in a rotating drum (hence, "drum-dyed" leather). Then stretch the hide out and dry by baking in an oven. Once dry, buff lightly to remove any surface imperfections.

Finish the leather by spraying it with liquid pigment and drying it in an oven. Emboss it to give it a uniform grain pattern. Spray on a clear protective topcoat, then tumble the leather in a heated drying drum to pummel it and make it soft. Iron the leather to remove any wrinkles.

You are now ready to mark the vest pattern on the leather, cut out the pieces and sew them together.

Yield: One leather vest.†

Historic sidebar
Published in *Lavender* #146 (December 29, 2000)

After the above appeared I received the following from Robert Davolt, former editor of *Drummer* Magazine:

"I read with interest your column on leather processing. I have never seen a leather column taken to such an entertaining and literal

---

*What about all the little bits of leather that have been scraped or shaved off the hide? They are combined with a glue or other binding resin, and the resulting mixture is rolled into sheets of so-called "ground leather," "bonded leather" or "reconstituted leather"—the leather equivalent of particleboard. Then there is "bicast" leather, which is often used in upholstering inexpensive furniture. This product is a thick layer of polyurethane applied to a backing of leather or, more probably, bonded leather. This material is so artificial that in some countries it cannot legally be marketed as leather.

† For much more about the practical aspects of leather, see **Appendix: The Practical Leatherman's Guide to Leather** on page 291.

end. I will be using your recipe on a few of the folks here in San Francisco — the prospect of making something actually useful out of old dinosaur hides is quite exciting.

"In one of those delightful blends of kinks, did you know that leather production in ancient times made human urine a valuable commodity? It took the urine of the entire city of Rome to supply the tanners who outfitted the Legions with leather armor and equipment.

"You can't imagine how long I have waited for an even vaguely appropriate application for this piece of historical trivia."*

Rubberwear and Latex
Published in *Lavender* #117 (November 19, 1999)

Of all the fabulous fetish fabrics on the Scene† today, rubber is second only to leather in popularity. When I talked recently with rubber and latex enthusiast B.D. Chambers, we started by defining our terms: Just what exactly is meant by saying someone is "into rubber"? According to Chambers, "Rubber, like leather, encompasses a broad range. There are people who are strictly into latex, and the more tight-fitting they can find the better. Other people are into industrial gear, hazardous-materials and other protective clothing, or diving suits. And some people do all of them. Basically it's an interest in clothing that is form-fitting and makes you sweat."

What's the attraction of rubberwear? Chambers says it offers "overall body stimulation. Particularly if you get into tight latex pieces and you use a good silicone lube underneath when you put it on, it will slide over your skin and hug your body in a way that even leather cannot. It's like getting a full-body massage as long as you're wearing it. Industrial gear, rain gear and gas masks summon strong,

---

*A sad update: Robert passed away in 2005, and I miss him tremendously. Robert was the author of *Painfully Obvious: An Irreverent & Unauthorized Manual for Leather/SM* (Los Angeles: Daedalus Publishing Company, 2003), for which I wrote the Introduction.

†Scene (with a capital "S"): Another word for the community that has evolved around leather, BDSM and fetish. The word "scene" without a capital "S" refers to an erotic encounter, often incorporating elements of BDSM, playfulness and/or fantasy. In other words, "the Scene" is on the level of the whole community, while "a scene" is on the level of the individuals involved.

aggressive, masculine images such as that of an oil rigger up on his rig—or, if you're into sludge play, the sewer worker down in the ground. There's also the sensation of the *lack* of sensation—when you get into gas masks and chemical-handling suits, you are cut off from the outside world, so you have the effect of a portable isolation tank. It creates its own bondage." There's quite a bit of crossover between those into rubber and those into bondage.

Chambers muses that the appeal of rubberwear can be almost primal: "You begin to recapitulate the womb. It's dark. It's warm. It's moist. It's constricted movement. All your sensations come to you second- or third-hand. It strikes some deep chord, some half-memory, of the womb. Especially the whole diving bit—when you start playing in a pool of warm water, well, let's just talk about rebuilding the womb right there! And if you've got a partner who's working with you in a scene and whom you can trust, there's a great sense of intimacy and trust, and feeling secure and safe."

Latex, unfortunately, can be expensive, and it demands a commitment to care and maintenance as well. A latex garment can tear, at which time there are two choices: "Invest in a good tire repair kit and learn how to repair it, or be prepared to buy new every time it rips." And, as we all know from condom seminars, oil (even skin oil) will eventually destroy latex. Therefore, steer clear of Crisco and other oil-based lubes, and wash and rinse your latexwear after you've worn it. Dishwashing detergent works well for the purpose, although Chambers speaks highly of Dr. Bronner's soap, an almond-oil-based castile soap available at health-food stores—"It cleans off the lubes and skin oils very nicely, rinses cleanly and leaves no residue, and it's a very neutral soap that's nice to work with."

What about body hair and rubberwear? The general assumption has been that if you have body hair you don't wear rubber, or else you shave, but Chambers disputes this. "If you have body hair, talc or baby powder will help get the latex on comfortably. Getting it off can be a challenge—I recommend, and this is my general recommendation for wearing rubber products—silicone lubes. A lot of people like Eros, which is from Germany. Another good one is Colt. Wet Platinum is the one I recommend overall, first of all because it's less expensive, and secondly because it adds vitamin E—which is an oil, so you'll want to rinse it off after you're through using your rubber. But I've noticed that the strictly silicone lubes tend to evaporate, so you can get the rubber on, but to take it off you have to step into the shower. The vitamin E in Wet Platinum keeps the silicone from evaporating, and it does wonderful things to moisturize your skin. Apply the lube to the garment and just slide it on, and when you're done wearing it the garment slides right off—even with body hair."

Because latex clothing must be form-fitting, shopping can be difficult. Stock items are made to standard sizes, and if they don't fit properly the only option may be to have pieces custom-made. For industrial and chemical-protection gear, check out army surplus stores and second-hand shops on a regular basis. You'll probably find pieces that appeal to you at prices that won't empty your wallet.

Uniforms

Published in *Lavender* #118 (December 3, 1999)

Many members of the leather community are attracted to uniforms. Some folks like collecting and wearing them; other folks simply gaze approvingly when someone else is wearing one. Uniforms seem to be a gender-neutral attraction, enjoyed equally by both men and women.

It's natural that uniforms should be a turn-on for the gay and lesbian leather community, considering that the community was initiated in large part by servicemen and servicewomen returning from World War II. They had come from small-town America where they lived in isolation, often feeling like they were the only person alive with these supposedly "unnatural" urges toward members of their own sex. Suddenly they were in the military, in same-sex living quarters, and they typically found out quickly that there were many, many others like them. Friendships were made that continued long after the war was over. Uniforms, being a big part of their coming-out milieu, acquired powerful symbolism.

Today, military uniforms remain popular and have been joined by police uniforms, medical uniforms (especially in medical fantasy roleplaying), prison guard uniforms . . . and the list goes on. Fire-fighting uniforms, with their rubber coats and boots and their fire-protection facemasks, have a special crossover attraction to lovers of rubber and industrial gear. And even to non-uniform lovers, a bright-red Royal Canadian Mounted Police uniform turns heads.

All these uniforms remind us of military or paramilitary systems dependent on hierarchy, authority and subordination; that gets fantasies going for many people. (Think drill-sergeant or prison-guard scenes.) Uniforms represent a masculine, rugged look, a splendid display of machismo that looks great on and can be appreciated by both leather-men and leatherwomen.

Uniforms can be procured at estate sales, second-hand shops and military surplus stores. Some people will feel fine wearing whatever uniform pieces they can find; other, more detail-oriented souls wouldn't think of wearing an incomplete or non-regulation uniform themselves, and wouldn't understand how anyone else possibly could.

And then there's a group of people who don't need to search for uniforms: real servicemen and servicewomen, who wear them every day in the service of their country. Every year the Olympus Leather Contest/Pantheon of Leather ceremonies feature a tribute to those patriotic members of the leather community who have served or are currently serving in the various branches of the Armed Forces. It's an impressive sight: a line of sharp-looking, proud men and women in uniform stretching across the stage. It makes a splendid illustration of the fact that the tradition of gay men and lesbian women (and kinky ones at that) proudly serving their country continues to this day.

Is it illegal to wear a uniform? The American Uniform Association is a nationwide group of uniform devotees, i.e. people "who share the pride, integrity, loyalty, and spirit that uniforms symbolize." Here's what they have to say about the topic: "AUA does not encourage illegal acts. Common sense dictates that the attitudes of law enforce-ment agencies be respected. But for the most part, collectors and enthusiasts are free to display what uniforms they choose. Laws vary from state to state and country to country. In some places owning certain uniform items is illegal. In others, the question in a confron-tation with the law may come down to whether there is an intent to misrepresent. AUA encourages its members to be discreet." The AUA has established a Legal Defense Fund to assist members who might be unfairly prosecuted.

Not everyone enjoys uniforms—certain aspects of uniforms make some people uncomfortable. What is sexy, they ask, about a police uniform when there's so much police hatred of, and brutality against, the GLBT community? Pacifists may feel uncomfortable with the militaristic, war-centric overtones of military uniforms. And certain types of uniforms and uniform scenes (for example, anything with a Nazi theme) are viewed by many members of the community as going too far and meet with almost universal disfavor. Police scenes combined with race play (such as white cop/black criminal, or vice versa) also are not exactly politically correct. Of course, some people find excitement in being politically incorrect. Everyone is entitled to their own opinion of what's appropriate and what's beyond the pale in such matters; your humble columnist was planning to be a conscientious objector rather than fight in Vietnam (or anywhere else), but he still finds something exciting about uniforms and about people wearing them.

And now for a column combining leather and uniforms:

Everybody in Leather (Bomber) Jackets
Published in *Lavender* #161 (July 27, 2001)

Are you in the mood to buy another leather jacket as an alternative to your black leather biker jacket? Perhaps you're a uniform aficionado who values authenticity, or maybe you just want a jacket that fits well, looks great and exudes masculinity. Maybe what you're looking for is a leather bomber jacket.

The quintessential black leather biker jacket that we all know and love became popular after Marlon Brando wore one in the 1953 film classic *The Wild One.** The leather bomber jacket's history and notoriety go back much further, almost to the dawn of aviation. The rigors of open-cockpit flying called for a leather jacket and often a leather helmet with goggles. (Early motorcycle riders adopted the same apparel.) During World War I many a French, British, German or American military pilot was photographed wearing his leather jacket standing beside his plane, looking every inch the glamorous (i.e., homoerotic) war hero. Actually, it worked for women, too; the

---

*See page 23 for more about *The Wild One*.

few women fliers of the day wore the same outfit and still retain their status as lesbian heartthrobs.

The United States Army Air Corps standardized the design for its Type A-1 "Summer Flying Jacket" in 1927 and for the more famous Type A-2 in 1931. These are the jackets seen on American fighter pilots in photos from the World War II era. The fit was trim and snug (and flattering) in both torso and sleeves. The leather was usually horsehide, although some A-2s were made with other hides, including goatskin. Horsehide is extremely strong and durable and, unlike other hides, is naturally waterproof.

The early 1940s saw the U.S. military abandon these leather-shell jackets for newer cloth-shell designs. The U.S. Air Force started issuing A-2s again in the late 1980s, but these modern jackets have a fuller and less flattering fit and are made of lesser-quality leather. Horsehide jackets are rare today because in the 1950s the U.S. government banned the slaughter of horses for leather; the only way to get horsehide leather today is from an animal that has died of natural causes.

If you're looking for a leather bomber jacket you have a wide array of choices. Fueled by "Greatest Generation" nostalgia, the subculture that has grown up around these jackets and other WWII-era clothing and memorabilia is truly amazing.

For around $200, you can buy a version of the modern A-2. It won't have the trim fit or quality of the original, but it will be serviceable.

At the other price extreme, you can search for a genuine original A-2 and own a piece of history. Sources include military-equipment collectors' shows and eBay; some manufacturers of reproduction jackets also buy and sell originals. Depending on the manufacturer, condition, artwork, patches and traceable history, you can expect to pay $500-$4,000 or more. Once you've paid that much, though, you might not want to wear it on a regular basis. And unless your stature is on the small side, you might have a hard time finding an original jacket that fits you.

Learning to Appreciate the West

Published in *Roundup* #9 (May, 1996)

The cowboy way of life has been a continuing theme in American popular culture. During my formative years, for example, stories of the Wild, Wild West were featured on such television shows as *The Lone Ranger, Davy Crockett, Maverick, Gunsmoke, The Rifleman* and *The Big Valley,* to name but a few. Country/western music was being featured more and more on the radio and in jukeboxes. Cowboy toys and clothing were prominent in the pages of the Sears, Montgomery Ward and Penney's Christmas catalogs. All the neighborhood kids would get together and play "cowboys and Indians" as a favorite way of passing a summer afternoon.

All the neighborhood kids except your humble columnist. TV shows, toys, clothing, music — it didn't matter. When I was growing up, anything country or western left me totally uninterested.

I've learned to appreciate a few things since then, starting with those television shows. After years of non-interest, along came a show called *The Wild, Wild West* that was and is a camp classic. All the heavy-Victorian sets were overdone (like so many of my childhood friends' living rooms), and star Robert Conrad had rugged good looks and a stunning physique, which he displayed whenever the scriptwriters could give him an excuse to remove his shirt. I started to appreciate the West in a new way.

I also began to appreciate the men of the Marlboro ads, and while they did not succeed in getting me to take up smoking, they gave me a powerful hankerin' to put something else in my mouth.

When I started visiting cowboy/cowgirl gay bars I noticed they were refreshingly different from many other gay bars. There was more mixing of men and women, and the mixing felt easy and natural instead of enforced by political correctness. There was a lack of attitude; people didn't stand around posing all evening with a serious look on their face. Instead, I saw people smiling as they got out on the dance floor, having fun and enjoying each other's company.

When I went to my first gay rodeo I found I actually enjoyed it. I have never been that interested in sports such as baseball, football, basketball or hockey, and the only parts of the Olympics I follow are the summer gymnastics and winter figure skating. But everything about gay rodeo is thrilling. The traditional events in the ring, the "camp" events (steer decorating and goat dressing — look them up if you don't know what they are), the antics of the rodeo clowns, the antics of fellow spectators in the bleachers — it's all wonderful.

At one of my first rodeos I witnessed something that captured the essence of what makes gay rodeo so special. A friend had decided to try his hand at chute dogging (holding a steer's horns and wrestling, or "dogging," it to the ground). He'd never done it before and wasn't quite sure how to go about it. But he was soon getting tips on how to do it—from the other contestants, the very people against whom he would be competing.

Well, my friend and the steer got in the rodeo ring, and the other contestants watched as he tried in vain to get control of the steer. But instead of jeering and belittling him they were yelling advice and encouragement from the sidelines, telling him what he was doing wrong and what he should do instead. He took their advice and finally wrestled that steer to the ground.

I appreciate how gay rodeo embraces that frontier spirit of co-operation and camaraderie. That spirit was powerful enough to build the West—imagine what else we could do with it.

Motorcycles

Published in *Lavender* #191 (September 20, 2002)

Why do motorcycles have such a hold on the imagination of the leather tribe? Why did the contestants in the 2001 International Mr. Drummer contest make their entrances on bikes? Why are the Dykes on Bikes such crowd-pleasers at Pride parades? Because motorcycles are butch—they are probably the butchest form of transportation available to the average person without access to a tank, Stealth bomber or Humvee.

There's a romance (a very butch romance, mind you) connected with the image of bikes, bikers and biker culture that was a seminal influence on the early leather scene, and that continues to influence leather culture to this day. In post-WWII America, bikers were gangs of modern-day cowboys on their internal-combustion-powered stallions following the lure of the open road, independent souls who lived life as they pleased, adventurous rebels who followed their own rules rather than conform to society's norms.

That reputation was splashed all over the silver screen in 1953 when Marlon Brando appeared in *The Wild One* wearing black leather and leading a motorcycle gang that terrorized a small town. The gang/

rogue imagery was a bit intimidating and off-putting to most Americans, and was so pervasive at the time that motorcycle sales suffered as a result. Honda tried to counter that image by running ads full of clean-scrubbed, Ivy-League riders and non-threatening, upbeat Beach Boys-style voices singing "You meet the nicest people on a Honda."

Homosexual men returning from military service in World War II, however, embraced the rebel image—which fit their feelings of being rebels and outcasts from the rest of society—and used it to build their own culture. Gay male leather clubs like the Atons and the Black Guard grew out of gay motorcycle clubs like the Satyrs, founded in Los Angeles in 1954 and now the oldest continuously operating gay organization in the country.

Although most of heterosexual society was too polite to mention it, or was perhaps too repressed to even notice, the erotic appeal of bikes and bikers was not lost on gay men. The image of the biker represented masculinity and power. ("My, look at that big powerful machine between your legs!") A biker's chaps were a perfect frame for interesting areas of the body both fore and aft. The experience of riding with a buddy, holding on to him or having him hold on to you, was a permissible public intimacy. One attraction of a bike couldn't really be seen but could certainly be felt: the vibration of the engine on the areas framed by the chaps.

When I was just getting into leather, one of the most impressive sights I remember seeing on a visit to San Francisco was the long row of bikes parked outside the San Francisco Eagle. At closing time I stood in front of the bar and watched as each bike was mounted (notice the imagery) by one or maybe two men who proceeded to ride off into the night.

No matter how fascinating motorcycles are, though, there's no escaping the fact that they are not always the most practical method of transportation. One almost has to be something of a rebel and an outlaw, or at least stubborn, to ride a machine that has so many disadvantages.

Downside: Motorcycles are not cheap transportation—the bike itself can cost as much as a car, and then there are the accessories: helmet, saddlebags, and all that leather riding apparel. If you want cheap transportation, buy a used Hyundai. Upside: Bikes are cheap to operate, although few American riders care. In Europe people ride motorcycles or motor scooters because the streets are narrow and gasoline is expensive. In America, land of wide-open spaces and relatively cheap gasoline,* these aren't major considerations.

Downside: Motorcycles offer no heating, no air conditioning and no weather shielding. That makes them spectacularly unsuited for places like Minnesota, where good days for riding are vastly outnumbered by bad ones. Winter is too cold and icy, and black leather can get awfully hot and sticky on a sweltering summer day. If it happens to rain while you're riding, you have a choice: duck under a freeway overpass and get out the rain poncho (which is even hotter and more stifling than your riding leathers), or keep going and get soaking wet. Possible erotic upside: If the leathers, and you, are rain-soaked (or perhaps better yet, sweat-soaked) when you get home, perhaps there's someone waiting there who will sensuously peel off all that wet leather and other clothing.

Downside: A motorcycle actually produces more exhaust emissions than a car—if you really want to be environmentally friendly, ride a bicycle. Upside: Because there are so relatively few motorcycles on the road, the total emissions produced by motorcycles are basically insignificant in the overall air-pollution picture. Currently the government is more concerned with emissions from power lawn equipment and outboard motors.

Downside: Motorcycles obviously aren't as safe as automobiles. Riding leathers and helmets offer some protection, but in a contest between the driver of a car (or an SUV or an eighteen-wheeler) and a motorcyclist, guess who's going to get hurt worse? Upside: Of course, in some cases that very danger is part of the excitement and thrill of riding; in that sense, cycles can be viewed as another form of edgeplay.

Automobiles and motorcycles have been around for about the same length of time, but there are practical advantages to automobiles that have allowed them to become the basic form of personal transportation in this country. Motorcycles, meanwhile, are transportation that's anything but basic. They're fun, and they make any journey an adventure. Oh, and—did I already say this?—they're butch, too.

---

*Well, cheap compared to European gasoline prices, anyway.

Modern Body Mod
The past, present and future of body modification
Published in *Lavender* #115 (October 22, 1999)

Like VCRs, microwave ovens, PCs and cell phones, body modification (piercing, tattooing, etc.) has recently become commonplace in western culture. Unlike those newfangled devices, however, body modification is not even remotely new. In ancient Egypt a pierced ear was the mark of a slave, and for about five thousand years circumcision has been one of the world's most popular body modifications. (Never thought of it that way? It qualifies.) But while circumcision has been accepted and even mandated by the Judeo-Christian culture, most other forms of body modification have been seen as sinful (defiling the temple, you know) and down through the years people who practiced body modification have been viewed with suspicion.

A few hundred years ago, the only men who either wore tattoos or had pierced ears were pirates. Such body modifications were the mark of an outlaw or outcast, someone who didn't play by society's rules. Pirates were feared and reviled; paradoxically, they were also romanticized at the same time. Oh, to be so swashbuckling and to live so dangerously! Women swooned and men were subtly envious.

Even in more recent times, tattoos still carried a less-than-savory reputation. The stereotype was that a tattoo was something drunken sailors (notice the nautical connection again) got while on shore leave, and supposedly regretted when they sobered up. They especially regretted it if they broke up with their girl after having her name tattooed on their arm. (Today's drunken sailors can have their tattoos removed by laser technology, assuming they can come up with the money to pay for the removal.)

Body piercing got even less respect. While it was all right for a woman to have her ears pierced, it was still an outlaw thing for a man to wear an earring. As for piercing other parts of the body, for either sex it was completely unacceptable. If tattoos were the mark of an outlaw, body piercing was the mark of a savage. Certain American Indian tribes, notably the Nez Perce (which in French means "pierced nose") had septum piercings, and certain African tribes did fascinating things with ear and lip piercings. But body piercing was something a "civilized" person simply wouldn't think of doing.

Except, of course, for Prince Albert and his Prince Albert,* which in Victorian times was known as a "dressing ring." It was all strictly practical, of course—men of that era used dressing rings to keep their penises strapped tightly against their legs, thereby minimizing unsightly bulges in the fashionably tight trousers of the day. In Albert's case the dressing ring offered a second benefit: supposedly he was un-circumcised, and by keeping his foreskin pulled back the dressing ring cut down on odor (wouldn't want to offend the Queen, would we?)†

Well, that was then. As the world's odometer prepares to roll over to another big set of zeroes,‡ body modifications like piercing (not just ears—anything and everything) and tattoos have become positively mainstream. Rather than being the mark of an outlaw, for some people they have almost become a statement of conformity. In today's leather world your humble columnist, who has no piercings and no tattoos, finds himself becoming the nonconformist.

Why do people get tattooed or pierced anyway? The most frequent reason I hear is "It's a way of asserting" (or "reclaiming") "control over my body." If someone is raped, or survives cancer, or gets out of a bad relationship, or comes out of the closet, they get a tattoo or a piercing as a symbol of celebration to themselves that they survived the ordeal, they're still here, and now they're in control. People also tell me they enjoy the natural high caused by the anticipation of getting the piercing or tattoo, and the excitement while it's being done. That high can be quite addicting, leading people to do it again and again. Many people like the decorative and creative aspect of tattoos and piercings, and they also can be markers for what a person likes sexually. Having a nipple pierced, for example, can make it more sensitive, and the jewelry also draws amorous attention to the area.

If tattoos and piercings are becoming commonplace, what's a person to do if they want to shock? The next hot thing—literally—in body modification is branding. Following the analogies above,

---

*Ring through a piercing in the head of his penis.

† Or maybe not. Some or all of this paragraph might qualify as "urban legend" dating from the 1970s. But isn't it more fun to think it might be accurate?

‡Well, I guess that dates this column, doesn't it? That, and the reference to VCRs at the beginning.

branding goes beyond outlaw and beyond savage, all the way to animal. But I'm hearing more and more about it, and at least one advertiser in *Lavender* is already offering branding services.

Scarification (cutting) is also becoming more popular. Cutting, knives and blood sports in general seem to hold more attraction for women than for men. I never quite understood why until a local group of leatherwomen explained to me that women are forced by menstruation to become extremely familiar with blood—bleeding is a normal part of their life in a way that it isn't for men.

If you're contemplating some sort of body modification, use common sense. These procedures are not for amateurs; people have showed me tattoos they claimed they did themselves using a ball-point pen, but this is not recommended procedure. And don't try to experiment with branding by grabbing the rosette iron out of the kitchen drawer. Borrowing from the "this is your brain on drugs" frying-pan ads, consider what happens to an egg (or a hamburger) if you throw it in a cast-iron frying pan that isn't hot enough, or that isn't seasoned well. It sticks, and it's a mess. Any questions?

Before you surrender to your passion, learn about what can go wrong (hepatitis from contaminated tattoo needles or ink, piercings that become infected or are rejected) and what can be done to avoid problems. That way you'll be able to select a good practitioner instead of a questionable one. For all forms of body modification, sterile procedure, expert technique and scrupulous attention to detail are the essentials that make the difference between a fantastic, fulfilling experience and a tragic one.

Continuing our discussion of body modification:

Our Autobodies, Ourselves
Published in *Lavender* #116 (November 5, 1999)

Why, after so many thousands of years of getting no respect, has body modification suddenly become so acceptable? What follows is certainly not the total answer to that question, but rather one facet of the answer.

When you were a kid, did you build model cars? I did. If you remember, most of these model cars came in kits that could be built in various ways: "stock" (as originally manufactured and seen on the dealer's showroom floor), "custom" (customized with a different grill, wheels, taillights, etc.) or drag-racing (oversize slick tires, mag wheels, and a supercharger sticking out of a hole in the hood). And every model car kit came with a sheet of decals, so you could decorate it in your own unique way.

I always built mine stock and never used the decals—I wanted authenticity. I had a friend, however, who plastered the decals all over every car he built. And for another friend, simply putting the model together and applying decals wasn't enough—he had a heated X-Acto knife with which he could cut plastic like butter. He did radical modifications to those kits and constructed some one-of-a-kind creations.

If the three of us guys got together today, and found we were all into "alternative sexualities," I predict that the guy who loved applying decals would be tattooed from head to toe, and the guy with the hot knife would be into piercing/cutting/branding. And me? True to pattern, I have no piercings and no tattoos.*

Almost since automobiles, trucks and motorcycles were invented, the American male has been carrying on a love affair with them. Sometimes the vehicles themselves are the "mistress," the object of desire, while at other times they serve as "chick magnets," an advertisement and declaration of a man's masculinity. Despite efforts by the major auto manufacturers to build cars that are seductive to women, car culture has for the most part remained a "guy thing" over the years.

Whether it's young boys with model cars or grown men with real ones, many of us tend to project a lot of ourselves onto our vehicles, and we want our wheels to make a statement about who we are, or at least who we wish we could be. A current ad for a new sports car challenges the reader to "be the person the chatroom thinks you are." The Jaguar XK-E and the Corvette Sting Ray are two of the most unabashedly phallic cars ever built. It's no coincidence that the colloquial term for a customized, sporty car is a "hot rod." We wash them, we polish them, we decorate them with flames coming out of

---

*And then recently I met a man who shot this theory to smithereens. He also built model cars growing up, and he also built them "stock." When I met him he sported two nasal piercings, both his arms were completely tattooed, and he even had an ornately tattooed "fairy charm necklace" around his neck. His explanation: "You start out stock, but after 40 years living in California, this is what happens to you."

the hood as an advertisement for the power that's in there. Come to think of it, there's not that much difference between the bulge of many car hoods of the 1950s and the bulge in a pair of men's briefs in a Calvin Klein underwear ad.

Well, maybe there's one difference. The automotive stylists of the 1950s knew there was an element of sexuality in their designs — Cadillac was famous for "Dagmars," bumper guards that looked like female breasts and got their nickname from a buxom female beauty of the day. And Freudian psychiatrists had a field day analyzing the myriad ways Detroit decorated the rear ends of its cars, especially the way the exhaust pipe openings were enshrined. (Can you say "anal compulsive"?) But it was all very furtive and very hetero. By contrast, the Calvin Klein underwear ads are purposely and unabashedly erotic and, more specifically, homoerotic. And they feature a real, albeit covered, human body — they don't displace their sexuality onto a motor vehicle.

For centuries western civilization has been an environment where the human body has been viewed simultaneously as a temple (which must be kept pure) and as a cesspool (so dirty we're ashamed of it). For most of that time the human body has been hidden from view under huge amounts of clothing. As Cole Porter wrote in the 1930s, "In olden days a glimpse of stocking/Was looked on as something shocking." Since it wasn't proper to publicly acknowledge that we had bodies, or that those bodies had a sexual component, sexual feelings and imagery were projected elsewhere. A few examples: automobiles, airplanes, skyscrapers, and even space missiles and bombs.

Of course, the next two lines of that Cole Porter song are "But now God knows/Anything goes." Nowadays it's hard to think of anything of which a glimpse would be shocking. One popular counter-cultural motto from the 1960s was "Let it all hang out." The free-thinking, pioneering members of the early leather community took that idea and expanded it to include not only letting it all hang out but decorating it as well. Thanks to their efforts, it's becoming more permissible to use our own bodies to make the statements that formerly had to be displaced onto our cars. Instead of re-sculpting the sheet metal on our vehicles using acetylene torches, arc welders and body putty, we remold ourselves using liposuction, weight lifting and plastic surgery.* Instead of decorating our motorcycles with custom pin-striping, we decorate ourselves with custom pinstriping. Instead of driving chrome-laden cars, today our brightwork is the body jewelry in our piercings.

Is this healthy? Unhealthy? It can be both. Increased body-consciousness can be liberating for one person and enslaving for another. But the leather community has always valued authenticity, and it seems to me admirably straightforward to make one's personal statements using one's person, rather than through more oblique means.

One of the characteristics of the Aquarian Age (1960s counter-culture again) will be that humanity won't require mediators to make contact with divinity. Some people think of this as not needing popes or priests or shamans to act as middlemen between God and us. But perhaps, on a more mundane but practical level, it also means that we won't need to go through the convolution of making our cars act as stand-ins for our real selves.

A Visit to an Erotic Trade Fair

Published in *Lavender* #103 (May 7, 1999)

In 1999 I attended an exhibition in New York called Erotica '99 that outraged many New Yorkers, including then-mayor Rudy Giuliani. He had just devoted major effort to "cleaning up" Manhattan by closing or relocating sexually oriented businesses. And now this kinky exhibition had come to the city-owned Jacob K. Javits Convention Center, effectively putting New York City in the porn business. Making matters even worse was a second exhibition at the Javits Center at the same time: the sixth annual International Gay & Lesbian Business Expo and Entertainment Festival, the largest event of its kind in the world. (A church group that had booked an event at the Javits Center pulled out rather than be surrounded by all these evil, twisted people.)

I spent an entire Sunday at the Javits Center attending both exhibits and drew some interesting comparisons and conclusions. Erotica was very kinky but very hetero, while the Gay & Lesbian Business Expo was very gay but not terribly kinky. I found myself wishing for a combination of the two.

---

*And steroids.

My status as a media representative allowed me to explore the Erotica show before it opened to the general public. I was able to explore the booths, view the sizable art gallery, and talk to vendors without having to shout over huge crowds. I left just as the floodgates were about to open—I counted 1,500 people standing in line waiting to get in. Expected attendance for the four-day run of the exhibition was 50,000—the city had to bring in extra police for crowd control. When I went back later in the afternoon it was difficult to move through the crowds.

What was the attraction? I suspect for many attendees it was curiosity about all these things that had been forbidden for so long. The exhibits and vendors seemed to be targeted at people who were predominantly hetero and not "into the Scene" at all. There seemed to be an air of "Oh, this is so naughty!" to many of the exhibits that didn't work for me. Nonetheless, I found a few interesting displays.

A company called Healthy Life Resources had several cutting-edge sex toys for sale. For men there was the "Bonerman," which could best be described as a milking machine's evil child. A Bonerman was custom-fit to each customer after that customer supplied five different measurements—four circumferences and an overall length. For bottoms of all genders there was the "PoniRocR," an upholstered hump containing mechanics that could vibrate and move your choice of over 160 different combinations of flexible attachments. If you've ever heard the limerick about the man who invented a screwing machine*—this is what he would have invented. Neither machine was inexpensive, but alone or in combination they looked like they could be great fun. Unfortunately, they weren't set up to offer free trials at the show.

And once you had your wonderful new sex toys, it was even possible to share the experience with a loved one who was far, far away. Remember those "Reach Out and Touch Someone" long-distance ads? Now, with the emerging brave new world of "cyberdildonics," you really could. Your computer's mouse would give new meaning to the word "joystick" as you controlled your lover's PoniRocR, Bonerman, vibrator or other "marital aid" from any Mac or PC with

*See the next column.

an Internet connection and a Web browser—while you watched their reaction via webcam, of course.

Best of all, according to a press release, it was healthy: "You'll never catch a sexually-transmitted disease at SafeSexPlus.com. Nobody will die of AIDs [sic] through SafeSexPlus.com." To find out more, you could have visited (you guessed it) www.SafeSexPlus.com. The software was free and the service was free. You also could have visited remotecontrolsextoys.com, the website of the originator of this technology.

Seven years later, more about sex machines:

Sex Machines Book Features Local Celebrity

Published in *Lavender* #279 (February 3, 2006)

"There once was a young man named Gene
"Who invented a screwing machine . . . "

So begins a very old, and very famous, bawdy limerick. The fascinating sexual subculture of "screwing machines," and the people who build and use them, is the subject of *Sex Machines: Photographs and Interviews,* a new book by Timothy Archibald.*

Sexual devices can be as simple as cock rings or as ubiquitous as phallic "personal vibrators" ("for soothing, relaxing massage on any part of your body!"). *Sex Machines* shows us more extreme, heavy-duty contraptions, designed to function as a sex partner that can truly last all night if necessary.

The machines shown in the book give new meaning to singer/songwriter Ann Reed's song that proclaims, "Power tools are a girl's best friend." One of the devices pictured in the book is, in fact, a power tool—a Sawzall with a dildo attached where the reciprocating blade would normally be.

Some of the machines are sleek and elegant, while others run the gamut from high-tech to crude. But all of them represent American ingenuity at its best. If nothing else, the machines certainly work as interesting sculptural creations (this is probably helped greatly by Archibald's photographic skills).

The inventors in the book are all men, and apparently all heterosexual. Many of them build the machines for the pleasure of the women

---

*Archibald, Timothy. *Sex Machines: Photographs and Interviews.* A Daniel 13/Process Original. Port Townsend, Wash.: Process Media, Inc., 2005.

in their lives, although the fact that a gay male (especially a closeted one) could put them to good use is mentioned often throughout the book.

These would-be Thomas Edisons are variants on the classic American garage inventor/basement tinkerer. For some it's a business, for others a hobby. Some of them hope to build the Next Big Thing, while others are satisfied if their creations can give someone pleasure.

What is most striking about the men who build the machines, and the women who use them, is their very ordinariness. You could run into any of them at the grocery store, the post office or (especially) the hardware store, and have no inkling of what they're doing in their garages or in their bedrooms. They don't look like either perverts or sexual pioneers; they look like their neighbors.

Throughout the book Archibald's photography is brilliant. His photographic style is documentary, colorful, deadpan, stark and honest. His portraits of the inventors are unblinking, often brutally realistic—and very revealing; he almost appears to be channeling Diane Arbus, only in a friendlier way. The photographs of the machines rise to the level of still lifes, skillfully capturing scenes of ordinary, mundane suburban or small-town settings—except for that odd-looking machine with a dildo (or two) hanging off one end.

In much of the book's text, author Archibald lets the people in the book tell their stories in their own words. As with the photographs, the reader is struck by the combination of the relentlessly ordinary and the outlandish—foolish dreams, innocent naïveté, triumph and disappointment and disillusionment, all leavened with a healthy dose of folk social commentary and sexual wisdom. A short afterword by A.D. Coleman puts the photos and interviews in context, and discusses the brave new world of machine sex in the twenty-first century.

Is machine sex good, or is it dehumanizing and isolating? Based on the interviews in this book it seems that, like so many other things, machine sex can be a very pleasurable blessing or a social impediment. Again, like so many things, machine sex is not for everyone—several of the inventors in the book were told by their wives in no uncertain terms: "You're not touching me with that thing."

In less skillful hands, this book could have been merely a voyeuristic exercise in shock and sensationalism. Instead, Archibald has crafted a thoughtful book with depth and integrity. Archibald's greatest contribution may be that as he introduces us to the topic of sex machines, he makes us think about that topic.

The publication of *Sex Machines,* as well as an accompanying exhibit in New York at the Museum of Sex,* is causing great excitement among members of the Twin Cities BDSM community. One of the machines in the book, "Huskette," was created by "James" of St. Paul, known locally as Charger. Another inventor in the book, Scott Ehalt, is from Champlin, Minn.

Huskette is one of a family of three machines, the other two of which are named "Husky." The machines have become legendary after making appearances at local parties over the years, and have even inspired a Royal Order of Husketeers club for those who have had the pleasure of riding them. Members wear Husky pins, and at parties join in singing the Husketeers song (to the tune of the old Mickey Mouse Club theme).

It was recently announced that the original Husky has been added to the permanent collection of the Museum of Sex. To fill the void left by its relocation to New York, Charger is designing and building a new, and radically different, sex machine. No doubt it will soon be coming to a party near you.

Woof! A Dog's Life

Published in *Lavender* #164 (September 7, 2001)

It's a charming scene: A dog and his master return from their evening walk. While the master sits in his easy chair by the fireplace, the dog dutifully fetches the master's slippers. Then the dog lies down by the fire and lays his head on his master's lap. His master lovingly pats the dog's head and they both drift off to sleep. Next morning, his master fills the dog dish; the dog eats breakfast and then heads for his job as a corporate-events planner.

Welcome to the "dog play" or "puppy play" section of the leather/BDSM community, where studded leather collars and leashes take on whole new dimensions.

If the idea of getting into the role and headspace of a dog doesn't suit you, pick another animal. Dog play is popular with gay men,

*See page 80.

and so is (what else?) pig play, while pony play is more popular with the pansexual BDSM community. Or maybe you've always been fascinated by unicorns—what would it feel like to be one?

If this all seems strange, consider that much of BDSM is built around roleplaying and fantasy, of which animal play is just another flavor. It can be enjoyable to experience "a dog's life" for a while— nothing to do but nap, frolic on the lawn and just spend time being faithful and adorable. And there's a shamanistic element for some animal players: what qualities does this animal want to teach them?

It should be noted that we are concerned with roleplaying by consenting adult humans here, not with exploitation of real four-legged animals. Bestiality is never condoned or tolerated by the BDSM community because it violates the safe-sane-consensual rule (animals are by definition unable to give consent).

"What's The Deal With SM?"

Published in *Lavender* #31 (August 2, 1996)

A recent leather event featured a flogging demonstration—several concurrent flogging scenes happening on stage with suitable lighting and music. After watching the action awhile, one of the people standing in front of me asked the person to his left: "So why are they doing this? What's going on? What's the deal?"

Perhaps you're asking yourself the same question—"How can pain and bondage and torture and humiliation be pleasurable?" Perhaps you'd like to ask someone else for an explanation but would feel silly admitting that you don't "get it" when it comes to SM (shorthand for sadomasochism—also called "S&M," usually by people not in the Scene).

SM sex is a way of exploring and growing in areas of sexuality and relationships that people often have problems with, such as trust (before I let someone flog me, I really have to trust them) or negotiating and respecting boundaries and limits (for example, a "safeword" is negotiated between top and bottom before the scene begins; during the scene if the bottom—or the top—says that safeword the action comes to a halt). And SM sex can be a way of discovering new feelings and sensations, of going where you've never been before.

If you've investigated SM and have concluded that it just isn't your cup of tea, that's okay. Not everyone who wears leather is into

SM, and not everyone into SM necessarily wears leather. No one has the right to make you feel like a second-class leatherman or leather-woman if you choose not to play in SM settings. However, respect is a two-way street—just because you choose not to indulge doesn't mean you have the privilege of judging other peoples' participation in SM as healthy or unhealthy.

If, on the other hand, you think you might want to start exploring SM, keep in mind that you get to choose how and when. Remember that the SM mantra is "safe, sane and consensual." No one has the right to coerce you into doing something you're not ready to do. If you feel like someone is trying to, remember that the ultimate safeword is "No!"

With that said, read on:

SM: It's About Respect, Not Abuse

Published in *Lavender* #50 (April 25, 1997)

Is SM: a) a sexual orientation, or is it b) a system of internalized violence?

The answer is: c) Neither of the above.

Is SM a sexual orientation? No, at least not in the way the words "sexual orientation" are generally used these days. The SM community refers to itself as "pansexual" because it is made up of members of every sexual orientation: lesbian, gay, bi, transgender, queer, and straight. (It is worth pointing out, however, that just because the community as a whole is pansexual doesn't necessarily mean that every individual member is pansexual. It is also worth pointing out that, when asked, some people *do* describe their sexual orientation as "kinky.")

To understand why SM is not a "system of internalized violence" requires a closer look at what SM is—and what it isn't. Imagine three groups of three people each. In each group, one person is being flogged by the other two. A person unacquainted with the dynamics involved in SM situations might see exactly the same thing happening in all three groups. Yet one of the groups is involved in SM, and the other two are not. What's the difference?

In the SM group, the motivating forces behind the action are respect, trust and love. The floggee asked to be flogged by the other two people because the floggee respects them, trusts them and knows it will be pleasurable to be flogged by them. The floggers, in turn, love and respect the person they are flogging and are pleased they can help this person achieve pleasure.

Notice that everyone in this group is being motivated by the same forces: respect, trust and love. There is no conflict here. This mutuality is the reason why SM scenes can be so powerful and so pleasurable for all concerned. This is how and why SM sex can be described by the SM community's mantra of "safe, sane and consensual." Because of the respect and love every group member feels for each other and for themselves, none of them would want to do anything that was not safe, not sane or that might endanger anyone. Because every group member trusts the other members and trusts themself, consent is possible.

Now let's look at the second group, where the picture isn't quite the same. Here, instead of unity of purpose, there is conflict. The two people doing the flogging are motivated by anger, hatred and vengeance. They want to damage the person they're flogging. The person being flogged did not ask for the flogging and does not want to be injured. This person is feeling threatened and fearful. Attacker does not respect victim, victim does not trust attacker. This is violence. This is abusive. This is not SM.

In the third group, the person being flogged asked for it. But he asked for it because his self-image is so poor he feels he deserves to be abused. While he may or may not respect the people he asked to flog him, he doesn't respect himself. This, then, is internalized violence, and it's not about SM. This is about martyrdom.

Some people may find SM offensive because they have been on the receiving end of abusive or violent behavior, and they may mistakenly associate SM with what they endured. They might be surprised to find that many members of the leather/SM community are also survivors of sexual abuse, childhood abuse or domestic violence. These community members have found SM to be helpful in learning to trust again, and in reclaiming their personal power and self-respect.

The hallmark of SM is respect for oneself and others. But respect, or the lack thereof, is not easy for a casual onlooker to judge. Therefore, casual onlookers who think SM is degenerate and who therefore want to avoid it and its practitioners may try to find a more visible marker.

Unfortunately, this doesn't work very well. The big butch stud dressed head-to-toe in leather may not be into SM at all. Not all leatherfolk are into SM, and not all SM players are into leather. Just as you can't always tell who's gay and who's straight by looking, you can't always tell who's kinky and who's not by looking. You can't always judge a sexual situation by looking, either.

Saying that SM "represents a system of internalized violence" is quite possibly the same as someone affiliated with an "ex-gay" ministry saying that gay sex is a sin, a perversion and an abomination in the eyes of God. In each case, the person casting disapproval on certain sexual practices may be trying to deal with their own fears by projecting them onto others. If you think SM sex is violent and therefore people in leather make you fearful, ask yourself why—it may be your own capacity for violence you really fear.

SM is based on love, trust and respect. SM is always, by definition, safe, sane and consensual. And SM is not for everybody. If you don't understand what the words love, trust, respect, safe, sane and consensual mean, I would encourage you to find out before you try SM. If you can't be safe, sane and consensual in your play, don't indulge your fantasies. You or someone else may get hurt.

Bondage
The difference between black and gray
Published in *Lavender* #39 (November 22, 1996)

True or false: a leatherman displaying a gray hankie in his right pocket thinks it would be fun to be tied up and beaten.

Answer: False. Although "tied up" and "beaten" may seem like a natural kinky sex combination, bondage and domination or B&D (gray hankie) are not the same as SM sex (black hankie). B&D covers a wide range of activities, some of which overlap with SM but many of which don't. The gentleman in the above example may indeed want to be tied up or otherwise dominated, but that gray hankie says nothing about wanting to be beaten.*

Being tied up or otherwise restrained may be followed by a flogging session, tit clamps and hot wax. But it could as easily be followed by a long, slow blowjob, full-body massage session, or a tongue bath— things even non-kinky types might find pleasurable. If you think of

---

*For more about the hankie code and its many colors, see page 141.

bondage only in connection with SM activities, think again; you may be missing something very enjoyable.

The theme of bondage runs through modern society, although most people don't consciously think of it that way. A wedding ring is a symbol of being bound to another person, and the fact that one needn't get pierced to wear one doesn't change that fact. And a necktie can symbolize submission to a multinational corporation just as much as a dog collar can symbolize submission to a master. Many people turn to bondage and domination play as a way of understanding dynamics that the rest of society often would rather not discuss.

For a person playing the "bottom" role, part of the thrill of bondage may come from being, literally, "out of control"—having turned control over to the top. The top, in turn, gets a thrill from being in total control of (and responsible for) another person. Some people even practice self-bondage (harnesses, corsets, cock-and-ball toys, butt plugs, or even tall boots laced up tight) and experience a combination of both feelings.

Safe, sane and consensual applies to bondage just as much as to SM. In SM sex the giving and receiving of pain is a major source of pleasure. Pain in bondage, however, is often a sign that something's wrong. For instance, ropes or handcuffs that are too tight can cut off circulation; uncomfortable positions maintained for long periods of time can lead to tissue or nerve damage. Duct tape-and-Saran-Wrap devotees can cause all kinds of problems by staying wrapped too long. Being bound in whatever fashion should not mean being in physical discomfort or danger.

Another safety point: Just as a good SM scene has a safeword that instantly stops the action, a good bondage scene has the Houdini-like escape provisions necessary to ensure safety in an emergency. Some examples: a knife or scissors to cut rope (use them carefully!); extra handcuff or padlock keys; quick-release buckles on restraints.

If bondage sounds interesting to you, explore it. Start slowly, and take the time to learn to do it safely. Although there are many excellent books available on various bondage techniques, please remember that no book can substitute for person-to-person mentoring.

Whip It Good

Published in *Lavender* #218 (October 3, 2003)

When vanilla folks describe SM, one phrase they're likely to use is "whips and chains." Let's examine the fascinating first part of that pairing.

Whipmaster Robert Dante holds people spellbound as they watch him handle a whip. He makes it look easy. It seems as if all he does is casually wave his arm and the whip responds like a magic serpent — cutting a playing card in half, extinguishing a candle or plucking a single leaf off a tree. He can snap the whip at a person with an ear-splitting crack, only to have the whip wind lazily around a leg or wrist. He can even use two whips at the same time, one in each hand.*

Whips have been a part of every culture since time began. They appear in ancient Egyptian art — and what do you think Jesus used to drive the moneychangers out of the temple? They are useful for herding animals — not by actually whipping the animals, but by virtue of the tendency of animals to run away from the loud cracking noise. Whips have been used for hunting, too; according to Dante, "In Indonesia they still hunt tigers with a whip in one hand and a spear in the other. If they lose the spear, the hunt continues. If they lose the whip, the hunt is over and everyone goes home."

Apart from their practical applications, whips are sensually satisfying. The crack of a whip, in Dante's words, "is wasabi — it wakes you up. It commands attention." In addition, there are all the other swooping and whooshing sounds a whip makes, along with the hypnotic sight of the whip flailing and writhing.

And then there's the feel of the whip, which is not always what you might expect. Dante explains that "a whip is the only SM toy, besides a TENS unit, capable of producing a range of sensations that goes from 0 to 99." The sensations produced by a whip can range from the breeze felt as the tip goes past, to a buzz as the tip gets closer, to burn, and all the way to bite.

There's an element of magic to a whip. Sometimes a whip almost seems like a living thing, but it's really an extension of you, your arm

---

*Dante is the author of *"Let's Get Cracking!" The How-To Book of Bullwhip Skills* (CreateSpace, 2008).

and your hand. It's *your* energy being channeled down the length of the whip, finally exploding at the tip with a satisfying crack. To quote Dante, "This is magic. The whip is the key, and the crack is the gate." Dante describes the spiritual dimension of his art: "Whipping sets up a cycle of energy. I draw energy from the universe and send it out through the whip toward my submissive, who receives it, feels it, processes it, and sends it back out to the universe. This is the magical alchemy that turns the lead of ordinary time into the gold of what could be."

On the other hand, a whip is really just applied physics, and an understanding of some basic scientific principles is necessary to use one effectively. For instance, a shorter whip is more accurate because you're standing closer to your target. A longer whip gives you more reach and more energy amplification but less accuracy.

More physics: As the whip moves through the air the tip gains momentum until it reaches supersonic speed. When a whip cracks, the tip is breaking the sound barrier. That means it is going at least Mach 1 — 761 miles per hour — 1400 feet per second. And it may go faster, up to 900 miles per hour. That's a lot of violent energy being released in a shockwave, and the whip is therefore capable of doing great damage to whatever it comes in contact with at that moment.

But once the whip has cracked, the energy has been expended. The whip can then gently brush a person's back or wrap around an outstretched arm without doing any damage at all. Obviously it takes skill and precision to be able to time the crack of the whip, and to acquire this level of skill takes practice. Dante practices every day and has been doing so for a long time. Practice, in his case, has made perfect.

People new to whips almost always find that the whip snaps back and bites them — perhaps in the leg or the arm, maybe nicking an ear, possibly across the face or in an eye. That's why one of the rules of whip practice is to wear eye protection, a hat with a brim to protect the face and ears (a motorcycle helmet is even better), and long pants and a long-sleeved shirt.

A whip is a three-dimensional instrument, so the next rule of whip practice is to keep a "bubble" or clear zone in all directions around and above — Dante suggests a clear zone of twice the length of your whip plus six feet. It's almost impossible to find a decent whip-practice space in the average home. Practice in a basement with a low ceiling and you will quickly develop bad habits that will be hard to break later on—not to mention the light bulbs you'll break in the process.

But outdoor practice spaces, such as public parks, present other problems. It's a good idea to have one person patrol the space and prevent intrusions while another person practices with the whip. And keep the ground as clear as possible. A pebble brushed by a speeding whip can turn into a bullet—all the more reason for eye protection, hats and long sleeves.

Dante suggests that you experiment and extend your whipping skills during practice sessions on inanimate objects. As with other forms of SM, when you play with a whip, play below your level of capability.

Fascinating facts that didn't make it into the article as published in *Lavender:*

A whip is an implement that has been painstakingly braided out of leather or nylon by a master craftsperson and is constructed to have a definite curve and coil to it. Using a whip properly is simply letting the whip uncoil the way it was built to uncoil.

A bullwhip has a rigid handle. A snake whip is flexible over its entire length.

Care and feeding of whips: Keep them clean. Dust and grit are death to a whip because they interfere with the constant flexing of the whip, and grind it apart with each flex. Also, don't share crackers (the string at the end of a whip, also called a "lash" or "popper") between bottoms. Crackers are cheap, so use a new and clean one every time.

According to Dante, there are only three basic whipping strokes: the overhand, the circus and the cowboy. All whipping consists of variations on these three basic strokes.

Dante demonstrated a "Wells Fargo" whip crack for me, and said that in frontier days different stage lines had different whip cracks, so even before people could see a stagecoach they knew which stage line was coming (see: song, "The Wells Fargo Wagon," from *The Music*

Man by Meredith Wilson. That's how the singers knew "The Wells Fargo wagon is a-comin'.") Also, if you've ever heard the phrase "riding shotgun," it comes from the fact that the guy sitting next to the guy holding the reins held a shotgun, and was therefore "riding shotgun." The guy holding the reins also held a whip that was used to control the horses, and he was therefore "riding whip."

If you've ever heard the term "throwing a whip," Dante says that's a misnomer. He prefers to think of it as "pushing" rather than "throwing."

When handed a whip, most novices will have trouble making it crack, going either too fast or too slow. If they then hold the whip in their non-dominant hand, often they will suddenly be able to make the whip crack almost every time. Dante explains that we all have preconceptions we've gleaned from TV and movies of how we think whips work. When we put the whip in the non-dominant hand we avoid those preconceptions and we let the reality of the whip shine through, and it tells us how it wants to be handled.

Close your eyes and you'll find you can still be reasonably accurate with a whip. Wear earplugs and you'll suddenly become terrible. A white cracker on the end of the whip is good, while trying to whip in red dungeon light is bad because it can interfere with depth perception.

And finally: According to Dante, "Excitement and fear are the same, except with excitement you breathe—with fear you don't."

Shiny Sharp Things
The erotic uses of knives
Published in *Lavender* #156 (May 18, 2001)

Cristo Webb is a nationally known knifemaker whose business, Cristo's Blades of Indianapolis, Ind., sells his own custom-crafted knives as well as other knives, antique and modern straight razors, and all kinds of knife accessories. He is an expert in all aspects of knives and razors and has been featured in the pages of *Blade* Magazine and *Knife Illustrated*.

Cristo describes himself both as "a big lovable farmboy who refuses to leave the Midwest" and a "dyke tranny* Sirboy switch who prefers

---

*Tranny: Shorthand for "transgender." Not meant in a disparaging way.

male pronouns." He is Sir to his long-term bottom boy, Corky. His BDSM talents and interests include anything to do with knives, razors, blood, boots, mind-fucks, fisting, uniforms, interrogation, canes, singletails, and breathplay. Cristo has spent many weekends traveling to leather-community events around the country as an activist, presenter, and vendor.

Knifeplay is generally regarded as an extreme form of BDSM play, even by many in the BDSM community. And it certainly can be intense — one breathtaking demonstration at a workshop I attended recently involved using a knife to remove some temporary piercings by cutting them out.

But knifeplay can also be stimulating without breaking the skin or drawing blood. Lightly dragging a sharp knifepoint across the skin can create intense sensations (and artistic welts). Different sensations come from dragging the edge of the blade across the skin at various angles, or thumping or scratching with the knife handle. For some people, something as simple as the feel of a cold, hard steel blade being rubbed flat against the skin can be a turn-on.

Just the sight of a knife can be intimidating. And then there are the sounds that go with knifeplay: the click-and-lock of a folding knife being snapped open, the whoosh of a fixed-blade knife being drawn from its sheath, the metallic scraping of blade against sharpening stone, or the splash of a knife going into (or coming out of) a jar of disinfectant solution.

A lot of the excitement of knifeplay comes from the head trip generated by these sights, sounds and sensations. According to Cristo, "For scene purposes, a dull knife can be just as effective as a sharp one." All sorts of tricks can be played once the appropriate mood has been created and a scene is underway, especially if the bottom is blindfolded; a letter opener, butter knife or even the edge of a credit card (Cristo asks, "Why do you think they call it MasterCard?") can feel like the sharpest blade ever.

Cristo's knifeplay workshop covered a wide range of knife-related topics, including different types of knives; how to buy a knife; knife care, storage and sharpening techniques; and knife safety, cleanliness and sterilization. Here are a few interesting points Cristo made:

- Where should you not do knifeplay? Avoid the area around the eyes (heed the voice of your mother: "It's always fun until somebody loses an eye") and ears, as well as areas of skin that have rashes. Be extra careful around key artery areas. And don't start right off by working on erogenous areas; Cristo suggests you "explore your partner's body—knives are wonderful objects for foreplay and teasing."
- Buy knives that feel comfortable in your hand—that comfortable feeling translates into better control when you're using them, whether you're doing knifeplay or deboning a chicken breast.
- Don't store a carbon-steel-blade knife in a leather sheath; the leather holds moisture, which will cause the blade to rust.
- Cleanliness and sterile procedures are absolutely essential for safe, sane, consensual knifeplay. Barbicide and other disinfectants are good stuff, but nothing kills hepatitis on a knife blade short of autoclaving—and many knives can't be autoclaved without being ruined. So for safety's sake, unless a knife can be properly sterilized it shouldn't be shared. Cristo's rule: "You get blood on it, you own it."
- Serrated knives are great for cutting off clothing during a scene, or as an emergency dungeon tool for cutting rope. But they are not recommended for knifeplay scenes. According to Cristo, a serrated blade is "a saw, basically, and it will maim a body."
- Knife laws are confusing, chaotic, and quirky. They vary from state to state, and state law is often overridden locally by cities or counties. Here are some highlights of the four-page knife law summary that was handed out at the workshop: In California, pens may be illegal because they are potential stabbing weapons; in Mississippi, threatening actions with a knife in the presence of fewer than three people may be acceptable; the one state people associate with Bowie knives (Texas) expressly forbids them; and Virginia state law 3.1-370 states that your knife must be cleaned daily.
- Before you ever touch a knife to someone else's skin (or your own, for that matter), be absolutely sure you know what you're doing—and polish your technique by practicing on inanimate objects. At the seminar, Cristo had us experiment on plum

tomatoes, but you can also use skin-on chicken breasts. Or practice cutting the surface of a pan of clear gelatin, where you'll easily be able to see how far the blade has penetrated.

The workshop ended with a hands-on exercise—a birthday surprise for bottom-boy Corky, who was not told about this beforehand and didn't know what to expect. In a creative combination of hot wax play and knifeplay, Cristo and members of the audience first dripped hot wax on Corky's back until the wax was about ⅛″ thick. Then, guided by a stencil, they used their knives to carve "HAPPY BIRTHDAY" into the wax. A little aerosol whipped cream, a few birthday candles, and presto—a human birthday cake.

Shiny Sharp Shaving Things
The erotic uses of razors and shaving
Published in *Lavender* #157 (June 1, 2001)

Sex and shaving in the 1960s: In a classic television ad for Noxema Medicated Shaving Cream, pouty Swedish model Gunilla Knutson gave the command: "Men—take it off! Take it all off!" Then viewers were treated to a good-looking man shaving his face while David Rose's "The Stripper" played in the background. Back then, that commercial was considered risqué.

Sex and shaving in 2001: On a recent Saturday afternoon, nationally known knife maker Cristo Webb presented a seminar called "Shaving: From Pleasure to Terror" that dealt with the erotic uses of razors and shaving.

For many people shaving is anything but erotic. Men traditionally shave their faces every morning, either without thinking about the ritual or cursing the drudgery of it all. Women in our society are faced with the more delicate tasks of shaving their legs and underarms; while they may feel it makes them more attractive, it usually is not something they look forward to.

But certain elements of society are increasingly playing with non-traditional areas of hair in non-traditional ways. Many more men are shaving their heads. Bodybuilders shave their body hair to better display their physique. Many men prefer the look and feel of a shaved scrotum or shaved pubic hair. Some men, instead of shaving, prefer to trim body and pubic hair neatly ("topiary," as my friend in New York calls it). Certain BDSM practices, such as fireplay and waxplay, are made safer and more comfortable by removing body hair.

Shaved skin can provide many wonderful and ever-changing sensual experiences. Whether you're touching your own newly shaved skin or letting someone else touch it (or even if you're touching newly shaved skin on someone else), the sensations are incredibly intense. As the hair grows out you are treated to a series of new sensations: first stubble, then bristle, then velour, and finally silk.

The experience of being shaved by someone else can be very sensual. First comes a hot towel on the area to be shaved, maybe an exfoliating scrub with a warm loofah sponge (to prevent ingrown hairs), hot lather to soften the hair and lubricate the skin, and a soothing or bracing lotion applied after shaving. It's nice to receive this kind of pampering, and it's also nice to be able to give it. According to Cristo, "Shaving and using a straight-edge can be a wonderful service and an important skill for a bottom or submissive to learn." Whether shaving Mistress' legs or doing a daily shave on Master's face or head, "learning to shave in a sensual manner can leave the person being shaved feeling relaxed and refreshed."

On the other hand, being shaved with a straight razor can be terrifying, or at least intimidating. The thought of such a sharp piece of metal (sharper than almost any knife) so close to the neck, face or pubic areas—and with no safety guard—can take shaving to new heights of excitement and stimulation. As with knifeplay, a shaving scene with a straight razor is a multi-sensory experience: the sight of light glinting off the blade, the smell of shaving cream, the rhythmic sound of the razor on the sharpening strop, the feel of the cold, sharp blade and the scrape and vibration as the razor is dragged across the tightly-pulled skin.

Straight razors are hard to come by these days, but they're still available if you know where to look (start by talking to Cristo). A close substitute is a hair shaper with a removable blade; these are used by beauticians for razor haircuts and are available at beauty-supply outlets. With both a straight razor and a hair shaper, the blade folds into the handle when not in use. A tip from Cristo: Always allow your razor to dry in the open position to prevent rusting, pitting, and weakening the blade.

A dull razor will pull. It won't give a clean shave, and it can nick or cut the skin. It also can cause rashes and aggravate ingrown hairs. A straight razor's edge is maintained by the use of a strop, preferably a two-sided strop consisting of a strip of canvas on one side and a strip of leather on the other. The canvas puts the edge on the blade and the leather hones the edge. (Hint: You also can hone the edge on your leather jacket or chaps.)

We've all seen a strop being used on TV or in the movies—usually incorrectly. Here's the right way: Hold the razor flat against the strop and drag the edge away from you. When it's time to change direction, turn the razor over by rotating it on its back, not by flipping it over on its edge as you've probably seen on TV. Never raise the back of the razor off the strop while it's moving; doing so will rake off the edge.

Besides straight razors and hair shapers, other types of razors include the traditional double-edge safety razor, newer multi-bladed types (Cristo's favorite—and mine—is the Gillette Mach 3), disposable razors (use them for only one shave), and electric razors, either plug-in or battery-operated. Electric razors pull hair and won't give a good clean pubic shave—but according to Cristo, they're wonderful for genitorture!

All the safety rules about not sharing knives apply equally to razors: Unless you can autoclave a razor without ruining it, don't share it. Here are some other safety tips relating to razors and shaving:

- Razors are very sharp and dangerous objects. Never become complacent with a razor, especially a straight razor. While shaving, pay attention to the entire length of the blade.
- Treat razors gently. The blades are so finely tooled or machined that the metal is brittle. Don't drop them. If a razor's blade becomes nicked or damaged, don't use it—it will mutilate whatever (or whomever) you're shaving.
- Always be in control of the razor, the person you're shaving, and your surroundings. Make your shaving area as sanitary and controlled as possible. In a bar or at a party, rope off an area so the person being shaved doesn't get jostled by passersby.
- Have a first-aid kit handy with a tube styptic or styptic pencil for minor cuts and nicks.

- Limit your play partner's movement during shaving—especially during pubic shaving.
- Feedback and communication with your partner are very important to get full enjoyment out of a shaving scene.
- Cristo likes Lubriderm lotion as a shaving cream for sensitive skin. There's less lather, which makes it easier to see what you're doing. Cristo also likes a men's shaving cream by Aveda.

If you've never used a straight razor, practice on an inanimate object and perfect your technique before trying to shave someone. The television cliche is to lather up a balloon and practice removing the shaving cream with a razor. Cristo doesn't like that approach for two reasons: 1) if you make a mistake, the balloon startles you when it pops; and 2) because the balloon just popped, you can't even see your mistake, let alone correct it. Instead of a balloon, Cristo ended the workshop by having us use straight razors to shave the fuzz off— no, not a peach—a kiwifruit. I did better than I thought I would, although I won't be trading in my Mach 3 for a straight razor anytime soon.

The Fascination of Fireplay

Published in *Lavender* #170 (November 30, 2001)

"How about a little fire, Scarecrow?"

Anyone who has seen *The Wizard of Oz* remembers that scene— it's almost like the Wicked Witch is coming at *you* with that fiery broom. Fire induces panic and fear, yet it can be fascinating at the same time. Fire seems to take on a life of its own as the flames jump and dance capriciously. And then there's the romance of sitting in front of a roaring fire, safely contained in a fireplace.

Panic, fear, fascination, and romance—no wonder fireplay is attractive to folks into BDSM. At a fireplay workshop I attended recently, in addition to learning about the passion and spectacle of fireplay, audience members also heard useful information about fire safety, first aid for burns (more about this in a moment) and the scientific aspects of fire. The workshop was conducted by a top wearing jeans and a t-shirt with nine fire-breathing dragons on it, and a bottom who spent most of the workshop naked—a sensible way to avoid setting clothing on fire.

The workshop started with some safety precautions—here are just a few of the caveats discussed:

- Fireplay should not be done on the face, around hairy areas (head, armpits, genital area, hairy chests or backs), on cut or infected skin, or around moles.
- Avoid fireplay on inappropriate surfaces, such as carpets, mattresses, or plastic surfaces. Beware of clothing and long hair.
- Mood-altering substances and fireplay do not mix. In the words of the demonstrating top, "You need a clear head and undiminished reaction time."
- In a fire situation, do your best to remain calm. Panic only makes the situation worse.
- Have a wool blanket handy to snuff out fires. Wool does not support combustion at normal levels of oxygen and temperature. Wet towels are an alternative, but they can be messy.
- Have a fire extinguisher available (the proper type, in good working order) and be familiar with how to use it.

Disclaimer: The descriptions of fireplay that follow are for illustrative purposes only; they are not complete instructions on how to do fireplay safely. Fireplay is edgeplay, and injury or death is possible. Do not play with fire unless you have had proper training and supervision from a fireplay expert.

Now that the disclaimers have been presented, here's what the audience saw during the demonstration portion of the workshop:

After a warm-up session in which the top caressed his bottom's skin with a burning, fragrant stick of incense (to her obvious delight), we moved on to flash cotton, which is simply cotton that has been treated to make it highly flammable. The top placed multiple bits of flash cotton of varied sizes all over the bottom's back. Then, at irregular intervals, he used a small butane torch to ignite the pieces one by one, each time causing a bright, quick burst of flame. The cotton was so light that the bottom couldn't feel it lying on her skin; she never knew where, when or how big the next flash would be.

What did it feel like for the bottom? She explained that when the flash cotton was ignited the heat was brief, intense and localized. Often the sudden intense heat was immediately followed by a chill. She also said the element of surprise made the sudden combustion of the cotton feel almost like an impact.

To demonstrate alcohol play at the seminar, the bottom leaned against a stepladder so that she was bent slightly forward. With his hand, the top applied isopropyl alcohol (other kinds of alcohol don't work for this) to the bottom's back. Then he literally set his hand on fire (drawing gasps from the audience), and used his human-torch hand to ignite the alcohol stripe on the bottom's back. There were more gasps as we watched blue streaks of flame run from the bottom's waist to her shoulders. For the bottom, the sensation was the cool feeling of the alcohol on her skin, followed by the intense heat from the fire, followed again by a comparatively cool sensation when the flame burned out.

As with other forms of edgeplay, fireplay is not for everyone. Even though fireplay done correctly does not cause burns or other injury, a person who cannot overcome their fear of being burned is not a good candidate for fireplay because they won't enjoy it. For those who think they might enjoy it, however, let me stress again that the best first step is finding a mentor who will show you how to properly and safely play with fire.

First Aid for Burns

Here's some information from the fireplay seminar about first aid for burns. This is good to know even if you never intend to do fireplay.

- First, remove the person from the burning situation, either by putting out the fire or getting the person away from the fire.
- Second, cool the burn with cool water until it feels better. Don't use ice or ice water, which can contribute to shock.
- Third, bandage the burn loosely with sterile dressings.
- "Critical burns" are burns that must receive attention as soon as possible from medical personnel. These include second- and third-degree burns (marked by blistering or charring), burns to the face, hands or feet, burns over more than 10% of the body, or burns sustained by infants, children, or elderly people. Do not apply ointments, salves or anything other than cool water and sterile dressings to a critical burn, and do not try to remove burned or charred skin from a wound.

Part II:
The Life

Word cloud: *Life, Leather and the Pursuit of Happiness,* Part II

Chapter 2

Past Life
Leather history

Intertwined Histories
The gay, leather and pansexual BDSM communities
Based on an article published in *Journal of Bisexuality* (Volume 1, Number 4, 2001)

There was a time in American history when the only valid gender identity was either male or female and the only valid kind of couple was made up of one male and one female. Any deviation from this standard was so threatening to the rest of society that it was looked upon as "sick" or "perverted" and was considered something to be stamped out by any means necessary. This could mean locking up the perverts in prison or sending them to hospitals for the mentally ill and administering electroshock therapy or other "cures."

This view was so prevalent that people who knew they were "different"—attracted to people of their own sex—also knew it was best not to be open about that fact. It was better to keep that part of themselves "in the closet." Many men and women grew up thinking they were the only person in the world who had ever had feelings like these.

Then along came World War II. Suddenly men (and, to a lesser but still significant extent, women) found themselves in the armed forces—in same-sex barracks. And they found that there were other men (or women) who shared their "difference." They weren't so alone in the world after all. Suddenly the closet door wasn't completely shut anymore. And suddenly the military, which was supposed to extinguish someone's individual spirit and turn them into one impersonal cog in a fighting machine, paradoxically became the setting where countless homosexual men's and women's spirits were set at least partially free.

Even when the war had ended, once these soldiers had tasted life among their homosexual peers, they didn't want to give it up. Homosexual men and women tended to congregate in larger cities such as New York, Chicago, San Francisco and Los Angeles, and staked out their territory: bars and coffeehouses, restaurants, bathhouses and other spaces for cruising (looking for sex or romantic partners) and public sex. Some people (who would later be referred to as "vanilla") wanted to get as far away as possible from reminders of their military past. But, especially among men, the rough-and-tumble, almost hyper-masculine comradeship of their military days held a romantic and even a sexual attraction.

This was the genesis of the gay male leather community, and many of the traditions of today's gay male leather community have their roots in WWII-era military traditions. Leather clubs were formed; some were bike clubs and required a motorcycle for membership, while others were simply fraternal social, service or charity fundraising organizations. Toward the end of the 1970s, the male beauty contests that had become entertainment staples at leather bars evolved into an elaborate system of leather title contests, culminating in the establishment of both the International Mr. Leather Contest in Chicago and the International Mr. Drummer Contest in San Francisco.* The International Mr. Drummer contest grew out of *Drummer* Magazine, one of the first visible published voices of the gay male leather community. It took its name from the famous Henry David Thoreau quotation, which appeared on the table-of-contents page of every issue: "If a man does not keep pace with his companions, perhaps it is because he hears a different drummer. Let him step to the music which he hears, however measured or far away."

Many of the men who formed the gay male leather community, or who joined it later, seemed to be attracted to extreme forms of sexuality (such as bondage, sadomasochism and fisting—to name a few) that found their fullest expression in the pre-AIDS 1970s. The

---

*See Chapter 9, page 156, for much more about leather contests.

community even evolved a "hankie code" in which the color of a hankie (or hankies), and whether the hankie was worn in the right or left rear pocket of one's jeans, signaled what kind of sexual action the wearer was looking for. (This is a convenience that has yet to be adopted by other communities.)

Some of the words and terminologies these men used to describe their sexual activity were grittier and more blue-collar than the words and terminologies commonly used today. When they talked about SM activities they spoke in terms of "work" ("working on someone" or "being worked on"), and they called their SM implements "tools." In a variation on the question ("Are you a traveling man?") posed by a member of a Masonic lodge to another man to see if he also was a Mason, a leatherman might ask a similar question ("Are you a working man?") of another man in whom he was sexually interested. If the other man responded favorably, negotiations could proceed. Today, instead of work most people speak of SM "play" and refer to their SM implements as "toys."

Stonewall and "Gay Liberation"

Things began to change with the Stonewall riots of 1969, which are considered by many a breakthrough event for the modern Gay Liberation movement. Suddenly gay men and lesbians were marching in the streets, saying there was nothing wrong with them just because they loved someone of the same gender and demanding an end to being treated as "sick" or "perverted."

In the late 1960s and throughout the 1970s, the increasing visibility and solidarity of the Gay Liberation movement coincided with (and probably contributed to) the increasing visibility and solidarity of the gay male leather community. But the attitude of many in the gay male leather community at the time was that they didn't want to interact even socially with lesbians, or male or female "breeders" (a derogatory term for heterosexuals), much less play with them in an SM context. For some gay male leathermen this attitude continues today; their dungeons are male-only space, and quickly empty if a female should happen to walk in. One leatherwoman likens it to the "He-Man Woman-Haters Club" portrayed in an old Little Rascals film.*

---

*See "Leatherwomen Speak Out," page 110.

Leatherwomen

In the early 1980s, lesbians in leather joined leathermen as a recognizable element of the gay leather community. The women's leather community resembled the men's leather community in some ways (they formed leather clubs and chose leather titleholders), but in other ways it was different (as far as I know there has never been a leatherwomen's bar). The AIDS epidemic seems to have been a major catalyst in bringing gay leathermen and lesbian leatherwomen together. Many gay leathermen were among the first people infected with HIV/AIDS. When AIDS devastated the fabric of the men's leather community, the women were there to help, both by becoming care-givers for men stricken with HIV and by raising funds for AIDS research and care. This is starting to be reciprocated; leathermen now commonly raise funds for breast cancer research.

By the 1990s, the gay men's and women's leather communities were for the most part no longer underground. In 1992, International Mr. Leather Lenny Broberg even was a guest on a daytime television talk show (although in the end it turned out he was there only to be mocked).

Heterosexuals

Also in the 1990s, another group was making its presence known: kinky heterosexuals, who were coming to the realization that even though they were heterosexual, their sexual preferences made them anything but "straight." They had been forced to keep their kinky predilections underground to avoid consequences such as losing their jobs or having their children taken from them. They realized that in certain ways they were just as much "in the closet" now as gay leathermen and leatherwomen had been. If the sexual practices of the gay leather community were now becoming known and some-what accepted, maybe it was time for kinky heterosexuals to follow the example set by the gay leather community and stop hiding.

Suddenly what had once been unthinkable for many kinky people, both gay and heterosexual, was becoming commonplace: Hetero-sexuals and gay people were talking to each other, getting to know each other, attending each other's parties. And they were finding that the dynamics were moving from "us" and "them" to just "us." The thinking behind this joining was that some of us are gay and some of us are straight, but we're all kinky, and it's in our best interest to work together to fight society's oppression of kinky sex practices of all kinds.

Bisexuals and Transgendered People

Because of the efforts of the early Gay Liberation movement American society went from a unipolar view of sexuality, in which heterosexuality is the only valid sexual orientation, to a bipolar view in which a person is heterosexual or homosexual, *either* one *or* the other. Unfortunately, this pretty much left bisexuals and transgendered people out in the cold.

In the early years of the Gay Liberation movement, bisexuals found themselves in the awkward position of having to choose sides in this debate; they had to be on one side of the fence or the other. Any bisexuals who let it be known that they could be quite comfortable on both sides of that fence soon found themselves distrusted and considered traitors by both heterosexuals and homosexuals.

The situation for bisexuals was no better in the leather bars and the newly forming gay leather/levi/motorcycle clubs than it was elsewhere in society. Bisexual leathermen have told me stories of how they kept quiet about their bisexuality when they were in the bars because they knew they'd be shunned if it became known they occasionally played with women.

Similarly, I have known several transgendered people who for many years presented a public front of "drag queen" or "drag king" simply because it was more acceptable, less threatening, and easier for their gay friends to understand. Only recently have the concepts of sexual preference and gender identity as ranges, spectra or even bell curves gained any sort of acceptance. Sometimes it's easy (or convenient) to forget that the community formerly known as "gay," and later "gay and lesbian," only became the "gay-lesbian-bisexual-transgender" or GLBT community in the 1990s.

Pansexual Kink

In sexual matters, members of the kink community tend to be more adventurous and less judgmental. This mindset creates sexual spaces where it's safe to experiment with and stretch personal boundaries, and to experience forms of sexuality and intimacy that have heretofore been kept off-limits. A self-identified gay man, for whom sex with a woman would be anathema, might suddenly find himself flogging a woman's back—and enjoying it. One of the boundaries with which a person can experiment is their sexual orientation—experiencing sex and/or intimacy with people of varying gender identities. Thus, the pansexual BDSM community has evolved into a place where people of all gender identities and all sexual preferences—gay, lesbian, heterosexual, bisexual and transgender—are welcome and can participate.

That's a capsule history of the flowering of all the modern flavors of the leather/BDSM/fetish community. But kink, and kinky people, were around long before the gay men's leather community started after World War II:

The Last Two Centuries of SM
Published in *Lavender* #287 (May 26, 2006)

The image was arresting. On the screen, in black and white, a naked woman was bent over a fainting couch while a naked man was poised to swing a switch at her buttocks.

What made the image more arresting was the fact that it was from the 1800s. And the man was, as they might have said in the nineteenth century, in full arousal.

Thus began "History of the Development of Sadomasochism in Twentieth Century America," one of the final presentations of the tenth annual Leather Leadership Conference (LLC) in New York in April.

One of the presenters was Robert Bienvenu, Ph.D., a sociologist who wrote his doctoral thesis on the development of SM as a cultural style in the nineteenth and twentieth centuries. The other presenter was Chuck Renslow, a man who lived (and made) some of the history Bienvenu included in that doctoral thesis.

In the first part of the presentation, Bienvenu described SM practices of the nineteenth century and how SM practices changed in the early twentieth century. Nineteenth-century SM imagery was built around "soft," essentially feminine materials such as silk, lace and fur. Participants in SM scenes either wore everyday clothes or were nude.

Nineteenth-century SM implements were simple, natural and uncomplicated—canes, switches, whips or birch rods. SM practices of the time were narrowly focused (on the buttocks, for example), ritualistic and predictable (starting with ritualistically exposing the buttocks), and endlessly repetitive (flagellating the buttocks, then flagellating them some more). Creativity and spontaneity were not the objects of nineteenth-century SM.

By the 1920s, SM had changed to a predominantly "hard," masculine aesthetic. SM imagery of the time revolved around polished leather, latex and metals. When SM participants in the images shown by Bienvenu wore anything, it tended to be specialized fetish attire, following an aesthetic that came to be known as "bizarre." Photographic backgrounds were urban and industrial. SM implements and situations showed a broadened focus and increasing creativity, ingenuity, spontaneity, complexity and unpredictability.

Bienvenu discussed three major categories of SM culture in the twentieth century: European Fetish (c. 1928), American Fetish (c. 1934-1938) and Gay Leather (c. 1950).

The European Fetish style, which first became identifiable in 1920s Germany, quickly spread to France and Britain, and then around the globe as far as India and Australia.

The American Fetish style started in New York in the 1930s but also had outposts in California. Originally an offshoot of European Fetish, it soon developed its own distinctly American look.

Both European and American Fetish were predominantly heterosexual, and the two styles shared many elements: bizarre costumes, uniforms, high-heeled shoes and boots, long black gloves, piercing and tattooing, and every sort of sexual apparatus imaginable. Practices included elaborate roleplay, cross-dressing, female domination, wrestling girls and human ponies.

Twenty years after the development of the American Fetish style, and with essentially no connection to either European Fetish or American Fetish, Gay Leather developed. It was at this point that Bienvenu turned the presentation over to Renslow, who shared his first-person account of leather's development and history.

Renslow founded Kris Studios and began photographing and publishing male "physique" or "beefcake" photos in 1950. He and his lover, Dom Orejudos (the leather artist known as Etienne), opened Chicago's legendary Gold Coast leather bar eight years later. In 1979, they founded the International Mr. Leather contest, of which Renslow is still Executive Producer. Following Orejudos' death, Renslow and former *Drummer* Magazine publisher Tony DeBlase were co-creators of the Leather Archives & Museum in 1991.

Renslow told of being brought up on obscenity charges, and subsequently acquitted. He told of the original group of Chicago leathermen and their search for a place to hang out. They finally found a club that welcomed them, the Gold Coast Show Lounge. Renslow eventually bought the business, shortening the name to "Gold Coast." The rest, as they say, is history.

When the presentation was over, I was in awe. We have a history—a history that's fascinating. But because it has been so hidden over the years, most people don't know it exists.

There's strength and power in discovering and uncovering that history. No matter what nasty names mainstream society may call us, we now know there have been other people through the years with the same feelings and interests we have.

Knowing we have a history makes it harder for us to accept being marginalized by mainstream society. Knowing we have a history makes it easier to carry on the fight for our own sexual freedom, and for everyone else's as well.

That's why this presentation was so affecting. That's why the Leather Archives & Museum is so important. That's why studies like Bienvenu's are so valuable. That's why Renslow and his contemporaries, and all the other people who have blazed leather/BDSM/fetish trails down through the years, are such treasures.

Bienvenu is currently at work on a scholarly book, *American Fetish,* to be published by Duke University Press. His doctoral thesis is available on the Web as a downloadable PDF file in either compact or expanded multimedia versions.

And our history goes back even further than the nineteenth century:

Who Put The "M" in SM?
Leather and SM in history
Published in *Lavender* #40 (December 6, 1996)

SM, in leather circles, stands for "sadomasochism." It is relatively common knowledge that sadism (achieving sexual pleasure by inflicting pain) takes its name from the Marquis de Sade. However, the origin of the name of the opposite practice, masochism (achieving sexual pleasure from receiving pain), is much less well known.

According to *The New Joy of Gay Sex*,* masochism takes its name from Leopold von Sacher-Masoch, "a historian and novelist. All his novels contained whipping scenes, and he himself preferred to be whipped by women wearing furs, especially if the women were older." It's an interesting comment on society's values that the Marquis de Sade has become a household name and archetype, while von Sacher-Masoch languishes in relative obscurity.

Some other items of historical interest from *The New Joy of Gay Sex:*

- The flagellants were a twelfth-century mass movement within the Catholic Church that encouraged people to flog themselves until they bled.
- Saint Margaret Mary Alacoque was a seventeenth-century nun who "carved the name of Jesus on her chest with a knife." Because the carving didn't last long enough, she subsequently burned it in with a candle. (She was canonized in 1920.)
- Saint Mary-Magdalen dei Pazzi "used to roll in thornbushes in the convent garden, then go into the convent and whip herself. She also forced novices to tie her to a post, insult her, whip her, and drop hot wax on her."

(The above examples are not intended to be disrespectful of the Catholic Church, but rather to show that SM impulses have been around a long time and in many different and unexpected segments of society.)

---

*Silverstein, Dr. Charles and Felice Picano. *The New Joy of Gay Sex*. New York: Harper Perennial, 1993. *The New Joy of Gay Sex* is a fascinating gay-sex encyclopedia covering everything from "AIDS" and "Bars" to "Wills" and "Wrestling." While not specifically targeted at the leather community, it contains a wealth of leather- and SM-related information (as well as some spectacular illustrations).

• The Chicago Hellfire Club is an organization of men who are into heavy SM play; their annual Inferno run* is a social and sexual highlight of the SM scene. Where did the name of the club come from? It was "probably borrowed from the Hell-Fire Club organized by Sir Francis Dashwood in late eighteenth-century England."

On a more local note, the Atons leather club of Minneapolis takes its name from Akhenaton, the Egyptian Pharaoh just before Tutankhamun. His theory was that there was just one divine being instead of a myriad of gods. He called that god the Aton, the Sun God, and symbolized it as a sun disk with rays streaming from it. He closed the old temples and built new ones for the Aton. After he assumed the throne he installed a man named Smenkhare on the throne of Queen Nefertiti, his wife. Smenkhare was given all Nefertiti's royal titles, and the inscriptions that remain make it clear that Akhenaton and Smenkhare were lovers.

Eventually the old priesthood overthrew Akhenaton, installed the boy prince Tutankhamun (whose name was originally Tutankhaton) as his successor, and tried to obliterate Akhenaton's name from the earth (primarily because of his religious heresy, not his sexuality).

Now you know.

And now, as history marches on, a few melancholy columns about things our community has seen disappear, followed by a few more hopeful columns on preserving our community's history.

Sic Transit Leather *Mundi*
Published in *Lavender* #208 (May 16, 2003)

When I think of all the famous and fabled places of leather's days gone by, and realize that I will never (or never again) be able to experience them, it makes me a little sad. This was brought home to me quite vividly on a recent trip to New York City. My host and former partner Ken Binder, who moved to New York several years

---

*Run: A term that originated among motorcycle clubs and referred to a club's motorcycle riding and camping trip. Now the term has broadened to include any (usually annual) weekend social event presented by a leather club and attended by members of other clubs. See page 150 for a more complete description of a run.

ago, pointed out to me that the leather scene there, at least for gay males, is in a period of either decline (pessimistic view) or transition (optimistic view).

Much of New York's leather scene has historically been in and around the notorious (and appropriately named) "meatpacking district," which was the area south of 14th Street between 9th Avenue and the West Side Highway (now renamed the Joe DiMaggio Highway). The docks and piers that used to be cruising grounds have long been cleaned up, and the truck trailers that served as sex shelters haven't been there for years. Fabled leatherspaces including The Anvil, The Mineshaft, The Ramrod and The Toilet (yes, it really existed) closed their doors long ago.

Until recently, the meatpacking district still was home to several leather venues — but now all but one of these are gone, too. The Eagle and The Spike closed in 2000 (after 30 and 20 years, respectively). That left only Johnny-come-lately LURE (an acronym that stood for Leather/Uniform/Rubber/Etc.). But in April LURE also closed its doors after nine years of operation. (LURE's website says that a 500% increase in their insurance costs forced them to close.) The Eagle recently reopened under new management a few blocks from its former location, making it currently the only leather bar in the area.

J's Hangout, which recently closed, used to host a variety of sex parties; some of the parties have moved and some have disappeared with J's. Two other neighboring establishments, Hellfire Club and Manhole, were forced out by their landlord, according to a website named "Peter Boots' Gay SM Leather Fetish Guide to New York City." Wallyworld, another sex-party venue, disappeared with the death in 1999 of local party impresario Wally Wallace, who also was associated with both The Mineshaft and later LURE. The meatpacking district has gotten so squeaky clean that, in Binder's words, "Even the tranny* hookers are gone!"

What happened? Until recently the answer was often politics, most recently in the guise of former mayor Rudy Giuliani's efforts to "clean up" (his words) or "sanitize" and "Disney-ize" (some other peoples'

---

*Tranny: Shorthand for "transgender." See page 44.

words) the city by tightening and enforcing regulations on sex-related businesses. Fighting political battles is tough enough, but it's almost impossible for leather to win economic battles, and money is what was at the root of the most recent round of closings. As one of the last remaining "ungentrified" areas of Manhattan, the real estate in the meatpacking district became too valuable. Buildings that formerly housed bars, dungeons and playspaces now are home to upscale restaurants, clothing shops and art galleries. Millions of dollars are being spent to turn the meatpacking district into the next TriBeCa, which itself was the next SoHo.

(Those with long memories will recall that SoHo, the area of Manhattan "SOuth of HOuston St.," at one time attracted an influx of artists who appreciated the neighborhood's great loft spaces and cheap rent. But that influx of artists made the neighborhood attractive, it became trendy, real-estate prices went through the roof, and the artists who created that wonderful neighborhood couldn't afford to live there anymore.)

New York, like any major city, is constantly changing, but Binder is one of many who aren't sure they like these most recent changes: "Even if I didn't spend a lot of time at LURE or J's Hangout, those kinds of places were one of the reasons I moved to New York. I was just glad to know those places were there—and now that they won't be there, I'll miss them."

It's not just the leather scene in New York that has been changing lately. Christopher Street, the epicenter of the Stonewall uprising that gave birth to modern gay culture, is no longer the gay Mecca it once was. The Leather Man Inc. store is still there, but many of the other gay shops have closed. After dark, Christopher Street isn't even a terribly safe area anymore, according to Binder: "On weekend evenings, young street thugs come in on the PATH trains from Jersey and take over."

The gay life that used to be on Christopher Street moved north to Chelsea (between 14th and 34th Streets around 7th and 8th Avenues), a neighborhood that then went from rough and raw to buffed and beautiful with the influx of the city's most gorgeous gay men. But even that neighborhood is changing. Binder, who lives in Chelsea, says his co-op building was until recently entirely gay-owned, "but all the recent sales of apartments in my building, apartments that were bought and fixed up by gay men, have been to straight couples who are pregnant." I asked him where he thought the next gay neighborhood in New York would be, and he told me that the general feeling among gay New Yorkers is that there might not be one: "Maybe the concept has outlived its usefulness. As we become more accepted and integrated into the fabric of society, that's what happens—there's less need for a gay ghetto or enclave."

These kinds of changes are not unique to New York, of course. On San Francisco's Castro Street, which has long been one of the most visible gay neighborhoods in the world, area residents must share the sidewalks with gawking tour groups. Many leatherfolk moved from the Castro to the South of Market area in the early 1990s, only to have that neighborhood then stolen from them by the dot-com crowd— who later slunk out of town once the dot-com craze bombed.

By way of postscript: The unfortunate fact is that nothing lasts forever, and I will never be able to visit legendary places like The Catacombs in San Francisco or The Gold Coast (in any of its incarnations) in Chicago. But we can all be thankful that leather historians at The Leather Archives & Museum and elsewhere have made it a mission to collect and preserve memorabilia, pictures and stories of these wonderful, vanished places.

Drummer Magazine: End of an Era
But the Mr. Drummer beat goes on
Published in *Lavender* #114 (October 8, 1999)

San Francisco recently held its annual leather bash culminating in the International Mr. Drummer contest on Saturday, Sept. 25, and the Folsom Street Fair on Sunday, Sept. 26. By all reports, the 1999 edition of the contest was a rousing success; it was a crowd-pleaser and, according to *Drummer* Magazine editor Robert Davolt,* the basket auction raised $7,000 for the winners' travel fund. But even as the new International Mr. Drummer and Drummerboy were being chosen, the magazine that started the contest and gave it its name was nearing the end of its run.

---

*See footnote, page 8.

Publication of *Drummer* has been sporadic for some time now; the magazine has been for sale, but no buyers have come forward. The International Drummer contest has been sold to Mike Zuhl of Pittsburgh, Pennsylvania,* and at this writing negotiations for the other *Drummer* assets are continuing, but the outcome of it all will probably be that *Drummer* Magazine no longer will be published in its current form. It seems to me a rather ignominious end to what was once the leather magazine against which all others were measured.

Leather publications (and, to a certain extent, all gay publications and all publications in general) have been experiencing lean times recently. But how can a leather institution like *Drummer,* which has been around for years and which has been so instrumental in shaping our whole concept and culture of leather, be on the brink of extinction?

Here's a history lesson about a seemingly unrelated topic: At the dawn of the twentieth century most homes had pianos in the parlor, and people bought sheet music at the local five-and-dime store so they could play the popular songs of the day. The music industry made money from the sales of sheet music, and a song's popularity was measured by how many copies of its sheet music were sold.

Then the phonograph became commonplace, and the popularity of a song was measured by how many phonograph records were sold; sheet music sales took a nosedive from which they've never recovered. Along came radio, and (for awhile, anyway) record sales suffered—why buy the music when you can hear it for free? Today, of course, the music industry is again in turmoil over the same idea, only this time it's MP3 files over the Internet (legally or illegally) cutting into CD sales.

Other parts of the entertainment industry have seen the same thing happen. Television had an adverse effect on both radio and movies. And now, in an ironic twist, cable is slowly killing network television, which proves that "Why buy it when you can get it for free" only goes so far. Sometimes people would rather pay for quality than settle for free mediocrity.

---

*The International Drummer contest was later renamed International LeatherSIR/ Leatherboy. The contest's ownership changed hands again in 2007.

Could it be that *Drummer* and other leather publications are the sheet music of the 1990s? Much as *Playboy* proclaims itself "entertainment for men" (or for some men, anyway), leather magazines are entertainment for the leather community—as are leather contests, leather events, even leather bars. All these forms of entertainment are being affected by the brave new Internet-driven world, but right now magazines like *Drummer* are being hit especially hard.

For one thing, the Internet and chatrooms drastically cut into the phone-sex business, and fewer phone-sex lines mean fewer phone-sex advertising dollars for the magazines. But even more damaging, from the magazines' point of view, is the fact that what people used to get from magazines—pictures, articles, one-handed fiction, personal ads— is now available for free (or at least for the yearly cost of AdultChek) on the Web. Davolt also points out that the Internet is basically unregulated (i.e. uncensored) with respect to both content and geographic distribution—Internet data can be sent almost anywhere and show almost anything.* Meanwhile, *Drummer* and other publications must operate within a straitjacket of local, state, federal and postal regulations that limit both what they can include in their magazines and where they can and cannot sell them.

Maybe it's just me, but personally I'm an ink-on-paper kind of guy. Reading text off a screen just isn't as comfortable as reading a magazine or a book, and even the best on-screen images don't have the fine, crisp resolution of print. And you don't have to wait for a magazine or book to download—just open it up and there it is.

There's also the matter of how long something endures. I have a large personal collection of *Drummer* and other leather magazines, and someone recently bestowed upon me their collection of vintage "physique" magazines and other pioneering gay- and leather-related printed materials from the 1950s through the early 1980s. As I looked through the collection, I knew I was holding history in my own two

---

*Well, it could until the advent of 18 U.S.C. § 2257, a federal law ostensibly aimed at curbing child pornography. The recordkeeping requirements imposed by the law also can be used as a legal bludgeon against the production and distribution of other sexually explicit images even if no underage performers are involved. Many people believe the law therefore impermissibly impinges on constitutionally protected speech.

hands. When the day comes that I'm done with all these printed pieces they will, of course, go to the Leather Archives & Museum to be preserved as part of our leather history and heritage. How will we preserve our heritage when it's composed of something as insubstantial, ephemeral and vaporous as a Web page?

But I see the signs of change all around me, and I can't stop evolution. After spending many years in the printing/publishing/advertising industry doing ink-on-paper graphic design and production, I find my career has taken a turn for the Web in the last few years—many of the documents I design and produce now will never see a printing press. I've had to adapt to changing technology many times during my career, and the pace of change is quickening rather than slowing down.

The folks at *Drummer* have evidently seen those same signs of change, and decided not to fight it any longer. *Drummer* has been a magnificent invalid for several years now; in 1997 alone it posted major business losses. Davolt was named editor in January 1998, and during his 21 months at the helm the balance sheets improved dramatically, but in the end it just wasn't enough.

Maybe it's good that leather has embraced the Web. Maybe all that information flowing so freely will allow more people to follow their instincts, to learn, to participate, to enjoy, to build a stronger community. I hope so. But it's sad that *Drummer* won't be along for the ride.

When Men Were Men and Videos Were Films
Joe Gage's Kansas City trilogy
Published in *Lavender* #186 (July 12, 2002)

In the modern age in which we live, if you want to enjoy an all-male erotic entertainment you simply pick one up at the video store, bring it home, pop it in your DVD player or VCR, and proceed to get your rocks off. It's easy, convenient and cheap. It's the video equivalent of a frozen entree—all it lacks is flavor, texture and interest.

Compared with much of the gay male porn that's being made today, the films that make up Joe Gage's Kansas City trilogy are gourmet feasts. The films (*Kansas City Trucking Company*, 1976; *El Paso Wrecking Company*, 1977; *L.A. Tool & Die*, 1979) all were greeted with enthusiastic acclaim from critics and viewers alike when they were first released, and they continue to be revered today, selling well on both videocassette and DVD. They are widely considered to be among the finest products of the golden age of gay male erotic filmmaking and supreme examples of a lost art. They really, truly don't make them like this anymore. (What was it Norma Desmond said in *Sunset Boulevard* about the pictures getting smaller?)

Male erotic films made prior to the mid-1980s were very different from modern-day gay male videos. The process of making them was different, their content was different, the way in which they were viewed was different, and the society and the milieu in which they existed were very different from today's world.

In 1976, when *Kansas City Trucking Company* was released, Stonewall had happened only seven years before. Vietnam was still a raw nerve in the American psyche (and is part of the storyline of *L.A. Tool & Die*). AIDS had not yet exploded. Gay life was pre-condom, pre-video, pre-digital, pre-virtual and pre-Internet. Gay men could be found hanging out in tearooms* instead of chatrooms.

In those pre-VCR days very few people had their own film-projection equipment, which meant that watching what was then known as an "all-male" film was a communal experience. One went to a slightly seedy theatre with a name like "Adonis" or "Gaiety" or "Bijou" and watched the movie on a theater-sized screen in the company of other men. The action in the theater usually mirrored what was happening on the screen. The floors of the theater were sticky, and it wasn't just spilled soft drinks. (Oh, and the patrons of those theaters probably stopped at the newsstand to pick up the latest copy of *Drummer* on the way home. Just as video killed film, the Internet has killed many magazines.)

Gage and many of the other makers of gay male erotic films of the era took their task seriously. Their films were certainly drenched in sex, but they also strove to make both an artistic and a political statement. (In those days having sex, and lots of it, was a political statement.) Comparing these films to most modern-day porn videos is like comparing

---

*Tearoom: a public men's restroom having a reputation, in certain circles, as a place to have sex with other men. See also: "Senator Larry Craig."

the lushness, sweep and spectacle of *Gone With the Wind* with the crass coarseness of the latest reality series on television,* or like comparing a fine erotic photograph from Colt Studios to the type of amateur male nude snapshots with which the Web is awash.

The films in the Gage trilogy include such now-quaint notions as a plot, including a story arc that spans all three films of the trilogy; character development; more dialogue than just the occasional grunt or "Suck my big dick" line; artistic camerawork and lighting effects; scenic landscape and location shots; and a soundtrack that is for the most part a very complex aural montage of relevant sounds that forms a breathtaking backdrop for the sexual action on the screen. Watching the films it's obvious that Gage was a guy who paid attention to details and wanted to take the effort to get them right. (*L.A. Tool & Die* took 20 days to film, which was and still is an unheard-of amount of time to spend making a gay porn flick.)

The men in these films are very different from the twinks in so many of today's porn films. You'll see no gym bunnies or steroid queens here, and no shaved chests or trimmed pubes—just good-looking, unpretentious, often hairy, real men having real sex with real gusto.

The trilogy was dedicated to pioneering leather artist Tom of Finland, and it's a Tom-of-Finland world that the films portray. There are stunning scenes filled with leather and motorcycles. Alcohol is much in evidence, especially while driving. Guns are toys. There are fistfights with homophobes, and the homophobes always lose and slink away. There is lust aplenty, but also love, camaraderie and, at the end of the trilogy, romance and a fairy-tale (pun intended) happy ending. For the most part it's a laid-back, mellow world with a happy bunch of guys-next-door (don't we all wish?) who enjoy each other's company. They work hard, and when the day is done they play hard. There also is the occasional female, usually a girlfriend, because Gage evidently liked to include something for the heterosexuals and bisexuals in the audience.

Unfortunately, the years have not been kind to these films. Many of the hairstyles are almost laughably dated, as is much of the music. These, unfortunately, are things that can't easily be fixed. Other

---

*See "Torture TV," page 247.

problems cry out to be rectified, however: the VHS versions that I viewed started with prints of the films that were scratched, dusty and missing significant chunks of footage. These problems were compounded with some of the worst film-to-video transfer I've ever seen. I would hope the film-to-DVD transfers were handled with more respect. If you want to add these films to your collection, *caveat emptor.* It might be worth renting before you buy. Know what you're getting and be prepared to settle for some technical shortcomings.

Or overlook the technical shortcomings, the cheesy music, the bad (at times) acting, and just revel in the cinematography, the story-telling, the men and the sex. Those days may be gone with the wind, but we still have these movies by which we can remember them.

How History Disappears
Published in *Lavender* #305 (February 2, 2007)

This issue's column is about a leather pioneer. But it's not the column I thought I would write. And it's not the column I wish I could write.

This issue's column was supposed to be an interview. Instead it's an obituary.

This issue's column was supposed to celebrate one man's life and share his stories. Now he can't share his stories with me, and I can't share them with you.

Several years ago I received an e-mail from Bob Guenther, a long-time leatherman, asking a favor. He told me of a friend, Gus, who was one of the last surviving members of the legendary but now defunct Cycle MC, a motorcycle club based in New York City. Gus had been the club's last president.

Gus had retired from his job as a court administrator in New Jersey and was now living in a Twin Cities suburb. Would I be interested in interviewing him for the Leather Archives & Museum's Oral History Project?

I expressed interest and in return received an e-mail from Guenther with a list of things to ask during the interview. But then I received another e-mail: "He doesn't want to talk about years gone by." Gus evidently did not want the people he called his "appointed parents," who controlled his finances, to find out about some of his past activities.

I was sorry to hear this and felt bad that Gus was not in a position to savor his life, but instead had to effectively disown it. I filed the e-mail exchange for future reference, hoping Gus would change his mind and allow me to interview him.

Recently I received another e-mail from Guenther. His Christmas card to Gus had been returned as undeliverable. Would I please check my local resources and see if I could find an obituary? Sadly, I found one in the *Minneapolis Star Tribune*.

This is how our history disappears.

Over the years I have interviewed many people for this column. I have collected their stories on cassette tapes and published portions of the interviews in print. It's been a fascinating undertaking.

Other folks are preserving our stories and our history, too. The members of the Knights of Leather have devoted great attention and many hours to putting together scrapbooks containing the history of their club. Now I understand they are taking the next step: they're not just making scrapbooks—they're Scrapbooking, in the best soccer-mom tradition.

And, of course, the ongoing Oral History Project of the Leather Archives & Museum has been collecting stories and reminiscences from leather community members. This is the project for which I would have interviewed Gus.

This is how our history is preserved.

You, dear reader, also can help preserve history. Spend an afternoon, or even longer, getting your own stories down, whether on paper, audiotape or video. Then send them to the Leather Archives & Museum in Chicago. Do it now, while you still can.

Or ask someone else to share their stories with you, and have a tape recorder or video camera running while they're sharing. You'll both enjoy the reminiscing and you'll get their stories down for posterity.

There are stories in memorabilia and mementos, too. Perhaps you have photos, programs, tickets, t-shirts, title sashes or other artifacts that tell a leather story of years gone by. Those pieces of our history are too important to disappear into a dumpster when you're no longer able to enjoy them. Make your plans now—and I stress now—to get those treasures into trusted hands when the time comes.

We need these stories of the early years of our community. There are people coming after us who will need those stories, too. We have a community institution, The Leather Archives & Museum, set up to preserve them, conserve them and make them available to future generations.

I have no doubt I would have enjoyed interviewing Gus. And I'm sure, had circumstances been different, he would have enjoyed being interviewed. Instead, tragically, he found himself in a position where he couldn't be open about, and proud of, his life and his stories. In the words of Bob Guenther, "Who knows how much New York City leather history was lost as a result."

The Leather Archives & Museum (LA&M) has already been mentioned several times in this chapter. I've written about the LA&M many times over the years, because it's a cause I believe in. Here's the first column I wrote about it in 1997:

"They Paved The Leather Roads We Walk On Now"
Preserving our leather history
Published in *Lavender* #60 (September 12, 1997)

Where did leather come from? How did the leather community evolve? If you've ever wondered about that, there is an establishment in Chicago that can enlighten you. The Leather Archives & Museum is devoted to collecting, preserving and displaying our heritage. The 1997 International Mr. Leather souvenir booklet featured an article on the Leather Archives & Museum, from which I quote with permission:

"The Leather/SM/Fetish community as we know it dates from at least the early 1940s, although many aspects of it date from hundreds or thousands of years earlier. But these aspects of our lifestyles have always been hidden from public view. They have not been written about with any real candor. Information about them has not been preserved in libraries and the artifacts of our existence have not been gathered into museums.

"New members of a sexual minority cannot go to the family attic and find Uncle Henry's horde of *Rigid Bondage Roster,* Aunt Viola's tit clamp collection or the home movies of grandma and grandpa having an absolutely wonderful experience with bondage and corsetry! The items of significance in our sexual lifestyle are not added to the biological family's collection of treasured remembrances. Instead they are consigned to dumpsters and trash cans, either by our own anxieties or by our survivors' disinterest or outright revulsion.

"Every generation of leathermen and leatherwomen has had to reinvent itself or base its community knowledge on the remembrances of living individuals. The Leather Archives & Museum is dedicated to preserving a record of our lifestyle, our communities, our achievements and our history for present and future generations.

"In 1992, Chuck Renslow (creator of our nation's first leather bar, Chicago's Gold Coast, and the Executive Producer of the International Mr. Leather Contest) asked several leathermen and women to join him in forming the Leather Archives & Museum. In 1993, LA&M presented its first exhibition of leather artifacts in a conference room at the Congress Hotel during the International Mr. Leather weekend. These exhibits were repeated in 1994 and 1995.

"In November of 1996, the LA&M moved into new headquarters at 5007 North Clark Street and opened its first permanent public exhibit space. The new space also housed the archival and research collections and allowed them to be accessible to serious students, who immediately came to use them from institutions ranging from the Chicago Art Institute to the Kinsey Institute for Sexual Research at Indiana University."

During the recent International Mr. Leather contest, International Ms Leather 1996 Jill Carter spoke from the stage at the Congress Theater about the importance of preserving our heritage: "Those individuals paved the leather roads we all walk on now." She also discussed ways the community can assist the Leather Archives & Museum in its mission:

"See what piece of memorabilia your community can donate to the Leather Archives. Is your club's history on file for all to read? Are your club colors on record? Has each state or region recorded its traditions to be saved for the future? Has the oral history of your community's elders been recorded? If the answer is yes . . . does the Archives have a copy? If the answer is no . . . what are you waiting for? An invitation? Well, consider it given!"

The LA&M collects and preserves books, newsletters, magazines, photographs, letters, videotapes, organizational minutes and files, club and business logos, catalogs, posters, fliers, brochures, tickets, programs, club colors, patches, banners, buttons, run pins, original artwork, sketches, sculptures, dungeon/playroom designs and plans, equipment designs, photos and sketches, and titleholder sashes, medals and trophies. If you are aware of items that should be preserved, do what you can to see that the current owner knows about the Archives and what it is trying to accomplish. The Leather Archives & Museum is a tax-exempt charity under section 501(c)(3) of the Federal Tax Code. This means that all donations to LA&M are deductible from federal income taxes. Memberships are available, and monetary donations can be made above and beyond membership. (The silent auction during the 1997 IML weekend raised over $3200 for the Archives.)

Visit the Leather Archives & Museum the next time you're in Chicago. Once you've been there, you'll wear your hide with more pride. In the words of Jill Carter: "Who we are—what we stand for—and where we are going must never again end up as landfill. Our memories are far too precious for that."

Three years later, there was much progress to report:

What The Leather Archives & Museum Can Do For You

Published in *Lavender* #138 (September 8, 2000)

I've written before about the Leather Archives & Museum. (All together now: "Located In Chicago, Serving The World!" That's what a leather crowd always yells at the first mention of the words "Leather Archives & Museum.") But every previous time I've written about it I've written in the spirit of "What a great concept—let's all make it happen." Well, it's happening, and it's happening bigger and faster than anyone dared hope. The Leather Archives & Museum (LA&M) has become a multi-faceted, vibrant organization working in many ways to collect, preserve, display and perpetuate the leather community's unique heritage. The LA&M serves up a feast of leather culture, and you don't even have to go to Chicago to indulge.

In a speech to the audience at the International Mr. Leather (IML) 2000 contest in Chicago, Executive Director Joseph Bean was clearly and happily overwhelmed at how quickly the community has embraced the LA&M. In November, 1996, the archives occupied its first public space, a rented storefront on North Clark Street in Chicago. By 1997, it had already outgrown the space. Bean told the IML audience, "I first dreamed of us owning a building in December, 1997. That was yesterday, barely. I announced the Capital Campaign to buy a building in January, 1998, imagining that it would take you guys ten years to buy us a building. Well, it took you less than a year and a half. You'd think that the geniuses of finance would live on Wall Street. Instead we live on Leather Street, U.S.A.

"Last year [at the 1999 IML contest] I showed you a picture of a building that could be a home for the Archives—this year it's a reality."

Bean went on to say that his hope was that the LA&M would be able to make the transition from leather community charity to leather community resource, and this appears to be happening as the LA&M finds new ways to reach out to the worldwide leather community. In addition to the exhibits in the improved display space afforded by the new building, the archives has put together a traveling exhibition of leather community history and memorabilia that has been ricocheting from city to city for some time now.

If you have Internet access and a Web browser, you don't even need to leave home to enjoy an exhibit from the LA&M. At the museum's website you'll find an online Art Gallery presenting examples of "the many erotic works the Archives has access to." Also on the Web, The Colors Project is an ongoing effort to collect and display the patches, banners and logos of the organizations, motorcycle clubs, discussion groups and social clubs that, as the website puts it, "are part of the foundation of the leather community, part of the proof that we ARE a community." The website also features links to 30 other archives, academic institutions and resources. An online gift shop and catalog are in the works.*

If you're in Chicago, you can visit the Archives (6418 N. Greenview Avenue, Chicago, IL 60626) and see the exhibits in person. You

---

*No longer "in the works," the online LA&M gift shop is going strong.

can also participate in the Archive's SMarts program, a series of 30 SM classes held at the Archives and taught by Bean. Some are lectures and some are workshops; upcoming topics include hot wax scenes, mummification, clamps and clothespins, and the spiritual dimensions of SM.*

The expanded space provided by the new LA&M building means that the Archive's collection can continue to expand. Bean noted during his IML 2000 speech that the Archives has "gone from representing about nine countries when I spoke to you last year to more than 30 this year. We keep getting letters from people saying, 'Someone from Ohio wrote to me, I'm here in Morocco, and I thought you'd like this.' It happens, it happens all the time and it's because of you. You guys are making them do it." And, he told the IML audience, "Without you none of it would have ever happened. No government institution, no foundation, no public reservoir of money has been involved. Every penny that has made the Leather Archives & Museum happen has come out of the pockets of leatherfolk."

Bean noted that, while he might wish otherwise, the need for raising funds for the LA&M continues. "We have the building, but that means we have a mortgage. I'm dreaming of paying off the mortgage in 2004. . . . If we pay off the mortgage by the refinance date in August 2004 you, the leather community, will save $813,000." He concluded by saying, "That's worth the effort. Make the effort."†

What You Can Do for the Leather Archives & Museum

There are many ways you can contribute to the LA&M:

- Contribute financially by becoming a member or by making a donation to either the operating fund or Capital Campaign.
- Contribute your time and talents by volunteering to work in the collections or to do administrative work. The Archive's Vacationing Volunteer program gives you a chance to do this even if you don't live in the Chicago area. In some cases, you can even work from your home by computer or otherwise.

---

*The series ran through November, 2000.

† And it came to pass. The LA&M mortgage-burning ceremony took place February 20, 2005. The leather/BDSM/fetish community now owns the Archives building free and clear.

- Expand the LA&M's collection and knowledge base by helping to research the histories of local clubs and organizations or by collecting the colors (logos, patches, etc.) of those clubs.
- Be aware of the leather history around you. Help the LA&M properly record and preserve leather history by identifying individuals who should be interviewed and by discovering leather holdings and estates in your area that should be collected and preserved.
- Make a will, or add a codicil to your will, to ensure that your leather-related items, perhaps money from insurance or other holdings, and even saleable assets such as real estate are donated to the LA&M. Donations to a 501(c)(3) charity like the LA&M can be very useful in estate planning; contact the Archives for more information.

Finally, here's another museum that might be of interest:

A Visit to the Museum of Sex
Published in *Lavender* #278 (January 20, 2006)

There are many museums in New York City devoted to a wide range of topics. Since 2002, one of them has been the Museum of Sex (or "MoSex," in the same way that "MoMA" stands for New York's Museum of Modern Art). The Museum of Sex is devoted to preserving and presenting "the history, evolution and cultural significance of human sexuality."

Located at 233 Fifth Avenue (at 27th Street), the outside of the museum consists of display windows that highlight current exhibits. On the inside, just past the lobby and reception area, is a museum shop fully stocked with, in the museum's words, "an eclectic assortment of publications, home accents, clothing and, of course, the best selection of sex toys available."

The museum currently has three galleries. When I visited, Gallery 1 was devoted to "Men Without Suits: Objectifying the Male Body." A timeline wrapping around two walls of the gallery gave a history of how the male body has been portrayed from ancient through modern times.

The rest of the gallery was concerned primarily with the history of male nude photography. The walls were hung with examples showing how photographic depiction of the male body changed from the advent of photography (naive and starkly honest), through the romantic/macho portrayals of early bodybuilders, to the closeted homoeroticism of the middle twentieth century and the let-it-all-hang-out (literally) abandon of the sexual revolution.

"Stags, Smokers & Blue Movies: The Origins of American Pornographic Film" was on display in Gallery 2. Before DVDs, before Betamax, before sex could legally be shown on screens in theaters, these were the forbidden films viewed in smoke-filled rooms (hence "smokers" in the exhibition title) at clandestine male gatherings called stag parties (hence "stags").

The gallery walls were dark. The tops of large black boxes on the floor were actually screens, on which were projected 20 films made between 1915 and 1960. TV screens in booths along one wall showed interviews with men who used to watch these films (and, in one instance, run the film projector). Since the films themselves are silent, the gallery was filled instead with a soundtrack composed of whoops, cheers and raucous comments that would have been made by groups of men watching the films.

Gallery 3 held several exhibits. "Spotlight on the Permanent Collection" included a history of sex-education materials, a collection of antique condom packets, a male chastity appliance for use in asylums and institutions, and other assorted sex-related paraphernalia.*

The Museum of Sex at the time had two fascinating online exhibits. "U.S. Patent Office Sex Inventions" was a history and compendium of actual patents for various sexual appliances. One of the most diabolical devices, an "Electric Spermatorrhea Shield," was intended to prevent masturbation and was to be used "until the . . . habit is mastered or overcome."

Many of the devices were intended to prevent erections, masturbation and even nocturnal emissions, while some conversely were pre-Viagra attempts to induce erections. There are also various "marital aids" in the form of couches and slings. Two anti-rape devices, both

---

*Another exhibit in Gallery 3 when I visited was "Sex Machines: Photographs and Interviews by Timothy Archibald," based on the book of the same name. You can read about that—and the local Twin Cities celebrity featured in both book and exhibit—on page 33.

worn in the vagina, promised to give any would-be rapist an unpleasant surprise.

The Museum's other online exhibit (also an on-site installation in
Gallery 3) was "Mapping Sex in America." According to the Museum,
the aim of this interactive exhibit was to create an "ongoing archive
chronicling American's stories of sexual practice and the evolution of
America's sexual customs." Online visitors to the exhibit could click
on a map of the United States and post their own personal sexual
history, or read what other people have posted.

You can view the Museum's current online exhibits, as well as
details about their current gallery installations, upcoming special
events and other museum information, at their website.

Chapter 3

Family Life
Family, community, tribe or nation?
Yes, yes, yes and yes.

In this chapter are excerpts from some early columns examining and explaining the concept of community as I saw it applied to leather at the time. As I read them now, many years later, they're still pretty accurate. Not much has changed about the community, its values, and how it functions since these columns were written.

The Leather Community: Myth and Reality
Published in *Lavender* #6 (August 18, 1995)

Recently I was comparing leather philosophies with an experienced leatherman who was visiting from New York City. When the conversation turned to solidarity, relationships and politics in the leather community, he seemed to feel that these concepts are paid a lot more lip service than they're worth. At one point he made a comment to the effect that "If I hear one more person talk about their leather family I'm gonna puke."

I'm going to try to write this column so he won't need a barf bag if he reads it.*

It's been a little more than two years since the first time I went to a leather bar and felt I belonged there. In those early months, I was

---

*Unfortunately, he won't read it in this book; since the column was originally published he has become another victim of HIV/AIDS.

amazed and delighted to find how welcoming people were. I owe a lot to those people who (literally and figuratively) "showed me the ropes," explained how the community works, and introduced me to their friends, who introduced me to *their* friends.

Now I find myself doing the same kinds of introductions for others who are going through their second "coming out" and joining the leather community. I'm now answering the same questions I remember asking not too long ago. For example, in the past week I've had the same conversation with two different people when they asked: "Where's the best place to buy leather around here?"

My involvement in the leather community has led to my developing a "leather family" that seems to keep growing. It includes people from the Twin Cities and from everywhere else. I feel blessed to have such a family. As with all families it's not unvarnished wonderfulness, but it's still very satisfying.

Often I hear members of the radical right talking about their idea of "family values" and I feel like *I'm* gonna puke. But maybe the romanticized idea of a "leather family" from which my New York friend was recoiling, or the romanticizing of the leather community in general, is our version of this myth, in which we're all noble, stalwart, good-hearted souls and everyone always gets along with everyone else. On some level this is what everyone is looking for, whether they're in leather or not. But it doesn't exist.

The unromantic truth about the leather community is this: Leather can make us better, more honest, more compassionate human beings. But so far it hasn't made me, or anyone else I know, perfect. People in leather are still human, and are still subject to the same human glories and shortcomings as anyone else. We may be different in that we wear leather (or other fetishwear) and are into varying degrees of alternative sexuality. But among leatherfolk I am going to see the same gamut of personalities, and of personal strengths and dysfunctions, that I see in other segments of society.

The philosophy of the leather community encourages honesty, integrity, personal strength, and respect for oneself and others. Many in the leather community try to live by these principles; some don't. Just because someone is wearing leather does not guarantee they will be a wonderful person. A jerk who puts on leather is still a jerk.

Looking with unclouded and unsentimental vision at my "leather family" and the friends I've made in the leather community, I see quite a few who have alcohol or drug problems. I see people in abusive and violent relationships. I see people who desperately want a committed relationship but can never find one that works. I see politics, rivalry and power struggles. I see people with HIV/AIDS who are miserable, and I see people with HIV/AIDS who are living life to the fullest. I see people who are stable, who have forged lives that work. I see leaders who have an innate nobility about them. That's my leather family. And I love them and care about them all.

If a person newly into leather expects to find a totally harmonious community, and a leather family who will make up for all the short-comings of their family of origin, they probably will be disappointed. But if we don't imbue leather with this magical power to make people something they're not, we can look at people honestly and accept them as they are. We will naturally gravitate toward people with whom we feel a kinship. We will find ourselves part of a mutually satisfying leather family. And we'll understand what's truly valuable about the leather community.

The Leather Community: A Short Explanation
Published in *Lavender* #14 (December 8, 1995)

So what exactly is this "leather community"? Here's as good an explanation as I can come up with:

There is no exact definition of the leather community; in order to belong you don't have to join anything, or sign up for anything. You *can* join a club if you want, but you don't have to. That's where the term "GDI"—which stands for "God-damned independent"—comes from. Basically, anyone who desires to be part of the community can join it.*

So who are the people in the leather community? Members can be any age and any sexual orientation. There are gay men, gay women, bisexuals (people who feel attraction for both sexes), pansexuals (people who play sexually with both sexes), and even straights.† Some

*Debate has raged in recent years about whether this openness to all comers is a blessing or a curse.

† Well, that's the word I used at the time. See page 119.

people in the leather community don't even wear that much leather—they may be more into latex, or spandex, or other types of fetishwear. Some members are into heavy sadomasochism, some only slightly, some not at all.

It's a pretty diverse and wide-ranging group that happens to be united by several characteristics. We tend to be drawn to things and activities, sexually and in other areas of our lives, that general "polite" (also known as "vanilla") society frowns upon and says we should feel ashamed of. We tend not to feel ashamed of them, however, but to celebrate them instead. That makes us outlaws, but for a lot of us that just adds to the excitement. We may sometimes find ourselves ostracized and shunned by "polite" society for what we see as flimsy reasons. Because we don't appreciate being shunned, it behooves us not to shun anyone else just because they may see things differently than we do. That means the leather community, at its best, is a very open and accepting group of people.

Calling All Wannabes
Published in *Lavender* #17 (January 19, 1996)

During the time I've been writing this column I've been introduced as a leather columnist to quite a few people. There has been one curious reaction that I have heard many times over. It is this: "Oh, so you're into the leather scene? Me, I'm just a leather wannabe!"

I suppose it shouldn't surprise me that I hear this "leather wannabe" response so often, because for many years I was a leather wannabe myself. Shortly after coming out at age 19, I was doing—ahem—"research" when I discovered *Drummer* Magazine. It was unlike any other gay magazine I had ever seen until then; the men were different from the men I saw in magazines such as *In Touch* or *David* (and certainly different from the men in *Playgirl,* which was my primary source of beefcake at the time).

The men in those other magazines ranged from ruggedly handsome to overly pretty. The *Drummer* men, however, were in a class by themselves. I almost didn't know it was possible for anyone to be that rugged and that masculine. Even fully clothed in leather, they exuded more sex than a lot of the naked guys in the other magazines. Of course, the *Drummer* men got naked too, and that was phenomenal.

And then they started doing unspeakable things to each other's bodies, which was scary. ("Gosh, doesn't that hurt?") Scary, but also strangely, secretly, somewhat shamefully attractive; it repulsed me when I thought about it, but some of what I saw in *Drummer* kept showing up in my fantasies for years.

As I got older, I kept my leather fantasies to myself. The thought of a big, masculine leatherman even wanting to speak to someone like me seemed outlandish. And the thought that I could actually meet that leatherman on his own turf was beyond outlandish—it was impossible. If I would have had the gall to actually put on leather and invade their territory, I felt like I would have been recognized as the phony I was and laughed (or thrown) right out the door.

I wasn't even a leather wannabe. I was a leather wish-I-could-but-know-I-can't-be.

Well, obviously a few things have changed, the first and most fundamental being my attitude toward leather. Once I gave myself permission to actually interact with leatherfolk I discovered that those tough people in leather were actually friendly and accepting. And I discovered that leather is about inclusion, not exclusion.*

Moral of story: If something about leather attracts and excites you, you don't have to be "just a wannabe." Give yourself the freedom to explore all the facets of leather life, and you'll be amazed at the new vistas you'll discover. You may really get off on certain aspects of the scene; other aspects may not be to your liking. You get to choose what works for you and what doesn't—you don't have to buy the whole package in order to be a "real" member of the leather community.

---

*See previous footnote on page 85 regarding the blessing/curse of community openness.

Chapter 4

Married Life
and other forms of relationships

Before you start reading the first column in this chapter, please note the date it was published. At least a decade before marriage equality became the big political issue that it is currently, members of the leather community were already aware of the issue and were agitating for it.

Gay Marriage (and other forms of bondage)
Published in *Lavender* #38 (November 8, 1996);
portions reprinted in *Lavender* #347 (September 12, 2008)

The legalization of gay marriage seems to have become a "hot-button" topic for the entire gay community, and members of the leather community are no exception. This year's outgoing International Mr. Fantasy, J.D. Buchert, and his lover, David Gillis, renewed their vows onstage at the contest. And at this year's International Mr. Drummer contest, Mr. Southern California Drummer Kyle Brandon (who went on to win the International Mr. Drummer title) performed a "fantasy" that was not a fantasy at all, but rather a real-life marriage ceremony between him and his lover. In addition, many of the speeches at all three of this year's international leather contests contained references to the issue of gay marriage.

Fighting for the legalization of gay marriage is a good and noble cause; it will be a great day when society no longer tells us our love is second-class love. But gay marriage is really just the tip of the iceberg.

In one sense, relationships in the leather community run the same gamut as in the rest of the gay community, which run the same gamut as in straight society (where, by the way, currently half of all marriages end in divorce). Leather relationships run for varying lengths of time, from hours to years, and none of them come with a guarantee. But because they're not "normal," people tend to give them a lot more thought before entering into them, and that tends to make them healthier and more stable.

Relationships in the gay community in general and the leather/SM community in particular come in a rainbow of flavors the general straight public doesn't usually consider. The leather community, in addition to woman/woman or man/man (and even, on occasion, woman/man) spousal relationships, offers such esoteric relationship choices as daddy/boy (neither of which is necessarily male, by the way) and Master/slave. Adding to the richness of choices (or confusion, depending on your viewpoint) is the fact that one person may engage in multiple concurrent relationships; one person could theoretically be someone's boy, someone else's daddy, someone else's Master or slave, and someone else's spouse all at the same time.*

Certain elements of straight society find relationships like these threatening and subversive. They are so frightened by the form of these relationships they never get around to investigating the content; if they did they'd see the same kind of "traditional family values" they spend so much time talking about. The negotiations preceding an SM scene, and the trust necessary to bring it off properly, bespeak a respect for ourselves and the other person or people involved. The same can be said for a healthy and affirming daddy/boy or Master/slave relationship.

These relationships don't just happen—they require work and care and nurturing. But the work and care and nurturing pay off in learning what makes a healthy relationship and what doesn't. And generally, the good that's gained from these leather/SM relationships spills over into all the other relationships in which a person is involved, from work to family to casual acquaintances to people on the street.

If we let someone else's disapproval dampen our enjoyment of our culture and our relationships, we have only ourselves to blame. No one can oppress another without the other's consent. To the extent we are

---

*Some community members believe a scenario like this is possible; others in the community would say such mixing of roles is improper.

secretive about the nature of our relationships we reinforce to ourselves, and to the general public, the idea that those relationships aren't acceptable.

The Stonewall rebellion was about gays and lesbians questioning their oppression by straight society. It spawned a viewpoint that said, "We're tired of not having the same rights as straights. When is it going to be our turn?"

The answer to this question is simple. It's our turn whenever we take it.

But if we don't take it, no one will ever give it to us.

More and more gay people, both leather and non-leather, aren't waiting for society to legalize gay marriage, to "give us our turn." They're taking their turn right now. The leather/SM and non-leather GLBT communities have taken society's rulebook (in which marriage is defined as a lifelong monogamous union of a submissive wife and a dominant husband for the purpose of producing offspring) and thrown it away. We are no longer constrained by those rules—we are free to invent new kinds of relationships that meet our needs and the needs of those we love. If two people of whatever sex and/or gender decide that a traditional monogamous marriage framework (with or without children) is what they want, fine. If another framework better meets their needs, that's also fine.

Legalized gay marriage will offer certain benefits (and also will entail certain responsibilities). But legislation won't change peoples' hearts and minds—hearts and minds will have to change in order for the legislation to be enacted. And hearts and minds will be changed, one heart and one mind at a time, by enough of us being open and proud of our culture and our relationships—woman/woman, man/man, daddy/boy, Master/slave, whatever.

Leather pride—or any other pride, for that matter—means we can be open, honest and genuine about ourselves and our relationships, and not feel a need to apologize. And it's a self-fulfilling prophecy— over time society will get used to the idea that our relationships can be healthy, positive and satisfying. Finally, in a stunning example of anticlimax, gay marriage will be legalized.

But we don't really have to wait for that to happen. Remember, it's our turn whenever we take it. It's our turn right now.

One's Kinky, the Other One Isn't
Can this relationship be saved?
Published in *Lavender* #169 (November 16, 2001)

Dear Mr. Leather Columnist, Sir: I've just fallen head-over-heels for a real dreamboat. He's charming, intelligent, and kind, and I think he's equally smitten with me. But as far as I can determine he's completely, relentlessly vanilla. I, on the other hand, have a closetful of leather and a bulging toy bag. Oh, and they sing "Hello, Dolly" when I walk into the Eagle.

Should I tell him about my interest in leather? If so, how? Or should I even be pursuing a relationship with him? Is it possible to make a relationship work when one member of a couple is into leather and the other isn't? Do leather and vanilla mix?

Should you tell this seemingly vanilla person that you're kinky? Suppose you do, and the other person is horrified; it's probably better that you discover this incompatibility before investing a great deal of time and energy in a relationship that might be derailed when your interests come to light. On the other hand, the other person might say something like "Oh, thank goodness, so am I! I was wondering how I was going to tell you." In that case, you can take the discussion to the next stage: "Are you a top, bottom or switch?"

A third possible response, of course, is an even-handed "I'm not into that, but it's not a problem if you are." Before you let your hopes be dashed because the other person doesn't share your leather interests, consider that they may have an interest that you don't share—opera, for example. If the rest of the ingredients for a relationship are there, what's to say it can't work? Maybe they wouldn't be averse to at least seeing what goes on in a dungeon, and you actually might enjoy *Carmen.*

On the other hand, not being honest with the other person— about kinkiness or anything else—pretty much dooms any relationship that evolves. As I said in another column recently, it's the secrets we keep that get us in trouble.* You'll be living in fear that your secret will someday come out, and sooner or later it probably will. Whether or not the relationship survives the disclosure, the situation probably

---

*See "The Secrets We Keep," page 181.

won't be pretty.

Sometimes, though, it's not a matter of keeping secrets at the start—it's a matter of self-discovery along the way. Unfortunately, that doesn't necessarily make things any easier:

Dear Mr. Leather Columnist, Sir: I really love my partner. We've been a happy lesbian couple for many years and have been through a lot together. But I am becoming more and more aware that we've grown apart, sexually speaking. After years of denying my interest in BDSM, lately I've been feeling like it's something I need to at least explore. When I confided in my partner, however, she told me that in her opinion BDSM was all about the degradation of women (obviously I don't share her opinion) and she gave me an ultimatum: BDSM or her. I don't want to lose her, but I'm afraid if I let her control me I'll grow to resent her for keeping me from exploring this aspect of myself. And I don't want to sneak around behind her back. What do I do now?

First of all, you are to be commended for your honesty (and perhaps courage) in telling your partner about your discovery of this aspect of yourself. You also are to be commended for your integrity in not wanting to sneak around behind her back, and for your insight about the possibility of developing resentments if you let her control you.

It seems to me that your partner, on the other hand, is being rather inflexible about the situation and inconsiderate of you and your feelings.

There are many parallels between this situation and a married couple in which one partner can no longer ignore their homosexual tendencies. The couple may stay together or may break apart, but if they stay together "arrangements" usually are made as the relationship is restructured in some fashion. Couples in which one partner is interested in kink and the other isn't must face and negotiate the same types of issues: If the relationship is to be opened up, how open should it be? What constitutes fidelity or infidelity, monogamy or non-monogamy? (To illustrate just one possible example, is the relationship to be sexually open but emotionally monogamous?) What's considered sexual play and what's considered non-sexual? How much or how little does the non-kinky partner want to hear about the kinky partner's adventures and discoveries?

There's nothing wrong with being kinky. There's nothing wrong with not being kinky, either—it's not everyone's cup of tea, and that's okay. As long as everyone involved can accept both these tenets and respect the other person's point of view, even if they don't share it, there's no problem. Problems happen when someone expects everyone else to be kinky (just like them) or not kinky (just like them).

Chapter 5

Social Life

We're (Almost) Everywhere
Published in *Lavender* #348 (September 26, 2008)

There was a time when only a few large cities had any sort of organized leather community. But in recent years, with the help of the Internet, leather/BDSM/fetish activities have spread to many smaller cities and towns. It is a measure, I think, of how leather culture has spread over the years that currently some visible degree of leather/BDSM/fetish activity can be found pretty much coast to coast in the U.S. (with one major regional exception).

I make this conclusion based on several non-scientific and arbitrary data sources: 1) where leather clubs belonging to various regional club councils are located; 2) where the contestants have come from at leather contests I've been to lately; and 3) where nominees for this year's Pantheon of Leather Community Service Awards hailed from. My thinking here is that some degree of organized leather activity has to exist in an area in order to keep a club going, send someone to compete in a contest or nominate someone from the area for a Pantheon award.

Let's look at leather club activity first. The Atlantic Motorcycle Coordinating Council (AMCC) coordinates activities for 26 participating clubs in the eastern U.S., while the Mid-America Conference of Clubs (MACC) coordinates activities for 28 clubs in states in the middle of the U.S. (No similar council currently exists for the western part of the U.S.)

AMCC currently has member clubs in many of its constituent

states. The exceptions are Vermont, New Hampshire, Rhode Island, New Jersey, West Virginia, and North and South Carolina. MACC currently has member clubs in all of its constituent states except Indiana, Arkansas, Alabama and Mississippi. (Later on, we'll see if we can find other kinds of leather activity in these states.)

Looking at AMCC and MACC membership gives us information about gay male leather activity, as does my next example: the International Mr. Leather (IML) contest. This year there were IML contestants from 22 states (as well as six foreign countries). All of the eastern and midwestern states sending contestants to IML are already on our leather map because they have member clubs in AMCC or MACC. But in the west, looking at where this year's IML contestants came from allows us to add California, Oregon, Washington, Arizona, Oklahoma, Texas and Colorado to our list of states with a leather presence.

Now let's look at a contest whose titleholders represent the pansexual leather community: the Mr. and Ms Olympus Leather contest. Out of nine contestants this year, three were from states we can add to our leather map of the U.S.: Utah, West Virginia and Alabama.

And with the addition of the 2008 Pantheon of Leather award nominees, we can account for even more states. This year's nominees came from 35 states, including some that aren't yet on our map: Indiana, Kansas, North Carolina, New Jersey, New Mexico and Nevada.

After looking at these measurements of leather activity, some states still aren't on our map. Here's where I add another data source: 4) an online leather club directory maintained by *The Leather Journal*.

In the Northeast, we were still missing Vermont, New Hampshire and Rhode Island. *The Leather Journal* lists several clubs in Rhode Island and one in New Hampshire, but none in Vermont. At least Vermont, a small state, is surrounded by states with a higher level of leather/BDSM/fetish activity.

In the South, our map was still missing South Carolina, Mississippi and Arkansas. For South Carolina *The Leather Journal* lists clubs in Charleston, Columbia and Myrtle Beach, and for Arkansas it lists Leathermen of Arkansas and MAsT: Ozarks Region. But Mississippi has nothing listed. Again, at least Mississippi is surrounded by states with more to offer in the way of leather/BDSM/fetish.

What about our two newest states? Alaska has the Last Frontier

Men's Club in Anchorage, which serves both leather and bears,* and which several years ago sent a contestant to IML. *The Leather Journal* lists nothing for Hawaii, though.

That leaves us with five remaining (and neighboring) states, a large hole in the northwestern part of our map representing leather's last frontier: Idaho, Montana, Wyoming, and North and South Dakota. Checking my leather history book I see that only two of these states have ever sent a contestant to IML (Idaho in 1989 and 1991 and North Dakota in 1997). *The Leather Journal* listings are meager for Idaho (Boise Black Rose and a bear group) and South Dakota (Leather Spirits, a pansexual group). Nothing at all is listed for North Dakota, Montana or Wyoming. If leathermen were missionaries, these five states would represent fertile ground for saving souls.

That's our snapshot of what today's map of leather across the U.S. looks like. Of course, things have changed over the years and will continue to do so. Many fabled leather clubs of yesterday are no longer around, and leather/BSDM/fetish activity in local communities has been known to heat up or cool down for any number of reasons.

So what tomorrow's leather map will look like is anyone's guess. Who knows? If enough of us retire to Hawaii, Honolulu might one day be a leather hot spot.

Leather and "Social Capital"

Published in *Lavender* #272 (October 28, 2005)

Go to a munch†—you'll live longer.

The above oversimplification points to a truth that goes beyond the leather/BDSM community to society in general: in the words of Dr. Robert Putnam, "Our communities don't work as well, and our bodies don't work as well, when we're not connected."

---

*Bears: leathermen's hairy cousins. Bears are gay, they are male, they are hairy and they are unapologetic about it. They also may be on the husky side, but not necessarily. There is a high degree of crossover between the bear community and the leather community, resulting in some men referring to themselves as "leather bears."

†Munch: a term coming from the pansexual community for a social, non-play gathering of people sharing an interest in BDSM, fetish and other alternative sexualities. Usually held at a restaurant, which means food and drinks can be ordered if desired.

Dr. Putnam, a professor of public policy at Harvard, spoke in Minneapolis last May at a Town Hall Forum presented by Westminster Presbyterian Church. He has spent years studying "social capital."

Dr. Putnam defines social capital as "features of social organization such as networks, norms, and social trust that facilitate coordination and cooperation for mutual benefit." Note that word "trust"—an integral component of leather/BDSM relationships.

Social coordination and cooperation are produced by face-to-face encounters leading to trust, shared values, a sense of belonging and a sense of commitment or connection to others. These qualities allow people to build communities and to weave a social fabric. Strong communities and high connectedness lead to better health, less crime, more economic prosperity and higher educational achievement.

According to Dr. Putnam, connection and commitment are social tools that allow us to get more done in less time, and a social network has benefits and value both for those within the network and for bystanders. Part of the benefit of social networks is reciprocity—as Yogi Berra put it, "If you don't go to other people's funerals, they won't go to yours."

The picture Dr. Putnam paints of the current state of social capital in America is sobering. For the first two-thirds of the twentieth century Americans were becoming more connected, creating new organizations, new networks and new social capital. But from the 1960s through the 1980s, connectedness leveled, declined—and then plunged.

Putnam, citing data from the Roper polling organization, concluded that one-half of our civic infrastructure evaporated in the last quarter of the twentieth century. He also cited a more specific piece of data leading to the same conclusion: DDB/Needham, an advertising agency in Chicago, documented a 45% decline in "frequency of entertaining"—we simply don't invite people over as often as we used to.

In leather/BDSM circles, a frequent topic of conversation is "What's happening to our community?" Why are traditional gay leather clubs graying, with few younger members in sight? Why is it harder to find contestants for leather contests? Why does it seem as if people don't go out as often as they used to?

Every other community is asking the same type of question. What's happening to our schools? Are parents too busy to be involved in the PTA? Is there still a place for labor unions? Who will be the next generation of members for the American Legion and VFW? Why do fewer people seem to be involved in political parties?

What has caused this situation? Putnam cited multiple culprits, one of which is suburbanization—10 more minutes of commuting time equals a 10% reduction in socializing. The rise of two-career families didn't help matters, either.

But high on Putnam's list of culprits: television. In Putnam's words, "Most Americans watch 'Friends' rather than having them."

The Internet, Putnam notes, is not a large factor in the decline of connectedness because the years of massive decline predate the Internet in its current form. The Internet will either evolve into a Super Television, which will be very isolating, or a Super Telephone, which will be very connecting.

Although users of phone-sex services might not agree, Putnam notes that "You don't make new friends on the telephone"—it's part of our network for maintaining connections we already have. Likewise, with the Internet there is room for creativity. Society needs to figure out ways to use the Internet to strengthen real community instead of fostering further disconnectedness.

Creativity is a ray of hope, not just for the Internet, but also for the entire matter of rebuilding social capital. At the turn of the twentieth century, the situation was much the same as it is today at the turn of the twenty-first. America was undergoing a transition from an agrarian society to an urban one; many of the old ways of relating and connecting didn't fit anymore. The problem was fixed in a very short time, however, and new organizations were invented quickly to fit people's new needs and situations.

That's our challenge now, according to Dr. Putnam: "We need to invent new ways of connecting that fit the way we live—we need to reinvent the Kiwanis or the Y."

Hmm. Creativity—now who are some of the most creative people you know?

That's right: us. Who is better than the members of the leather/BDSM community at figuring out new and delightful ways to please each other? Who has more fun finding new uses for things from the hardware store? What other group takes such pleasure in pushing envelopes and blazing new trails?

Instead of worrying about where the leather/BDSM community is going, let's use our creativity and imagination to strengthen what works and reinvent what doesn't. In this era of social upheaval and rebuilding, the leather/BDSM community might one day find itself even more relevant, and to more people, than ever.

For further reading: Dr. Robert Putnam is the author of a dozen books, including *Bowling Alone: The Collapse and Revival of American Community** and *Better Together: Restoring the American Community*.[†] (Those with long memories will recall that the theme of IML 1994 Jeff Tucker's title year was "Better Together." They will also recall that IML 1996 Joe Gallagher's theme was "Get Linked.")

Virtual or Reality?

Published in *Lavender* #252 (January 21, 2005)

It's fashionable these days to talk about how technology is ruining leather and BDSM culture. Some say it started with the invention of the videocassette recorder—before which, since most people didn't have film projectors at home, it was necessary to leave one's residence, go to a theater, and actually mingle with other people in order to watch a porn film.[‡] With the VCR, one could watch a porn video in the privacy—and isolation—of one's living room.

Then someone invented telephone sex lines, which subsequently morphed into chatrooms—before which it was necessary to leave one's residence, go to a bar (or a bathhouse, park or dungeon) and mingle with other people in order to find, um, companionship.

Then came dial-a-trick, which became click-a-trick, which meant that one no longer needed to leave the house to cruise for sex or BDSM play partners.

But, so the argument goes, chatrooms are at worst a poor replacement for, and at best often a shoddy introduction to, actual real-life community experience.

To a great extent I agree with statements of this kind. But, on the other hand, technology and new inventions are not necessarily always

---

*New York: Simon & Schuster, 2000.

[†] With Lewis M. Feldstein. New York: Simon & Schuster, 2003.

[‡] For more on this, see page 70.

bad. I'm glad, for example, that somebody invented the technology that allows people to read this column over the Web.

In fact, I have a list of new inventions I'd like to see and technologies I wish would be taken further.

The first VCR I ever owned seemed great at the time. But my second VCR made the first seem primitive. Why? Because it had a remote control that allowed me to start, stop, pause, fast-forward and rewind from the comfort of my chair.

Let's take that concept further: I want a VCR remote control for my life. Just think—if I caught a fleeting glimpse of a handsome man in a crowd, I could put life on pause and get a better look. Or, if I had too much to do and not enough time to do it, I could put everything else on pause until I caught up.

Boring meeting? Fast-forward through it. Really great vacation? Hit rewind and enjoy it all again—fast-forwarding through the mundane parts, of course.

Another example of technology that needs to be taken further is a feature of Adobe Photoshop and other image-editing software: the cloning tool. Its on-screen icon looks like a tiny rubber stamp. It allows one to digitally sample a portion of an image and then duplicate ("clone") it anywhere else on the image.

To see the cloning tool in action is to watch magic happen. Perhaps there's a picture taken on a recent vacation that would be scenic except for the telephone poles and power lines. Simply sample the sky and clone away the wires going through the air. Then sample the trees and clone in some more trees in place of the telephone poles.

I want somebody to invent a cloning tool for real life. It would truly be a tool of a thousand uses. Imagine the infomercial: "Did you get mad and put your fist through the sheetrock? Simply sample another portion of the wall and clone away the damage! Teenagers: Did your face break out before a heavy date? No more Clearasil—clone away blemishes instantly! Also works on scars, wrinkles and bags under the eyes! Male-pattern baldness? Clone some hair into that bald spot! The possibilities are limited only by your imagination!"

Adobe Photoshop is based on technology that was originally invented by the innovative and creative folks at NASA for enhancing photographs from outer space. But not all inventions are technological ones—and when it comes to inventions, the innovative and creative people in the leather and BDSM communities have come up with some great ones over the years, too.

The invention of the hankie code, for example, adds interest and conversational opportunities to cruising while also being a great timesaver.*

Another great invention to come out of the dungeon is the safeword, a means of quick communication during a scene. One of the most common safeword scenarios is modeled on the metaphor of a traffic light: When asked, a response of "green" means everything is fine, so keep going. Say "yellow" and the action slows down or temporarily halts while people check up on you and see how you're doing. Say "red" and that's it—the action stops, scene over.

So, actually, in the dungeon one can have the real-life functions of some of the buttons on the VCR remote control. Saying "yellow" is like pressing "pause" and saying "red" is like pressing "stop" or "eject." Now if we could just figure out the fast-forward-and-reverse thing.

The problem is that safewords don't work outside the dungeon. Believe me, I have tried. But when the car is spinning out of control, or the doctor breaks the news that the lesion is malignant, or the pipes have burst and are flooding the basement, yelling "RED!" at the top of one's lungs doesn't do any good.

All of this, to me, makes the concept of dungeon play that much more valuable. We call it "play" to distinguish it from real torture experiences, like what happened in Nazi concentration camps or more recently at Abu Ghraib. A scene in a dungeon is like a scene in a play, except that it's participatory theater instead of happening on a stage.

Both live theater and dungeon play are "real" in that they involve flesh-and-blood humans, as opposed to the celluloid image of a movie or the video image of videogames and webcams. Both dungeon play and live theater are illusory in the sense that they are exercises in roleplaying. Both require what theatrical textbooks call "the willing suspension of disbelief."

---

*See 'The Nonverbal Language of Leather," page 139, and "The Zen of Hankies," page 141.

But illusory or not, once disbelief has been suspended both live theater and dungeon play can be profound and life-changing experiences. Someday virtual-reality technology may well evolve to the point where it can offer the same level of experience. Someday I might have real-life fast-forward and rewind buttons—and my real-life cloning tool, too.

But for now, technology only goes so far. Chatrooms and the Internet can offer only a shadow of the richness and transformational power of real-life involvement in the real-life leather/BDSM community.

If Everybody's Kinky . . . Nobody's Kinky

Published in *Lavender* #317 (July 20, 2007)

Someone, somewhere thinks you're kinky. And they think you're evil because of it.

They think Your Kink Is Not OK. They even have an acronym for it: YKINOK.

They may be a right-wing conservative extremist. They may be a "vanilla" member of the GLBT community. They even may be a member of the leather/BDSM/fetish community playing the MKIOK/ YKINOK game ("My Kink Is OK/Your Kink Is Not OK").

You may think their judgment of you is not fair, and you'd be right. But are you doing the same thing?

What exactly does "kinky" mean, anyway? Who gets to define what's kinky and what's not?

Everybody does. That's the problem.

"Kinky" is a relative term. Many people define as "kinky" what they don't like, don't identify with, don't feel comfortable with, or don't understand. Kinky is the opposite of "normal," whatever that is.

Many members of the leather/BDSM/fetish community self-identify as kinky individuals. They are the opposite of what they call "vanilla," which to them means conventional, "usual" sex—not that there's necessarily anything wrong with that. Sometimes even self-proclaimed kinky people are in the mood for vanilla sex.

At its most extreme, though, "vanilla" sex is fundamentalist: one man, one woman, missionary position, for the purpose of procreation. Anything outside that small, supposedly moral, scope is fair game for the disapproving "kinky" designation. Of course, some of the fundamentalist types who berate these "unnatural" sexualities are speaking most loudly to themselves, trying first and foremost to convince themselves of the evil nature of these practices.

In this context, there are people who classify all kinds of things as kinky: gay or lesbian sex, bisexuality, anything connected with transgender issues, polyamory, swinging, vibrators and other sex toys, and even sexually suggestive clothing. So if you've ever been associated with any of these, someone thinks you're kinky.

But there's good, clean, morally approved "vanilla," and then there's reality. And the reality tent is a lot bigger than the fundamentalists like to admit.

When I am introduced to people as a leather columnist, I often wind up finding out a lot about them. Often they tell me, "Well, I'm not kinky, *but . . .*" and then they name their predilection: "I like to be spanked." "I like to get tied up sometimes." "I like to have my nipples played with."

Who's kinky? Almost everybody, in some way or other. But if everybody's kinky, nobody's kinky. The concept of "kink" loses its meaning when the normality of many and varied forms of human sexual expression is recognized and even celebrated.

One man, one woman and the missionary position is not the one true way. Other societies have organized things differently: ancient matriarchies; multiple wives (in the Bible throughout the Old Testament, in many Middle Eastern societies today and historically among otherwise-conservative Mormons); the "walking marriages" of the Mosuo people in central China, a matrilineal society in which families of biological brothers and sisters raise the sisters' children, often without knowing or caring who their father was.

So could we all just lighten up a bit? Could we cut each other some slack? If I don't get off on something but you do, why should I deny you your right to the pursuit of happiness? Wouldn't it be better if I respected your rights and preferences, and in return you respected mine? There's an acronym for that, too: YKIOK/MKIOK ("Your Kink Is OK/My Kink Is OK").

That is nothing less than the beginning of world peace. Maybe if we can agree on that, we can agree on some other things as well. And, to paraphrase what an IML contestant a few years ago proclaimed during his speech: "World peace has to come from somewhere. What better place than this community?"

For a long time, leaders of the GLBT community have been saying that discrimination based on affectional preference or gender expression makes no sense. And it doesn't, any more than discrimination based on skin color, race or ethnicity. And discrimination on the basis of kink preference or disapproval also makes no more sense than, say, discrimination on the basis of ice cream preference:

"Well, I've often dreamed of trying the triple-mocha caramel, but I never actually would. What would people say if they found out? It's just not respectable. (But, oh, I bet it's delicious!)"

Or how about, "Watch out for that one—I hear he goes for tutti-frutti."

Or maybe, "She's so staid—she only ever eats vanilla." To which she answers, "Yes, I prefer vanilla—but only *really good* vanilla!"

As I sit here at the completely homosexual end of the sexual-preference bell curve, I clearly see the artificial and limiting nature of our society's current "vanilla" sexual paradigm. But what would a less enforced, less rigid, less vanilla world look like? Would kinksters lose that outlaw thrill? Would we be just like everyone else? Could we stand it?

No, we wouldn't be like everyone else, because our preferences are not everyone's. But we'd be like everyone else as far as human rights and human dignity were concerned. Wouldn't that be a good change?

We crusade for sexual freedom as a fundamental human right for everyone. That means freedom to consensually enjoy any sexual flavor *du jour*. Yes, even the freedom to be monogamously vanilla—which some of us think is the ultimate kink.

Fear of Leather

Published in *Lavender* #187 (July 26, 2002)

Who's afraid of the big bad leatherman? A lot of people, it seems, and sometimes that's part of the fun. Admit it—don't you sometimes derive just the teeniest bit of enjoyment from intimidating people? I was recently part of a group of leathermen and leatherwomen who caused heads to turn, and probably tongues to wag, as we walked to our table at an upscale restaurant.

On the other hand, sometimes it's not fun at all when people are afraid of you. Fear of people who are different has produced (among other things) the Crusades, the Holocaust, the troubles in Northern Ireland, perpetual war in the Middle East, and nuclear tension between India and Pakistan. It has produced Jim Crow laws and sodomy laws. And it fuels the recent and continuing vicious attacks by conservative Christian groups on members and organizations of the GLBT and leather/BDSM communities.

Incredibly and unfortunately, leatherphobia is found in many groups besides conservative Christians. Some "mainstream" GLBT folks cast a jaundiced eye at leather, as do some feminist groups who believe that all BDSM play constitutes abuse.

And then there is our community's own leatherphobia: gay leathermen who are hesitant about socializing with lesbian leatherwomen (and vice versa), gays who are suspicious of bisexuals or heterosexuals in leather (and vice versa), and everyone who feels uncomfortable around leather transsexuals and those into genderfuck.

What is everybody so afraid of? Where does all this fear come from, anyway? Why do so many people feel threatened by so many other people?

There could be many reasons why I might feel threatened by someone, and all of those reasons can be highly instructive if I can stop being afraid long enough to learn their lessons. Here are just a few possible scenarios:

If I am a closet case, ostensibly a heterosexual but who feels "forbidden" urges for members of my own sex, I might project those urges onto all the queers out there and then loudly decry their immoral ways. Ditto if I feel the "forbidden" urges of leather, BDSM or anything else that to me seems "kinky," i.e. attractive and repulsive at the same time. Those urges, and by projection the people I see "giving in" to those urges, are threatening to me—because if I took an honest look at what those urges were telling me, I might have to make major life changes. Never mind that those major life changes might make me a happier and more authentic person—I'm too threatened to allow that into my consciousness.

Fear does not always so neatly equate to projection and disowning parts of oneself. If I, as a gay leatherman, am threatened by conservative

Christian groups who are saying that what I am and what I do is evil, it might be that part of me suspects they're correct. This is internalized homophobia or leatherphobia rearing its ugly head, and I need to have a serious talk with myself. Or it may be that I am quite comfortable with who I am and what I do, but I fear the consequences of hate speech for me and for my tribe: oppression that can range all the way from the inconvenience of a canceled leather/BDSM event to hate crimes up to and including murder. One way of dealing with that fear is to become more involved politically and socially, to work to turn a climate of hatred into a climate of acceptance.

What about people into leather/BDSM who distrust not just conservative Christians but all "vanilla" society—anyone who's not as kinky and as much of a player as they are? Does everyone else have to be kinky in order to validate their own kinky proclivities? That could be shame, guilt and a sense of inadequacy talking.

What if you're one of those people who play the "My kink is okay but yours is disgusting" game? Maybe someone else's kink, or the way they practice it, really isn't safe—in which case some mentoring and education is in order. But more probably this game is another form of internalized kinkphobia. If their kink bothers you that much, ask yourself why. What buttons are being pushed? One of many possibilities: Maybe you secretly want to try it but are ashamed of your desire. What can you learn from your discomfort, and what can you then do with that knowledge?

To say that these types of fears are irrational and therefore should be ignored or "gotten over" is to sell them short. On some level, we must be perceiving a threat or we wouldn't feel fear. So to ignore our fears or to discount them is to miss their lessons. On the other hand, by looking at them unflinchingly we can discover why something or someone makes us fearful, and we can then make whatever changes are necessary so we don't have to feel that way anymore. Our lives will be better and we will be stronger for having had the courage to face our fears and deal with them.

What's Your LPT (Leather Personality Type)?
Published in *Lavender* #271 (October 14, 2005)

In an effort to understand the world and its inhabitants, psychologists have come up with systems for classifying human behaviors and personality types. Two of the most notable (and currently fashionable) are the Myers-Briggs Type Indicator (MBTI) and the Enneagram. The MBTI defines 16 basic character types using a 4x4 grid, while the Enneagram defines 9 types using a 3x3 grid (basically—the Enneagram is more complicated than that).

Both the MBTI and the Enneagram can profitably be applied to the world of leather. However, after intense observation and analysis, your humble columnist has created a more leather-specific system.

My new Leather Personality Type (LPT) classification system contains, at last count, twelve types. These could be put into a 4x3 grid—or a 3x4 grid—or a 6x2 or 2x6 grid—or even a three-dimensional array of 2x2x3, 2x3x2 or 3x2x2. Choose one. Or feel free to skip the grid entirely.

Before describing the types, a brief disclaimer: These are archetypes. Almost no single living, breathing human represents one type exclusively. Your personality, and the personality of everyone around you, most likely incorporates elements from several of these types.

Nonetheless, I find it's good to understand the various types and what makes them tick (and what doesn't). It helps explain why we don't necessarily all see things the same way, and why we don't always have the same likes and dislikes.

In other words, what flips our switch may not flip someone else's, and vice versa. And that's okay.

With that said, here are the twelve Leather Personality Types:

LPT 1. Leather Club Member: Team players all, LPT1s are committed to strengthening their community by working with other like-minded club members. LPT1s enjoy the camaraderie and family feeling of belonging to a group. Leather clubs were, to a very great extent, where today's leather community started, which is why they have the honor of being the first Leather Personality Type.

LPT 2. The GDI (God-damned independent): An independent member of the community but a solid member nonetheless, free-spirited LPT2s don't feel the need to join a leather club, although they are often supportive of the clubs and their LPT1 members. Perhaps LPT2s can't make the significant time commitment demanded by club membership. Perhaps meeting agendas and Robert's Rules of Order bore them to tears. LPT2s find many other ways to enjoy, be involved with, and contribute to the leather community.

LPT3. The Titleholder: The leather community's rock stars, LPT3s enjoy the spotlight. They are passionate about their community and their issues, and work tirelessly to raise awareness. Sometimes seen by other LPTs as living a glamorous, jet-set life, LPT3s know that under that thin veneer of glamour is a lot of work and a lot of inconvenience. (How glamorous is it to live out of a suitcase 48 weekends of the year?) But for LPT3s, the rewards of contributing are worth it.

LPT4. The Master or Mistress: Resolutely self-assured, strong and confident, LPT4s find gratification and fulfillment in dominating and controlling others. Other LPTs may be envious when they see a Master or Mistress being waited on hand and foot (often literally), and might see LPT4s as somewhat selfish. But the emotionally healthy LPT4 understands that with the pampering comes total responsibility for the submissives or slaves doing the pampering, which most people couldn't handle. Fortunately, the LPT4 can.

LPT5. The super submissive or super slave: Often seen as the polar opposite of the LPT4, LPT5s are surprisingly similar in many ways. LPT5s are often wrongly perceived as weak and lacking self-confidence. In reality, healthy LPT5s are every bit as self-assured, strong and confident as the LPT4s they serve—they simply choose a different way of expressing it.

LPT6. The Professional: LPT6s are so dedicated to leather that they make it their livelihood, and thank goodness they do. The leather community could not function without the merchandise and services provided by LPT6s. If you didn't personally make that leather vest you're wearing, thank the LPT6 who made it and the LPT6 who sold it to you. Ditto for other leather-related apparel, toys, dungeon supplies, videos and reading material, and so on. Some might unfairly criticize LPT6s for "taking advantage" of the community or "getting rich" at the community's expense. This is balderdash—if LPT6s were motivated solely by money, they could find many easier and more secure ways to earn a living.

LPT7. The 24/7: At any moment they could meet the dress code at any Eagle in the world. They are leather and leather is them, and they wouldn't want it any other way. Or maybe they can't always look the part, but even in a business suit they're still leather and proud of it.

LPT8. The Hobbyist: Sometimes derisively considered "Weekend Warriors," leather is one aspect but not the totality of an LPT8's life. Perhaps they're new to the Scene, or perhaps they've been around awhile and incorporated into their lives the aspects of leather that work for them. By their participation they strengthen the community, so they're always welcome at a bar, an event or a party.

LPT9. The Specialist: Their interests are narrow but deep. LPT9s may or may not be involved in other aspects of the community (and may or may not be criticized for it). But they are passionate experts at their chosen interest or fetish, be it flogging, singletails, motorcycles, or anything else. If you want to explore a new leather interest, the proper LPT9 can be an invaluable resource.

LPT10. The Exotic: Puppies. Ponies. Goth. Babies. Not everyone can understand why LPT10s get off on getting into an alternate headspace. But LPT10s enjoy it—and that's what matters, as long as they're not hurting anyone else.

LPT11. The Exhibitionist: You might see their image in a magazine or video, or you might see them live on a stage, at a party or in a dungeon. In addition to whatever else they get their kicks from, LPT11s get their kicks from being watched. For LPT11s, leather is a celebration—and they want to share the experience.

LPT12. The Journalist: Carefully observing everything going on around them, LPT12s savor it all, remember it, and write it all down. They do this to preserve the culture for future generations as well as to mirror it back to the rest of the community. Along with mirroring it back, LPT12s often try to analyze and explain things. Sometimes they even attempt to classify and categorize them.

Chapter 6

Variety is the Spice of Life
Leather subcommunities

Leatherwomen Speak Out
What leathermen need to know about leatherwomen
Published in *Lavender* #105 (June 4, 1999)

The Knights of Leather, a local women's leather group, recently presented their eleventh annual Tournament run. It was attended by a diverse crowd, half women and half men. (Historically, men outnumber women at Tournament, even though it's presented by a women's leather group.)

I spent a good part of the weekend asking this question of the women in attendance: What do leathermen need to know about leatherwomen? I got a broad spectrum of responses that ranged from "I never thought about wishing that the guys knew anything about us" and "I don't define myself by what men think of me" to "I've been waiting years for someone to ask me that question!" Presented here is a very small sampling of the opinions voiced during the weekend. We'll start with one leatherwoman's laundry list of things she wants leathermen to know:

"I'm tired of leathermen being afraid of leatherwomen. I'm tired of walking into a dungeon and having the dungeon clear out. I'm tired of not being included in men's events. I'm tired of not having equality between men and women. I'm tired of having Mr. Eagle contests and not Ms Eagle contests. I'm tired of being an afterthought. I would like to be included on a more regular basis.

"A lot of women don't even think of going to men's leather events because we don't feel welcome. I've been to men's leather events where there were only two women there. And we're always asked, 'Where are the women?' Well, all the advertising is geared toward men. There's nothing there to make women feel welcome, so why would we go to your event? I don't want people to ask 'Where are the women?' anymore. We're here, we're loud and we're proud— we're just over here, as segregated as you want us to be."

Many leatherwomen don't feel terribly welcome in leather bars, either. "I remember I was at the Eagle when they started Wednesday night women's space. There were guys at the bar who said, 'What are they doing here? This is our bar.' I said, 'This is women's night.' And they said, 'We're out of here. This is a men's bar, this is a leather bar, and we don't want women around us.' What I'd like to ask leather-men who don't want women around is 'Why not?' I don't get it." Another woman chimed in: "It's like the Little Rascals, the He-Man Woman-Haters Club."

Some leatherwomen have problems with leather contests: "Some contests should be open to either sex. I identify as a boy. I would love to enter a Drummerboy contest, but just because I'm anatomically female, I can't do it. I don't have a dick—my dick is in the drawer at home, but I don't have one physically attached to me. So I can't enter the contest. And I know some guys who identify as girls, and we don't even have a contest for them." Another woman said, with a devilish gleam in her eye: "I know we're going to have some woman run for Mr. Minnesota Leather one of these days, and it's going to cause a big stir. And I'll be glad."

Many women wanted more mixed playspaces: "We don't have as much money as men do, so we can't set up a dungeon. Especially in a town like this, where there aren't public playspaces, we end up with not as many places to play." The woman standing next to her agreed: "The gender-division thing kinda sucks. I like watching men play. You need to let women come and watch you. We're voyeurs too." While we're on the subject of play: "One thing that pisses me off is that guys think women can't play as hard or as raw as they can. I have a pussy, but I'm not a pussy."

On sharing playspaces: "The problem I have is that I want to respect men's choices, but I also don't want to be excluded. And balancing those two is really difficult. I think that it's not a bad thing to have a Tuesday night men's night in a bar, and a Wednesday night women's night. It's a level-of-comfort thing—that's what we're used to, it's what we accept—but I think we should strive to have a Thursday night 'together' night. It's valid to have men-only playspace and women-only playspace, but have a common playspace, too. That way you have the opportunity to watch both genders play. You have the feeling of camaraderie that comes with the mix, and it's a hell of an education. That's part of the way to knock the barriers down."

Another way to knock the barriers down is to learn to trust each other and to focus on what leatherwomen and leathermen have in common: "We both want to embrace who we are, and to be okay with being different. But it's hard to cross those bridges and break down those walls because they've been there for so long. As a young dyke I didn't trust men because at that time, in the seventies, women were jealous because men had more power, more freedom, more privileges. But after feeling that way for a certain amount of time, you get tired of it. As I became more secure with myself it didn't matter so much what other people had. I felt free to be myself and to let others be themselves."

Leatherwomen don't want to be patronized: "Don't give me the line about 'brotherhood' and 'sisterhood.' Don't feed me the line—show me that you are actually practicing what you preach."

Leathermen aren't the only group that leatherwomen would like to talk with: "The question about what dialogue we would have with gay leathermen is not as pressing to me as maybe what dialogue do we want to have with vanilla dykes? Not to say this isn't something we need to talk about, but when we start talking we have more in common with leathermen than we do with vanilla queer women."

A postscript: In other areas of the country this topic might not be as relevant as it is in the midwest. A visitor from the eastern U.S. said, "I find this whole conversation odd. When I first came into the community I had a mistress in Washington, D.C. and the first place she took me was The Playhouse in Baltimore, which is generally pansexual. So that's my norm."

Baby On Board
Leather lesbians on the mommy track
Published in *Lavender* #139 (September 22, 2000)

On Sunday afternoon, August 13, 2000, leather history was made when a baby shower was held at The Minneapolis Eagle — quite possibly the first baby shower ever held at any leather bar anywhere. The entire Twin Cities leather community had managed to keep the upcoming shower a secret from the two moms-to-be, PJ and Vicki Knight, and many leathermen and leatherwomen had braved the terra incognita of Target's baby department and lived to tell about it. Ed Hopkins, the owner of The Minneapolis Eagle, was at the shower and was clearly excited and pleased about the event. PJ and Vicki were completely surprised, and totally delighted as well.

This may be the start of a trend. Vicki is due to deliver a baby boy at the end of September. Another leather lesbian couple, Kay and Shelley, are the proud parents of a beautiful daughter born in 1999. Shelley is the birth mother and Kay is a legal guardian of the child. According to Kay, "she is still on the petite side at only 22 lbs. but her vocabulary and understanding of concepts and conversation are growing at a phenomenal rate. She is quite the interesting person." (At Kay and Shelley's request, their last names do not appear in this article, and neither does their daughter's name.)

While certainly there are folks in the GLBT leather community with kids, up to now most of them had their children in their "previous" lives, when they were still married to someone of the opposite sex. A relative few have become parents through adoption. What's new and noteworthy is that lesbians are coming out in both a GLBT and a leather sense, pairing up, and then deciding they want to raise kids, and to — ahem — make them "from scratch," even.

While it's revolutionary in one sense that leatherwomen are having babies, in another sense it's a non-issue. All these mothers agree that they are not raising "leather babies." Nor are they necessarily raising future leather daddies or leather dykes. "I don't know who this new little person is," says Vicki. "People come up to me and joke about the future leather daddy. I don't know if he's a future leather daddy or not. This kid is not waving any flags for the leather community, unless he chooses to do so when he's an adult. And that will be *his* choice—I don't have any control over it."

Kay says her daughter *has* waved a flag: "Our daughter rode the trolley at the head of the gay pride parade in Chicago, waving her little rainbow flag, and she went to the Pantheon of Leather this year and to the Michigan Womyn's Music Festival last year. But she doesn't really understand any of those things yet. I think our daughter will grow up more as the child of a lesbian couple than as a 'leather baby,' because in many respects we live a pretty dull, vanilla life, and she leads a pretty sheltered life, too."

Shelley isn't sure what she and Kay will tell their daughter about their sexuality and their leather/SM leanings—"That's the big unknown for us, both philosophically and practically. There's not much that she sees, of course: we keep our play and equipment well out of her consciousness. But for us, leather/SM doesn't begin and end at the dungeon door. The baby sees me in my collar at home, and hears me call Sir 'Sir'—I feel like now she's too young to understand, but soon that won't be true. I'm not interested in recruiting her for the International Ms Leather contest in 2025, yet I don't want to imply that there's anything shameful or wrong about her parents' Dominant-submissive relationship. I honestly don't know how we'll handle this one. I'm just glad I don't have to do it perfectly."

Like the rest of these women, Vicki feels that leather is for consenting adults and not for a child's consumption. "Leather/SM and child-rearing are apples and oranges to me—they're two completely different worlds. I don't personally want this kid to know anything about my sex life, or any lifestyle in that respect that I choose to follow. While we're raising our child, that part is in the background."

PJ believes it's possible to enjoy leather while keeping it separate from child rearing. "When I was young, my parents would allow me to go to a friend's house for a sleep-over. Well, I know full well *now* what they did the nights that I was gone—they were making babies. So while our child is sleeping over at a friend's, we'll be playing in the sling—what's the difference there? The point is that all the toys are taken out when the child is gone and they're all packed away nice and neat before the child returns home."

Still, parenthood brings inevitable changes. Kay describes a few: "We can't hop on the motorcycle or go to a movie or do any of the spontaneous things we used to do. Weekend visits to see friends are logistically more demanding because children are equipment-intensive. And we don't swear any more because our daughter picks up on words so easily. We now live a child-focused life, but we were ready to make that commitment."

Shelley says, with a sigh, "Becoming a parent has meant giving up a lot of the things I most enjoyed about being a leather dyke. We rarely travel to leather events anymore; it's hard to find the time and space for intense play; and I'm 15 lbs. too big for my hottest outfits." But she accepts the changes and says, "I've found I can't have everything, but I'm happy and blessed with what I have."

With the birth of their child getting closer and closer, PJ sounds like she's ready for parenthood. "Right now everything seems to be like it is for every other pregnant couple getting ready for childbirth. We've done birthing classes and I feel like all the rest of the fathers in the room—the anticipation, the extra work, the preparations, all of it." PJ says she needs to get a workbench together—just like her father had—so she can fix things like bikes and skateboards and Rollerblades.

Vicki has had a difficult pregnancy and says it will be a relief when the pregnancy is over and her child is finally born. But more than that, she is excitedly looking forward to being a parent. She sounds refreshingly enthusiastic when she says, "I want to be involved with the PTA. I want to do bake sales and all that kind of stuff—I do! This is not a mistake. This is a choice—I'm choosing this person to be in my life, so I'm going for it!"

Wouldn't it be great if every child could be born into such welcoming circumstances?

Follow-up: PJ and Vicki now have two sons, both of whom have the same father.

Bisexuals and BDSM
Bisexual people in a pansexual community

Published in *Journal of Bisexuality* (Volume 1, Number 4, 2001)

Introduction

For many gay, lesbian, bisexual and transgendered (GLBT) people, the Holy Grail and the New Jerusalem of sexuality will be a world where it's okay for everyone to be who they are and to love whomever they choose. This applies both to one's gender (male, female, or anywhere in between) and to one's sexual orientation (homo, hetero, or anywhere else on Dr. Kinsey's scale).*

Is it possible that such a wondrous community already exists? Well, sort of. In recent years the pansexual leather/BDSM community has been formed by the alliance of elements from the gay male leather/SM community, the lesbian (and/or lesbian/feminist) leather/SM community, and predominantly heterosexual BDSM/fetish groups. This new community describes itself as "pansexual," meaning it's okay for everyone to play with everyone else. Such a pansexual atmosphere, where it truly doesn't matter to anyone what the gender of one's play partner is, could be just the thing a bisexual or bi-curious person would be looking for. That's the premise, but is it the reality?

Bisexuals in Today's Leather/BDSM Community

Does a bisexual orientation mean a person will also be interested in BDSM? Not necessarily, although my own personal experience has been that many of the people I've seen at bisexual conferences are also people I see at pansexual BDSM gatherings. And perhaps this stands to reason, because when one throws away society's rulebook and roles in one area, it's easier to do it in others. Freed of the man-on-top-woman-on-bottom rule, it's easier to explore different types of relationships, different ways of relating, different styles of intimacy—and this can be a gateway to BDSM.

---

*Kinsey's scale: 0 = exclusively heterosexual, 6 = exclusively homosexual. Your humble columnist is a 6.

But how pansexual is the BDSM community in reality? How accepting is it of bisexuals? I asked those questions of several community members. Jerry (not his real name) considers himself a 2 on Kinsey's 0-6 scale for coming to orgasm. But for BDSM play, "It really doesn't matter. Well, there's one way it matters—it gives a particular flavor to the scene. The same scene with a man or with a woman will be different scenes, but they both can be wonderful."

There are many reasons why Jerry finds BDSM play interesting and fulfilling: "The thing about BDSM that excites me is becoming aware of my body. You become involved and intimate with it in ways that go far beyond plain sex. We've been so hung up about sex in our society—sex is something you do in a dark room, preferably wearing blinders. Now we're getting more acquainted with our bodies through things like massage or tai chi. BDSM is another way of accomplishing this. It may not always lead to orgasm but it's still pretty terrific. It's dealing with parts of the body that are highly sensitive and eroticized; it just doesn't always have the same outcome as what we think of when we think of sex."

Jerry also likes the way BDSM blurs the boundaries and definitions of what's sexual, what's erotic, and what constitutes intimacy. And, he continues, "There's a political dimension to this, too. Large portions of the country are moving to the political right, and the moralists are telling us basically to reject our bodies, except where they want us to—excuse the hyperbole—adorn them with output from the capitalist system. The autonomous knowledge of who we are gets erased in the process. But it's interesting that there's this countertrend of BDSM. It opens up the consciousness of who we are through roleplaying, costume, or sensation. You have the opportunity to do all sorts of things that bring awareness and consciousness of your body out into the foreground—you have the opportunity to try new things. Bisexuality is the same—you can switch top and bottom roles, you can switch the gender of your partner."

Jerry says he has never felt any disrespect or rejection in the BDSM groups he's been a part of. He cites as an example his membership in a men-only BDSM club that holds annual retreats. At the retreat grounds, the heterosexual men (10%) post a banner outside their cabin proclaiming it the "Het Ghetto." But they still have no problem engaging in BDSM play with the other 90% of the attendees who are gay. This seems pretty typical of Jerry's experience with the pansexual BDSM community: "There's a lot of goodwill toward me as a bisexual person. The attitude is 'We're here to have a good time playing, and the expectation is that you ought to have as good a scene as possible, whoever you are.' The measure is in the quality of the scene, not the orientation of the people in it."

A Visit to Two Play Parties

An examination of the action at two recent play parties is a good indication of how pansexual the leather/BDSM community really is. One party was staged by a gay men's leather club, and all of the 150 people attending were male. Many of these men are still squeamish about having lesbian leatherwomen or kinky heterosexuals in their dungeon. But others are grudgingly accepting and some enthusiastically accepting of pansexual play. Some of these men have had bisexual leanings but it hasn't been okay to express them until recently.

Two weeks earlier a predominantly heterosexual group threw a play party in the same space, and the energy was quite different. Men were topping women, women were topping men, and women were playing with other women. But the only male-male play at the party was by two self-identified gay men.

Even among people who self-identify with the pansexual label, it's still apparently a bit too much of a stretch for supposedly "straight" men to play with other supposedly "straight" men in public at a play party. When asked about this, Jerry's analysis is that man-to-man play is still taboo for the same political reasons that drag is taboo—because it's seen as a bit embarrassing. Heterosexual men are uncomfortable watching men play together, because "to admit interest in that is to give up that position of privilege which is accorded to the heterosexual man." It's okay for women to wear men's clothes, but when men wear women's clothes we have to make fun of it—if it's taken seriously it's too threatening. For the same reason, while BDSM play has recently become a staple feature of advertising and the media, all the media presence for BDSM is very heterosexual—it would be too threatening otherwise.

Jerry notes that among the men attending this party, man-to-man play has been known to happen in private. "BDSM opens people up to exploration, but more on a local level, one couple at a time. In a club setting or a gay leather bar the roles are fixed already, so it's harder to bend them. But in private it's easier to get people to drop their roles and expectations, and to experiment."

Conclusion

So, is the pansexual BDSM community the first harbinger of a world where gays, lesbians, bisexuals and heterosexuals all respect each other, and maybe even feel free to play with each other? My assessment of the situation: Champions of pansexual BDSM may be on the cutting edge, but to date that edge is still a small one. While people in the BDSM community are willing to talk about the concept of pansexuality and to explore it intellectually, personal issues and biases mean that for many people the label "pansexual" is probably a bit ahead of reality. But the leather/BDSM community must be given credit for at least seeing the possibility of the concept, and for being further ahead than anyone else in making it a reality.

New Queers On The Block: Heterosexuals
... and don't call them "straight"
Published in *Lavender* #96 (January 29, 1999), reprinted several times in other publications

"Queer" seems to be the new umbrella term that's been chosen to be inclusive of all sexual minorities, such as gay, lesbian, bisexual and transgender people. Is that umbrella big enough to cover kinky heterosexuals as well? Historically the gay (predominantly men's) leather/SM community and the community of kinky heterosexual folk have been parallel worlds, with little interaction between them. Some folks might like to keep it that way, but increasingly there are powerful forces inspiring a convergence of the GLBT and heterosexual kink communities.

I first heard about the concept of "het queers" from Jonathan Krall, senior congressional advocate for the National Coalition for Sexual Freedom. He was in the Twin Cities this summer to address a meeting of TIES, a local pansexual group of kinky people that bills itself as "GLBTH" (you can guess what the "H" stands for). He finished his talk with this admonition to the audience: "Don't let anyone ever call you 'straight'."

It's not easy for kinky heterosexuals in today's society. They are in a no-win situation: They may look "straight," but they aren't, because according to society's rules straight people don't engage in kinky activities. They therefore have a choice: By being "straight acting and appearing" they can avoid the oppression and disdain that society reserves for the queer community—but they will be ignoring an important part of themselves in the process. Or they can be open and honest about their kinkiness, and society will reward them with the same disapproval it gives queers.

Actually, the disapproval may even be greater than that reserved for obvious queers, as if society were saying, "Well, we *knew* they were queer, so we wrote them off a long time ago. But we had such high hopes for you. You have a lovely spouse, 2.2 children, a stable job, a house in the suburbs. How can you be such a traitor to our ideals?" Marriages may break up over the revelation of one spouse's kinky proclivities; even if both partners are kinky, there's always the question of what to tell the children—and how to keep the rest of society from finding out, lest the children be taken away.

As a response to these types of oppression, the national heterosexual and GLBT leather/SM communities have joined forces to form The National Coalition for Sexual Freedom (NCSF), a lobbying group that is "working to reduce the discrimination faced by adults who engage in, write about, study, or describe alternative sexual practices in the United States." The NCSF includes gays, lesbians, bisexuals, heterosexuals, the transgendered, and individuals who self-identify as "none of the above." According to Executive Director Susan Wright, "It's time that Americans realized that one of our First Amendment rights is freedom of sexual expression. No one should ever have to suffer violence or discrimination because of their sexuality."

In most places the infrastructure of the heterosexual kink community is not yet as well developed as that of the gay leather/SM community; there are few equivalents to gay leather bars where they can meet like-minded individuals. In the Twin Cities there are several organized groups for kinky heterosexuals, but TIES (an acronym for "Tremendously Intense Erotic Situations") is the only one that is public enough to mention in print; the rest of the groups are composed of people who, for various reasons, need to keep their private lives private.

TIES hosts a monthly gathering (called a "munch") for members and non-members; attendance at December's munch was somewhere around 150 people over the course of the evening. There are monthly discussion groups for dominants, submissives and switches. There also is a TIES quarterly play party with attendance by invitation only. And there is an e-mail listserv featuring interesting discussions about topics ranging from serious (how do I tell my husband/wife that I want to experiment with SM?) to lighter subjects (BDSM shopping at Ax-Man, a local surplus store).

It was through the TIES e-mail listserv that I first got to know some of the members of TIES—a varied group of interesting people of all ages, genders, orientations and interests. Having followed the list for many months, and having attended two monthly munches, I am finding I have a lot more in common with them than I expected. If I had just assumed that we would have nothing in common because they're het and I'm gay, I would have missed meeting some very nice people.

I know some male members of the GLBT leather community who are not happy about the coming of pansexuality to the leather/SM scene. For them leather is about gay men relating to other gay men, and they are allowed to make that choice. I'm sure there are lesbian feminist leatherwomen for whom leather is a woman-to-woman scene. And there are probably heterosexuals who don't feel comfortable with the label "queer." To all of these people, I have said it before and I'll say it again: The leather/SM community is pansexual, crossing all gender and orientation boundaries. The people who make up that community, however, are not necessarily pansexual, and that's okay too.

That's an important distinction to keep in mind. If a group hosts a playspace and wishes to designate it as exclusively for lesbian activity, for instance, that's not politically incorrect. That's their prerogative, and it would seem to me rude for a group of men to crash the party. On the other hand, no one group or faction "owns" the leather community; in order to thrive it must be open and accessible to anyone who wants to identify with it and with its traditions and values, regardless of their sexual orientation, identity or expression.

Transgender Leather

Published in *Lavender* #111 (August 27, 1999)

Okay, so you're a proud member of the leather/BDSM community. If you're reading this column, the probability is highest that you're a gay white male (as is your humble columnist). But you, like your humble columnist, understand that something as wonderful as leather-sex must be open to everyone regardless of age, race, sex, orientation, and so on. So you try to be open-minded and accepting, even of women at the Minneapolis Eagle or heterosexuals in a dungeon.*

You're even trying to be open-minded about transgendered people in the leather/BDSM community. Here you may fall into one of two categories: either "I don't know any, but of course they would certainly be welcome" or "My goodness, they're everywhere—where are they all coming from? But they're certainly welcome." Too often, however, either of these sentiments is followed in the next breath with this disclaimer: "But of course I would never play with one."

My first response to this is, why not? My second response is, how do you know you haven't? Considering that much SM play is non-genital in nature, how can you be absolutely, positively sure that the person who flogged you last night (or the person whom you flogged) was not a trans person? Have you checked the chromosomes of everyone you've ever played with to be sure they matched the person's outward appearance?

Suppose you found out the next day (or next month, or next year) that the person you played with last night was a tranny. Would you feel differently about the experience? About the person? Why or why not?

If you feel comfortable with trans people, congratulations—you can skip the next part of this column. If you don't feel comfortable having trans people around, however, let me say this as gently as I can: Get Over It. Here are two different (and somewhat opposing) viewpoints to consider that may help you adjust your attitude:

---

*See previous columns on leatherwomen (page 110) and het queers (page 119).

Viewpoint #1: Think of a transgender orientation as a special asset instead of a liability. Consider that trans people are an interesting and diverse group. I seem to be getting to know more and more of them, so I say this from personal experience: They've seen a lot and been through a lot, and they have the stories to prove it. Their experience of questioning something about themselves that most of us take for granted tends to give them a special insight into themselves (and others, and society in general) that can be refreshing to be around.

Viewpoint #2: The words "transgender" and "transsexual" are labels. People aren't labels; if I look at a person and all I see is a label, I'm not really seeing that person. Instead of thinking of a transgender orientation as a special asset (as described above), don't think about it at all. Focus on a trans person as simply a person, and try relating to them as you would relate to any other human being. You might be pleasantly surprised. Maybe you'll make a new friend. You might even play together. Who knows what chemistry you'll find once you get that pesky label out of the way?

One final note: If you are at all curious about gender issues—perhaps your own, or perhaps in order to better understand a newfound transgender friend—read *My Gender Workbook* by Kate Bornstein.* Before seeing this book I thought gender was basically either male or female, and transgender people either went from female to male or male to female. (And they always used hormones and surgery to make the transition.) I now realize it's not always that simple. Here's just one example of a "nontraditional" transgender person: Joe knows he is male, in spite of the fact that he was born with a female's body. Joe is so sure he is male, in fact, that he sees no need to bother with hormones and surgery. So just have respect for his gender choice—call him Joe, and call him "him," and he's satisfied.

Gender comes in many different flavors, and it will be a lovely day when people can taste them all and choose their favorite with no apologies, shame or stigma.

---

*New York: Routledge, 1997.

Masters/slaves: Let's Be Careful Out There*

Published in *Lavender* #57 (August 1, 1997)

Of all the types of relationships in the leather/SM community, the Master/slave relationship is among the most intense. The relationship can only be considered safe, sane and consensual if both Master and slave are familiar with themselves, their partner, and the unique dynamics of this type of relationship. It's certainly not for everyone. At its best, it can fulfill both partners in a way nothing else can. At its worst, it can be horrifyingly—and criminally—abusive.

It was not long ago that a man in Duluth decided he wanted to be a master and have a slave. He picked someone up, brought him home, drugged him and locked him in a closet, thinking this would be a peachy way to break the man's will and turn him into a slave. After two days, he checked on his slave and found him dead. This is an extreme example of the tragic consequences of someone trying to play master without knowing the first thing about it.

The Master/slave relationship is about love and fulfillment, not exploitation and abuse. A Master's main responsibility is to do everything within his power to help his slave grow and develop. A Master is responsible for every aspect of his slave's well-being, including physical and emotional safety. (In the era of AIDS, this is an especially important consideration.) That can become a huge responsibility that very few are able to shoulder.

A slave's primary function is to please and serve his or her Master. A slave's primary function is not to serve as a whipping boy upon which the Master takes out his frustrations. And a Master's function is not to punish a slave who, because of feelings of low self-esteem, feels a need to be tortured or humiliated. A slave also has a responsibility to communicate to his Master what he needs to take care of himself—if he doesn't take care of himself, what will he have left to offer his Master? (Again, this is especially important if the slave is HIV-positive or has AIDS.)

Neither Master nor slave should enter into their relationship lightly. A novice Master can inflict horrible abuse on his unwitting

---

*Please keep in mind as you read this that the term "Masters" is intended to include all genders.

slave; a novice slave, who has no knowledge of what makes a good Master, can be taken advantage of and badly treated by a so-called "Master" who is only in it to get his own jollies and who doesn't care what happens to his slave. When this happens, it makes the institution of Master/slave relationships look bad, and gives a black eye to the entire leather/SM community as well.

Remember, Master/slave relationships still fall under the leather/SM community's rallying cry of "safe, sane, consensual." If it doesn't meet all three of these criteria, it constitutes abuse.

For more on safe/sane/consensual Master/slave relationships, including an excellent essay entitled "When Your slave Has AIDS," visit the Masters And slaves Together website.

New Book about Black Men in Leather
What does it mean to be a person of color
in the leather community?
Published in *Lavender* #108 (July 16, 1999)

If you're reading this column on a printed page, and you live in the midwestern United States, the overwhelming odds are that you are of white European ethnic extraction. If you're reading it in a city outside the midwest, or you're reading it on the Web, the odds may be less overwhelming, but "white European" is still a pretty safe guess.

The ideal image of the leather community (at least as it's held in the minds of those of white European ethnic origin) is that everyone is welcome, regardless of sex, gender, sexual preference, kink preference, or any of the other politically correct things people are not supposed to discriminate against these days. That theoretically includes race.

Look around at any local, regional, national or international leather event in the United States, however, and you might notice that you see a rainbow of faces, but you see a lot more of some colors than of others. Black people, Asian people, Latin Americans, Native Americans—each of these groups constitutes a minority (ethnic group) within a minority (leather/SM community) within a minority (GLBT community). Females or trans people can add another level of minority to that list. As a white male, I think the community is pretty accepting. But how do members of these various subminorities feel about that statement? If I stood in their boots, would I feel accepted? Not accepted? Patronized? Tokenized?

Cain Berlinger, long-time leather community member, writer and activist, has recently published *Black Men In Leather*.* In this landmark book, Berlinger explores how black men fit into the leather/SM community—or how they don't. He also addresses the issues that black leatherwomen and Asian leathermen may have with the leather community.

In the words of the author, "I was anxious to see the Leather Community through the eyes of people of color in gay America." The book is the result of several thousand surveys Berlinger distributed to people of color both in the leather community and outside it; the book therefore rings not only with author Berlinger's voice, but with the diverse voices of many other people who responded to his survey.

I stopped counting the number of subjects dealt with in this book that until now have seemed to be off-limits in leather literature. Take interracial partnerships, for example: If a black man looks for a white partner because a white man is more liable to be skilled in SM practices, is that bad, good or neutral? How about if the black man wants a white partner as a "trophy wife"?

How about "snow queens" (black men who like white men), "dinge queens" (white men who like black men), and "rice queens" (men who like Asian men)—does a preference for a particular ethnic group constitute racism, or is it just another fetish? (Or perhaps it's just a preference.)

Then there's the extremely sensitive topic of race play. Is it okay within the context of a scene for a white man playing a plantation owner to "punish" a black man taking the part of the slave? What about a black "plantation owner" punishing a white "slave"? What about scenes involving white "cops" and black "criminals," or vice versa?

Especially up here in the northland, if we're white we're not used to thinking about issues like these. We'd rather believe the politically correct and comfortable notion that we live in a colorblind community where we've transcended the issue of race. This is a book that's

*Tempe, Arizona: Third Millennium Publishing. 2nd edition, 2006.

concerned with neither political correctness nor comfort—it's more concerned with being a reality check, and as such it pulls no punches. It doesn't pretend to offer easy solutions (of which there are none), but it does an excellent job of describing and illuminating the many complex issues regarding race and the leather community. I found it thought-provoking, fascinating, sometimes disturbing, but ultimately mind-expanding.

Even Daddies Need Daddies
Leather and aging
Published in *Lavender* #164 (September 7, 2001)

A question I constantly ask myself is "Why can't the rest of the world be more like the leather community?" Today's case in point: Age, aging and ageism.

So much of the world today is obsessed with youth. General-audience fashion and entertainment revolve around images of people (models, actors, entertainers, musicians) in their teens or twenties— and these already youthful images have been retouched to make them look even younger and more perfect. A huge cosmetics industry has been built on "reducing the appearance of aging." People want to deny aging, because they know that as they grow older they become less desirable and more disposable. But they grow older anyway, and they find themselves lusting after someone younger. Having a young, beautiful trophy wife (or husband) on their arm, they think, will say to the world that even though they've gotten older they still have what it takes. (That's what they think; actually, they often suffer from the comparison.)

Unfortunately, a large segment of the gay male community mirrors this behavior. There are certain bars, coffeehouses and other gay gathering spots where "older" is defined as over age 35. At the other end of the scale are establishments snidely referred to as "wrinkle rooms," hangouts frequented by primarily older gay men and visited by younger men only because they either want to find a sugar daddy or laugh at the—another unkind word here—"trolls." The trophy wife concept is mirrored in the gay male community by the concept of the "kept boy," whose sole function in life is to live at the gym and in the tanning booth in order to present a testament to his partner's virility.

Members of the gay male leather community (and the bear community as well) tend to think differently about the whole concept of age, whether our own or someone else's. A person's age tends to be just another physical attribute like hair color or shoe size. We notice a person's age, but we tend not to value or devalue them because of it. Instead, we as a community tend to celebrate all ages. We cherish our young men (some of whom call themselves "boys") for their beauty, their energy and their potential. But we also cherish our elders (some of whom call themselves "daddies") for their history, their experience, their knowledge—and their beauty, energy and potential.

Visit any leather contest, or flip through a leather-themed calendar, and you'll see hot men of all ages. Our community's elders are anything but disposable, as evidenced by the popular t-shirt that reads "Even Daddies Need Daddies."

Where else would other men realistically and respectfully consider a gay man of age 55, 65 or 75 to be beautiful, attractive, desirable and sexy? Where else could that man have an image of himself as a beautiful, attractive, desirable and sexy man—and not worry he was delusional? Where else can a man of age 55 get together with a man of age 30 and not be called a chicken hawk?* Where else can an older man pursue a younger man, or a younger man pursue an older man, and not set tongues wagging?

Something about the leather and bear communities encourages people to be real. It's okay to look our age and to act our age, whatever that age is. That quality of "real" can be very sexy. Gray hair or beards can be sexy. Balding or shaved heads can be extremely sexy. On the other hand, bad toupees, comb-overs, obvious dye jobs and other attempted deceptions aren't generally considered sexy. Trying to look 45 when you're 60 isn't real, and it isn't pretty.

Maybe, for purposes of perpetuating the species, an obsession with youth used to make sense. If I were a man who wanted to keep my genes circulating in the gene pool, I would look for a young partner at the peak of her childbearing years. Life spans used to be

---

*"Chicken hawk": an derogatory term for an older man who pursues "chicken," a derogatory term for younger men. Notice that in this scenario no one, regardless of age, escapes derogation.

much shorter, so we would want to start having children right away, so we could raise them to adulthood before we died. And if we lived on a farm we'd want to have a lot of kids because they could help with the chores.

Well, it's the twenty-first century. Life spans are longer; people are having kids later in life; and families are smaller. Maybe, in another couple hundred years, society won't be so obsessed with youth because it won't need to be.

In the meantime, I am thankful that I belong to such a non-ageist community. What a gift it is, what a luxury, to be able to enjoy men of all ages, and to know that as I get older I will continue to be able to enjoy them.

The Next Generation of Leather
Published in Lavender #194 (November 1, 2002)

Leather, like almost every other community these days, has to deal with a generation gap. Our version is called Old Guard vs. New Guard, and it can make the routine battles of parents and teenagers look like high tea. Here is a brief snippet of typical dialogue—or rather, two monologues—from the two camps:

Old Guard: New Guard, you say you're the future of leather? Boy, are we in trouble! You're undisciplined, you're disrespectful, you're slovenly! You think you know everything, but take it from me—you know nothing! You're hopeless! Why should I waste my time trying to whip you into shape—so to speak—when you show absolutely no interest in shaping up, getting your act together, and doing it right?

New Guard: Old Guard, you're old fogies! You're still fighting World War II, or at least Vietnam! The world has changed, but you haven't! People don't go for all that hierarchy and discipline stuff any more, and most of your vaunted protocols are just so tired! Why would I want to play those games? Just because I'm young doesn't mean I want to be your apprentice for the next 20 years! What do you have to teach me anyway? Who said your way was the only right way? Who made you leather god?

It didn't used to be like this. For the first several decades of the leather community's existence there was no Old Guard vs. New Guard.

Those expressing an interest in leather were mentored by those already in the community; in this way the community's knowledge, traditions and values were passed down from generation to generation. The AIDS epidemic destroyed this system of mentoring, as described by noted leather author and International Mr. Leather 1989 Guy Baldwin in a recent speech:

"... the old leather tribal elders ... became distracted by the need to help care for their own brothers who were suddenly fighting for their lives, and all too often, losing the battles ... the tribal elders simply no longer had the time or the emotional energy necessary to focus on bringing new 'children' into the fold. And just as in any culture, whenever elders can't make time for their children, those elders become irrelevant as children strike out on their own to explore their interests ... whatever they happen to be."

So that's the problem. What do we do about it? Here's a starting suggestion: You know all the advice and cliches about parenting and raising children that you've heard over the years? Some of us who didn't have kids thought we could safely ignore them. But—guess what—they apply now, to our community. The elders are parenting the community, and the next generation represents their leather offspring. They don't call them Daddies for nothing.

So, what do leather parents need to know? First let me say that your humble columnist writing about parenting is like a priest offering marriage counseling. So I am indebted to Stephen Covey's book *The Seven Habits of Highly Effective People** for this bit of parenting wisdom:

"There are only two lasting bequests we can give our children—one is roots, the other wings."

Ponder that for a moment. Let it sink in.

We can give the next generation of leather roots by remembering, respecting and honoring our leather traditions and those in leather who have gone before us. The Leather Archives & Museum in Chicago is so important because it's all about roots. So is the heritage of leather clubs. We also give the next generation of leather roots through

---

*New York: Free Press (imprint of Simon & Schuster). 15th anniversary edition, 2004.

education that goes beyond mere technique—by modeling and sharing our community's heart, soul and values. There's more to BDSM than just technique, and there's more to leather than just BDSM.

Because of the huge hole left in the community's structure by AIDS, the New Guard felt it was in the position of having to reinvent the wheel. A sense of roots lets the next generation of leather know the who and the how and the why of the community, so they don't have to reinvent the wheel—they just have to update it.

We give the next generation of leather wings by giving them freedom—by letting them update that wheel. They're not us. They will do things differently, and their leather community will reflect them, just as today's leather community is a reflection of us.

We can't know what the future holds—who could have seen AIDS coming? But we do know one thing the future holds: change. I've seen leather change since I started writing this column in 1995, and it will continue to change and evolve. It won't stay the same. If we try to keep it the same—if we don't let it change—it will die. We will kill it.

As we pass the leather torch to the next generation, we can't tie their hands—so to speak—by saying, "Here, we bequeath this to you—*but you must always do it like this.*" What kind of estate planning is that? Besides, we won't be around to check up on whether they're doing it "right." All we can really do is to foster a next generation who understands leather, respects it, cherishes it, and is smart enough to make good decisions about its evolution.

And now, a later reflection on . . .

Leather's Next Generation
Published in *Lavender* #318 (August 3, 2007)

"Where are the young people in the leather community? Where's the new blood? Where's the next generation?" Over the last few years I've participated in many discussions centering on these questions, and I've written at least a few columns that touched on them. I thought they were good and worthwhile questions to ponder, and ponder them I did. But did I have an answer? Nope.

Now I think I might have one, at least partially. But the answer I think I've discovered isn't what I would have expected.

The series of questions above are presented as three aspects of the same question, but they really aren't as related as they seem. If we as a community assume they are, we will not be doing ourselves any favors.

Since the beginning of the year I have been quite pleased to see several new faces at leather events. I have talked to many of these individuals, asking who they are and what brought them to that particular event. After hearing several similar stories I have come to realize a few things about the future of our community.

I'm happy to report I don't think leather is in danger of dying out anytime soon, any more than the GLBT community will be disappearing. In both instances, every day more community members discover and claim their membership. The process has been going on for some time now in both communities, and I believe it will continue.

But while the age at which people identify as gay, lesbian, bisexual or transgender seems to be getting younger, it appears to me this is not what's happening with leather. If anything, judging solely from the new faces I've seen in leather recently, many people are finding leather later in life. That's not what I personally would have expected, but that seems to be what I'm encountering.

Now that I've noticed this, I guess it stands to reason. Major life changes offer people opportunities for reassessing their personal history—where they've been, what they've done, where it's gotten them—and perhaps making some course corrections. The kids are grown; a job disappears; a relationship ends; suddenly there's a freedom and an opportunity to explore parts of oneself that formerly, for one reason or another, couldn't be explored. The start of my leather journey was triggered by just such a major life change, and I've talked to many others who can say the same thing.

But these kinds of life changes don't—can't—happen to people in their twenties. People in their twenties can't be empty-nesters. They can't end a decades-long relationship because they haven't lived long enough to have one.

Many, many years ago, your humble columnist came out as a gay man at age 19. I didn't get into leather until I was 37. Getting into leather took me almost twice as long as coming to terms with my gayness.

People discover leather when they're ready to discover it. Some people do it early, others do it later. Fortunately, there's no rush—

leather is one of the few communities where "sexy" is not necessarily linked to "young."

But even though our community prides itself on not being age-discriminatory, when we expect and assume our community's "new blood" and "next generation" will be young people—isn't that being a bit ageist? While we're busy wondering where the younger folks are, and worrying about reaching them and bringing them into the fold, we might be overlooking many, many people who may not be young but are certainly interested and enthusiastic.

Perhaps it's time we realized that "new blood" can be any age, and started to think a bit differently about the future of the community and how we reach out to leather's next generation.

For many years, one of the guiding principles of twelve-step recovery programs has been "attraction, not promotion." Noted leather author and speaker Guy Baldwin has suggested that this same principle be applied to leather, and I second the motion. Rather than trying to figure out how to get a younger crowd interested in leather, wouldn't our community be better served by simply 1) being who we are, and 2) being visible? If we do those two things, we will attract people—of all ages—who like what they see in us and want to join us.

At that point it doesn't really matter what mileage is on someone's odometer. Once they realize they're interested in leather—when they're 20 years old, 40, 60, whatever—what they need and want is someone willing to welcome them, show them the ropes and explain how leather works. If they are provided with that, they will be part of the future of leather.

"Circuit Boys in Rented Leathers"*

Published in *Lavender* #99 (March 12, 1999)

Is leather a fashion statement or a way of life? Warning: This is a trick question.

Leather is not one or the other. Wearing leather or other fetishwear is always a fashion statement, and a pretty strong one. The real question is whether, for a given individual, it's only a fashion statement, or if it

---

*When this column was first published the headline had been changed (not by me), in a fit of political correctness, to "Circuit Boys and Girls in Rented Leathers."

goes further and reflects a way of life. But even for the most hard-core and dedicated member of the leather community, the act of dressing in leather and other fetishwear makes a fashion statement.

What is the primary goal of fashion? At minimum, it's to look attractive. But those models strutting down the runway in Milan or Paris aren't stopping at attractive—they're going for sexy, seductive, alluring. Fashion is about sex appeal, and it's also about the power over others that comes with being sexually appealing. But, of course, nobody ever talks about it in such blatant terms—that wouldn't be polite. No, we spend huge sums of money on clothing because "we just want to look nice."

Leather and other fetishwear is about sex appeal and power, too, but it's not hidden behind a veil of politeness. When I wear leather or other fetishwear, I am sending a very distinct message about myself and my sexuality—what I have to offer and what I'm looking for. This is epitomized by the unashamed convenience of the hankie code, an invention that has yet to catch on in "polite" society.

For some people, wearing leather goes further. It becomes a reflection of a way of life, a set of values, a worldview, a type of spirituality. Other people use it as a fashion statement and nothing more. I've been at many large leather gatherings where at some point I've heard some of the former people trashing the latter. The old-guard, heavy-duty SM player will smugly and disrespectfully refer to the "circuit boys in their rented leathers." To be truthful, at one time some of you may have heard *me* refer to someone that way.

"Circuit boys in rented leathers" is the cliche, but it undoubtedly happens in women's, het and pansexual situations as well. Sometimes it's obvious that a person doesn't know how to wear the apparel properly; I once saw someone wearing their harness backwards, which many people in the bar that evening found amusing. Other times there are more subtle clues that a person isn't used to wearing leather—things just don't look right. Another giveaway: Everything they're wearing looks brand new and straight off the rack. To paraphrase the Saloon ads: "Your leather will betray you."* And when it

---

*This refers to an ad campaign run in *Lavender* by The Saloon, a Minneapolis gay bar. "Your body will betray you" was the tagline of the campaign.

does, reactions from "real" leatherfolk may range from mild amusement to an indignant tirade.

Lately, I've tried to be less judgmental. Hey, everyone has to start someplace. The first piece of leather I ever wore was a borrowed harness, and I was totally unprepared for the feeling I got when I put it on. I felt transformed. At the risk of being politically incorrect, it was like Cinderella must have felt as her rags were changed into a ball gown. Wearing that harness to the leather bar that evening (Rod's in Madison, Wisconsin) I got cruised like I had never been cruised before.* It was heady stuff. (Yes, I was wearing the harness correctly, smart aleck—see the final paragraph of this column.) Shortly thereafter I bought my first piece of leather. Now I've got a whole closetful.

Some of the people being ridiculed for their "rented leathers" are having experiences just like that. Some of them are in the process of their leather coming-out and will become tomorrow's leather community stalwarts.

And some of them aren't interested in discovering a deeper part of themselves—they're wearing leather because they know they look hot in it and they want to get laid. They may not fully realize the statement they're making by wearing leather, or they may not care. But just because they may appear clueless today doesn't mean they'll always be that way. If they aren't ostracized, they might eventually come to a fuller understanding and appreciation of leather as a culture and a way of life.

Rather than criticizing or ridiculing, how about mentoring? When I wore that borrowed harness, I wore it correctly because its owner showed me how to put it on properly. When a harness is worn backwards it shows a need for education, not ridicule.

---

*Sadly, Rod's, and in fact the entire Hotel Washington complex of which Rod's was a part, has since burned to the ground.

Chapter 7

Night Life

An Evening at The Minneapolis Eagle
Published in *Lavender* #216 (September 5, 2003)

Let's continue our journey into leather culture by visiting one of the places from which the leather community sprang: a bar.

Since The Minneapolis Eagle opened five years ago, I've heard many men say something like this: "Well, I've tiptoed up to the Eagle and stuck my nose in, but I could never actually *go in there!*" Evidently, quite a few *Lavender* Magazine readers have actually "gone in there," and they liked it so much they chose The Minneapolis Eagle as "OutStanding Bar to Meet Men."*

For many years bars have been an important social center for the gay male community. Gay bars were a safe place, a shelter from the outside world, where people could be themselves without fear of harassment. Bars were places to meet people of like mind, to converse, to dance, to watch a drag show or other entertainment, to cruise (or just to people-watch), or to hook up for a night or a lifetime. Bars were our turf, our territory.

For the gay male leather/biker community that evolved after World War II, bars filled the same purposes, and still fill them today.

There are many leather bars across the United States and Canada and throughout Europe and Australia. Their names are often some variety of masculine homoerotic double-entendre (such as "The

---

*The theme of *Lavender* #216 was the "OutStanding" awards.

Barracks" or "The Tool Box"), but probably the most ubiquitous name for a leather bar is "The (insert city here) Eagle." If you're in a major city and want to find the place where leathermen, bears and other masculine gay men congregate, the local Eagle is a good place to start.

The various Eagles are not members of a chain; each is independently owned and run and each has its own unique flavor. Here's a description of the flavor of The Minneapolis Eagle on a typical Friday night.

9:45 P.M.: Things are just getting going. The music is lively but not overwhelming. The bartender greets me with a friendly nod (he's the man for May in this year's "Men of the Eagle" calendar). The manager of a local leather store is setting up a leather vending area by the front door. Two guys sitting on one barstool are sucking face, oblivious to the rest of the world around them. And two other guys leave—they must have hooked up early.

The lighting, both from the art-deco fixtures behind the bar and the utility lamps hanging overhead, is almost all red. Two TVs are showing a tape of the 1996 International Mr. Leather contest, while a third shows a continuing series of what appear to be amateur near-porn photos harvested from the Internet.

The Atons leather/levi club of Minneapolis is having its monthly fetish night, this month's theme being rubber and latex. The club's president is sitting at a table, brushing layer after layer of liquid latex on a pair of waders. He was supposed to be having the liquid latex brushed on him, but he had an unfortunate depilatory accident that left his skin unfit for the exercise.

10:45 P.M.: Next door to The Minneapolis Eagle is another bar, The Bolt. Both bars are under the same ownership, and they're connected by a roll-up door that's open most of the time. But the roll-up door is closed now, and the bootshine area is set up in front of it. Fridays and Saturdays after 9 P.M., when The Minneapolis Eagle's dress code is enforced, the only way to get from one bar to the other is either from the street or through the outdoor patio in back that is shared by both bars.

I go back to the patio to check out what's happening there, but it's a sultry evening and the crowd on the patio is small. I return to

The Eagle, and suddenly I'm struck by the fact that there is very little traditional cruising going on here. The crowd is not lining the walls, quietly staring at every man who passes by. Everyone is engaged in conversation in groups of two, three or more, scattered gloriously helter-skelter around the bar. I also notice that the music is kept low enough that conversation is possible.

11 P.M.: It's hard to move. It's crowded—there are men everywhere. An intense game of pool is going on; several people are leaning against the back wall, watching and commenting. One of them is Mr. Minnesota Leather 1990 (the very first), who is watching his husband—"Yes," he says, "we're both husbands"—shooting pool. The line of quarters on the edge of the pool table indicates that it will be busy all night. Another gentleman leans against the back wall, watches the pool game, and smokes a cigar—"a Butera, with a B," he says when I ask him what kind of cigar it is.

I notice the club colors of the Atons and Black Guard, two local leather/levi clubs, decorating the back wall. There are also posters from other leather bars, some of them long gone. It's comforting to see our history on display. On a shelf toward the ceiling are many trophies and plaques for various Minneapolis Eagle softball teams.

11:30 P.M.: I make my way to the front of the bar. There are now two guys manning the leather shop area, helping a customer try on a leather vest. The on-site ATM is busy—a bearish guy in a sleeveless flannel shirt, cutoff jeans, a Van Dyke and a hardhat gets money while another guy stands in line watching him.

Midnight: It's even harder to move in the bar now than it was earlier. A buff gentleman with a shaved head and no shirt bumps into me. In the butchest of voices and without a trace of campiness, he very politely apologizes by saying, "Excuse me, dear." Chivalry is not dead.

I notice many non-white faces. It's about time. I also notice that everyone is interacting with everyone else rather than maintaining skin-color cliques. It's about time for that, too.

1:30 P.M.: One gentleman has stripped down to bare-ass chaps. The patio is jammed. The sound system is playing "Believe" by Cher (she's in town tonight).

This evening I've seen camo fatigues and I've seen a very impressive chain harness. Some guys have been wearing leather, some have been bearish, some have straddled both categories and some haven't fit into either. But regardless of what they're wearing, for the most part each man here has at least one thing in common—as one man puts it, "There's a little more maturity here than you find at some other places."

The Eagle stays active until 2:30 A.M., but I don't. On the way to the door I see a gentleman wearing a t-shirt that says, in large type, "This place isn't for everyone." In smaller type it says "(Thank God.)"

The Nonverbal Language of Leather
Published in *Lavender* #283 (March 31, 2006)

Leather's use of symbols for non-verbal social communication is conscious, intentional, creative, inventive—and relentless. A person in leather is a veritable billboard. If you know how to parse the symbols, everything means something.

Let's start with the basic concept of left and right. Items worn on the left (keys, armbands, wristbands, floggers, hankies sticking out of pockets) indicate the wearer is a top or prefers the active role. Such items worn on the right indicate the wearer is a bottom or prefers the passive role. Items worn in the middle indicate the wearer is a "switch" and can be flexible.

In social situations this left/right marking is handy. If you're talking to someone face to face, and their accessories are on the same side as yours, that means you might be a good match.

If their accessories are not on the same side as yours, you are talking to another person who prefers the same role you prefer. In that case there's nothing to stop you from switching your armband from one side to the other—unless they do it first.

One of leather's most celebrated methods of nonverbal communication is the hankie code—displaying hankies in one's back pocket whose colors correspond to various erotic activities in which the wearer is interested. According to one source, the practice comes from the San Francisco gold rush of 1849. Since the miners were mostly men, at evening dances they used back-pocket bandanas to indicate who was willing to lead (left pocket) or be a "girl" (right pocket). The modern hankie code started in the 1970s, when it was seen as a good way to visually signal sexual preferences in a noisy bar.

Communicating by using the hankie code is known as "flagging," as in "See that guy flagging red right? Maybe you should go talk to him."

If you see someone flagging a color that dovetails with your interests, go strike up a conversation and see what develops. You can also flag your interests, and maybe someone will strike up a conversation with you.

Ideally you'll both be wearing the same color, but in opposite pockets. This is no guarantee there will be any attraction or chemistry between you, of course. But if the attraction and/or chemistry is there, the hankies can make a nice conversation-starter.

There are readily available lists of the different colors of hankies and what they mean. A short list might contain the ten or fifteen most popular colors; the most complete list I've ever seen covered two full pages in a magazine.

If the idea of having to memorize all those colors seems overwhelming, just remember that a) you can always have a cheat sheet in your wallet, and b) you only have to memorize the colors that reflect your interests.

Regional variations to the hankie code exist, and in the dim light of a leather bar it can be difficult to tell the difference between certain colors. When in doubt, ask, and see where the conversation goes.

Other apparel items that communicate status include hats, harnesses, collars (padlocked or not) and even button-fly jeans (certain buttons left unbuttoned).

Almost every surface of every garment is open to decoration that reveals something about the wearer — club patches, run pins, a studded vest or belt displaying a leather title. Even the decorations on a person's skin — tattoos and piercings — communicate something.

This non-verbal language of leather evolved because it's an efficient method of communicating if you know the code, and it's hidden in plain sight if you don't. It lets us screen to see if another person is "one of us," if they "speak the language."

There was a time when this was necessary, and perhaps it still is. But some people are starting to wonder if this colorful and rich language is marginalizing us.

Might the codes and protocols of leather be a turn-off to people, especially younger people, who don't see the need to buy a new wardrobe and learn a new language in order to participate? If leather seems to lack an influx of younger people, that might be one reason why.

Victorian-era society had a rigid set of rules, codes and signs for courtship. Ladies of the era used their fans, gloves and parasols to signal interest, or lack thereof, to their male suitors. Someday the hankie code might seem as quaint.

On the other hand, author John T. Molloy's 1970s-era *Dress for Success* books were popular because they demystified the code of corporate business dress. Three decades later, not much has changed —it's still true that wearing the wrong clothes can get in the way of career advancement.

Codes come and go. Some say the hankie code and leather's other non-verbal signals are being made obsolete by the Internet. Yet a recent Internet search for "hankie code" showed that the idea is being appropriated by other people. (Christian hankie code, anyone?) Maybe the hankie code's ultimate destiny is to be yet another gift from leather to mainstream society.

The Zen of Hankies

Published in *Lavender* #324 (October 26, 2007)

> *Hankie haiku here*
> *The Zen of the hankie code*
> *Read and you will know*
>
> *Red hankie on left*
> *You want to shove your fist where?*
> *That sounds good to me*
>
> *Dark red hankie right*
> *I handle two fists at once*
> *Even both of yours*
>
> *Black right masochist*
> *Breathlessly says thank you sir*
> *May I have one more?*
>
> *Grey in right pocket*
> *I am a bondage bottom*
> *Tie me up tightly*

Charcoal hankie left
Rubber top looks for bottom
Latex is sexy

Mr. Businessman?
I'm flagging grey flannel right
Do you wear a suit?

Black and white checked left
I am into safer sex
I hope you are too

Yellow stripe on chaps
I am into watersports
I don't mean swimming

Mustard hankie right
Tonight I'll be a size queen
Got a big package?

Gold hankie on left
We are a loving couple
Looking for one more

Gold lamé flagged right
I like my men with muscles
Love your great physique

Apricot flagged right
Chubby means there's more to love
I like them beefy

Tan in left or right
Cigar is just a cigar?
Let's play and find out

Rust in left pocket
Cowboy seeking horse to ride
Yippee ki yi yay

Coral hankie left
Little piggies at market
Suck my toes, baby

Light pink right pocket
My tits are wired to my groin
Play with my nipples

Dark pink left pocket
I like to wield a dildo
Let me work on you

Fuchsia on left
Have you been a naughty boy?
Someone needs spanking

Lavender flagged right
You're looking at a drag queen
Worship the diva

Red and white striped left
I like razors and lather
Need a shave, mister?

Purple left pocket
Looking for a piercing scene
Where's my pincushion?

Olive drab on left
Military drill sergeant
Follow orders, boy

Hunter green on right
Stud muffin boy on a quest
Are you my daddy?

Hustler here for hire
Kelly green in left pocket
I'm yours for a price

Robin's egg blue left
Let us sing the glories of
The number 69

Medium blue left
Policeman wanting action
Obey the officer

White in right pocket
Brought to you by J and O
Simply the basics

Leopard hankie left
Let me show you my tattoos
I'm a work of art

Teddy bear flagged left
Want someone to cuddle with
Lots of big bear hugs

Tie-dyed hankie left
I'm a hippie and a top
Peace and love, brother

Cocktail napkin left
Wanna bed a bartender?
My shift ends at 2

Chamois left pocket
My motorcycle's outside
Wanna come see it?

Doily right pocket
I'm a tearoom toe tapper
Check out my wide stance

Stereo plug left
*Sound system will fuck your ears**
While I do the rest

Orange hankie left
I'm open to anything
What you got in mind?

For a rainbow tribe
A rainbow hankie spectrum
Now you understand

---

*I offered the magazine "rock your ears" in case they didn't want to use "fuck."
They published the column using "fuck."

When I submitted the "Hankie Haiku" column to Lavender *I included a photo of blue, red, black and black/white checked hankies stuffed into my partner Bill's left jeans pocket. I also sent them the following note with the photo:*

In a blinding flash of the obvious, I just realized that the photo, should you use it, might need a cutline—and why not haiku there, too? Choice of two:

Hankies shown above:
Top cop fisting S&M
And safer sex, too

Or, more generically:

What do hankies mean?
Study lines of poetry
Mystery is solved

Are Leather Dress Codes Discriminatory?

Published in *Lavender* #37 (October 25, 1996)

Lavender recently received a letter that asked:

"When I go into the LaFemme Show Lounge,* I don't have to wear drag. When I go into the Triangle Corral, I don't have to wear a cowboy hat. When I go into the Dance Annex, I don't have to wear dancing shoes.

"Why is it that when I am invited to *pay* for admission to the Men's Room for a Leather Community event, I am told that a dress code will be enforced. Does this mean that the Leather Community is excluding other factions of the total Gay Community? I'm especially interested because several times you have given the advice that if a person thinks he may be interested in the Leather Community he should attend a couple of events. That means I have to buy the leather *before* I make my decision."

Mention the words "leather dress code" and a heated discussion will probably ensue. Some people feel they're discriminatory; others

---

*A popular drag-show venue, part of the Gay 90s Entertainment Complex in downtown Minneapolis. All the other bars mentioned in this column are also parts of the Gay 90s.

wonder why the Twin Cities doesn't have a leather bar with a dress code enforced seven nights a week, not just on special occasions.

New York City is large enough to support a leather bar called LURE with a dress code that's always enforced. LURE is an acronym for "Leather, Uniform, Rubber, Etc.," which is the dress code that is very concisely spelled out at the entrance. No tennis shoes, no polo shirts, no chinos, no cologne or aftershave.

This is not the Fashion Police at work. This is a business trying to please its customers; the dress code is there in response to, and with the support of, LURE's primary clientele. This is no different from an upscale restaurant requesting that gentlemen wear neckties.

Leather events in the Twin Cities use the leather dress code for the same reason: to get more people to attend. The leather clubs and other organizers of these events don't want to exclude those who may be curious about the community but haven't yet acquired any leather; on the contrary, they want to encourage these people to investigate the Scene. This is why the dress code at most events includes "Levi/Shirtless." The combination of jeans and a bare chest is a masculine look appropriate to the event, and just about everyone already owns a pair of jeans.

A drag show is just that: a show. The performers are on stage to be slightly outrageous, to titillate and to entertain the public. To paraphrase Liberace, they don't dress that way to be ignored. The patrons at a leather bar, on the other hand, are there to enjoy the atmosphere and each other's company, not to be part of a floorshow. So leather dress codes *do* aim to exclude "tourists," i.e. people who don't understand or respect leather and its ethos—who think leather is just another form of drag show and who want to be scandalized by these "brutes who are fruits." People like this are pretty easy to spot in a leather bar, and they are not appreciated.

Dress Codes: "Because We Said So"
Published in *Lavender* #243 (September 17, 2004)

Leather dress codes are a perennial topic of discussion among both those who are into leather and those who are not. Some people resent being kept out of a popular gathering place because they aren't wearing the proper attire. It is their belief that this is America, and dress codes are an infringement upon their God-given right to go to any bar they damn well please. Others point to the regimented sameness of the attire and dismiss those inside as "clones."

Then there are those of us who are grateful for our leather community's spaces, such as The Minneapolis Eagle. We appreciate the effort that goes into creating the leatherspace and into formulating, maintaining and enforcing the dress code.

As dress codes at leather bars go, The Minneapolis Eagle's is pretty typical. You can find it at the bar's website, but I'll save you the trouble. Headlined "because we said so," here it is:

"Acceptable:
- Leather Jackets, Pants, Vests, Straps, Chaps, Dresses, Skirts, Shorts and Accessories
- Rubber, Vinyl, Latex and Plastic
- Law Enforcement and Fire Protection
- Military Uniform
- Construction Gear
- Western Wear
- You can also gain entry with a solid black, grey or white t-shirt, denim jeans (black or blue) and black leather boots.

"Unacceptable:
- Dress Shirts, Sweaters or Polo Shirts
- Dress Pants or Khakis
- Dress Shoes or Loafers
- Sandals or Tennis Shoes
- Suits & Ties or Tuxedos
- Disco Wear"

The Minneapolis Eagle's dress code is enforced Fridays and Saturdays after 9 P.M. and is encouraged but optional Sunday through Thursday nights. Even if you are not wearing appropriate attire, if you are already in the bar when the dress code takes effect you will be allowed to remain—you will not be asked to leave. But see below.

I've been thinking about the topic of dress codes quite a bit lately because the company for which I work (no, not *Lavender*— my other job, the one with a major national discount retailer) recently dropped their "Business Casual" code and ratcheted things up a notch to simply "Business." That means that Monday through Thursday

I have to wear either a sport coat or a tie, neither of which I have heretofore normally worn at work. For many years I was able to state proudly that my regular, day-to-day style of dress was such that at any given moment I could have met the dress code at any leather bar. One of the concessions I made when I started working at the major national discount retailer was to start wearing Dockers and polo shirts.

Under the new dress policy, should I someday show up at work without either a sport coat or a tie I can be "sent home to change." To me that's the same thing as being denied admission to the Eagle because I'm wearing dress slacks. I might not like it, but those are the rules.

As one might expect, the change in the dress code has sparked a certain amount of grumbling among my coworkers. I even contributed to the grumbling—before heading off to the-department-store-that-was-recently-sold-by-the-major-national-discount-retailer-for-which-I-work and buying up a storm. If government statistics show that the nation's economy improved in August, I'm the reason.

And why did I spend so much money to comply with the new dress code? Because I want to continue working there. That, and because I was able to take advantage of some really good discounts.

Why do I have a closet full of leather and related apparel? Because sometimes I like to hang out at the Eagle. That, and because I like wearing leather. I also like being around other people who are wearing leather. And I don't like feeling like a tourist. (In leather parlance, a "tourist"* is someone in a leather bar who sticks out because he or she is not wearing leather or other appropriate attire. If you are not appropriately attired and you stay at the Eagle when the dress code takes effect at 9 P.M. on Friday or Saturday, you risk being branded a tourist.)

Actually, now that I've been sensitized to the issue, I see that dress codes, both spoken and unspoken, are more pervasive than I ever realized. Just today, as I was walking from the parking ramp to my office at the major national discount retailer's corporate headquarters, I passed a construction site. There, in big, bold letters, was the following proclamation, a "dress code" of sorts: "100% Hard Hat Area/100%

---

*As noted previously on page 146.

Protective Eyewear/100% Fall Protection." I was wondering what constituted Fall Protection, and what made Fall Protection different from Summer Protection or Winter Protection, until I realized that they probably meant "protection against falling"—like cables and harnesses, for instance. (Hmmm . . . construction workers . . . cables . . . harnesses . . . .)

But I digress. In a heavy construction area there are good reasons— like health, safety and protection—to mandate what workers wear. Mandating dress elsewhere, whether in a corporate setting or a leather bar, is done for other reasons—primarily to create an atmosphere that represents and reflects what is most appropriate for what takes place in that atmosphere.

After years of too often being inappropriate (and suffering the consequences), I have learned the value of appropriateness.

So if the management and customers of The Minneapolis Eagle support the idea of a leather dress code, I will wear appropriate dress to the Eagle. And I will be rewarded by being surrounded by leather, uniforms and other butch attire.

And if the major national discount retailer decides that it wants to project a Fashion Forward image, I will appropriately spiff up my act. My reward will be that everyone else will spiff up their act, too, and I will be working in an upscale atmosphere with people who are nicely dressed.

On the other hand, thank goodness they're keeping "Casual Fridays" so I can wear my 501s* to work at least one day a week.

---

*501s: Levi's® 501® button-fly jeans, the most iconic jeans in leather circles.

Chapter 8

Club Life

Recipe for a Run
Published in *Lavender* #211 (June 27, 2003)

Most people who attend leather runs arrive at the beginning of the run, have a weekend's worth of fun, and leave when the run is over—probably without giving much thought to how much effort is involved in pre-run planning and preparation, actual operation of the run, and clean-up afterward. According to one long-time club member, "It's like planning and hosting a wedding—every year!" I beg to differ—it's actually more work than a wedding, unless your wedding plans include four dungeons.

Here's a recipe that shows what's involved in putting on a leather run. The Knights of Leather recently used this particular recipe to create this year's Tournament XV; the result served 75 people. But with a little tinkering and a few ingredient modifications the same basic recipe could be used to prepare a Black Frost (Black Guard), Gopher (Atons), or any one of the many runs that leather clubs everywhere present each year.

- Procure a place to hold the run by calling the State of Minnesota and reserving a group campsite in a state park. This must be done months in advance, and the call must be perfectly timed or you'll find that some Boy Scout troop or church youth group has already booked the site for the weekend you wanted.

- Come up with a theme for the run (this year's Tournament theme was "Little Dungeon on the Prairie"). You will be applying this theme to almost every aspect of the run.
- Make food and beverage plans—a Saturday-evening banquet plus four other meals, plus two early-riser breakfasts, plus round-the-clock snacks and beer, sodas and water for (in the instance of this year's Tournament) 75 people. Plan your menus (keeping the theme in mind, of course) and make your shopping list. Be sure to make arrangements for run participants who have special dietary restrictions.
- If your campsite doesn't have kitchen facilities, figure out how you're going to cook and serve all this food—and who's going to do it. (Tournament is blessed with two things: a campsite with a full food-service kitchen, and two caterers named Joy and Michelle d/b/a Rainbow Creations to handle the food-preparation duties.)
- Keeping your run theme in mind, design, produce and distribute advertisements, posters, flyers, press releases, registration forms, etc. Also get something about the run on the club's website. Arrange to accept registrations by mail or e-mail and payments via credit card or an online payment service like PayPal. Process registrations as they come in by mail or online.
- Find people to present run-themed workshops, seminars, demonstrations and other entertaining and educational events. To give just one example: plan a workshop on pony play, then design and build (from scratch) a covered wagon and arrange to have it pulled around the campsite by four (human) ponies.
- Line up other leather clubs to host evening cocktail parties (at Tournament XV the Chicago Leather Club hosted one on Friday evening and the Atons of Minneapolis hosted one before Saturday's banquet).
- Plan your dungeon layout and logistics. The Knights plan called for four different dungeons filled with varying equipment—one with electricity (for powered toys) and three lit only by candles and a fire roaring in the fireplace.
- Plan placement of tiki torches for nighttime illumination of the paths between the main lodge, bathrooms, cabins and dungeons.

- Make run packets, one for each participant, filled with a run booklet, run pin and/or run t-shirt (all of which you have previously designed and produced), safe-sex supplies and other sundry items. To hold the contents of this year's Tournament run packets the Knights sewed 75 burlap bags, decorated them with a stenciled run logo and tied them shut with gingham ribbon.
- Make table decorations for Saturday night's banquet. Members of the Knights made small covered wagons emblazoned with the run logo, floral centerpieces, and coordinated red-hankie-print table runners and party favors (foil-wrapped chocolate coins wrapped in a red-hankie-print paper napkin and tied with gingham ribbon).
- Prepare award plaques to be handed out at the closing ceremonies on Sunday. Include appreciation plaques for clubs that have hosted cocktail parties and awards for "pig" (weekend's most active male), "kitty" (weekend's most active female), and person who traveled the longest distance to attend. This year the Knights also prepared aprons with club patches to give to the caterers, who are now honorary club members.
- The caterers will buy the food, but you must still go shopping for beer, sodas, water, snacks, safe-sex supplies, insect repellent (!), tiki torches and fuel, and other supplies.

Once all the preparations are made and the supplies are procured, it's time to actually make the run happen. Here's how the Knights did it this year:

- Disassemble dungeon equipment in various members' dungeons. Rent a 26-foot truck and load it with disassembled dungeon equipment and tools for reassembly, beer, pop, water, tiki torches and fuel, safe-sex supplies, insect repellent (!!!), run packets, table decorations, covered wagon, etc. (Do you know how much stuff a 26-foot truck will hold? A lot.)
- Friday: Drive to run site. Unlock all cabins and other buildings and start settling in. Unload truck. Set up dungeons, reassembling all dungeon furniture (including three steel cages). Stock dungeons with firewood, candles and safe-sex supplies. Fill tiki torches and install throughout campground. Get beverages

iced. Check in guests as they arrive. Light tiki torches at sundown. Have dinner, welcome guests, present workshops and cocktail party, build campfire, open dungeons. Play if you have any energy left.

- Saturday: Present more workshops and seminars during the day. Replenish firewood, candles and supplies in dungeons. Refill tiki torches. Decorate main lodge for banquet. Light tiki torches at sundown. Present cocktail party and banquet, build campfire. No matter how tired you are, if you're going to get any use out of all that dungeon equipment, this is your last chance.
- Sunday: Have breakfast. Present awards and bid farewell to run participants. Take dungeons apart, disassembling all dungeon furniture. Load truck with all dungeon equipment and all the other leftover supplies. Sweep out dungeons and clean fireplaces. Collect tiki torches. Pick up trash from all cabins. Clean all bathrooms. Sweep all cabins and close up. Clean main lodge and kitchen. Drive back to city, unload everything from truck and return it to truck rental office. Reassemble members' dungeons.
- Start planning next year's run.

Of Magic and Mountaintops
Reflections on the Atons' 25th-anniversary run
Published in *Lavender* #62 (October 10, 1997)

The Atons of Minneapolis held their 25-year anniversary run, "A Renaissance—Renewing the Ties that Bind," at the Minneapolis Regal Hotel from Friday, September 26 to Sunday, September 28. Following is the text of some remarks I made at the Sunday morning closing ceremonies.

"This has been a magic weekend for me, and I hope for you all as well. I'd like to tell you a little bit about my experiences this weekend, and offer you a few things to think about during your drive or flight home.

"Of course I knew that this weekend was going to be a magical event, and that the Atons' 25-year anniversary was historic. But I didn't really appreciate how historic it was until I spent some time Friday night talking to a gentleman who is here for the weekend from Chicago. He is a professional librarian, and among other things he is currently the head librarian at the Leather Archives & Museum in Chicago. He gave me a new appreciation of how far back in the community the Atons' roots go, and how amazing it is that out of all the clubs that were started years ago, and all the clubs that have come and gone in the meantime—and there have been many—this club has lasted 25 years and is still here, strong and vital. That really is worth celebrating.

"And celebrate we have. Yesterday many of us went to the Minnesota Renaissance Festival. I had a wonderful time. I've been there many times before—years ago, when I was in high school, I worked it—but being there yesterday as part of this group, and at every turn seeing someone in leather, made the day magical. And yes, the evenings and nights have been pretty magical too.

"And then I woke up this morning and I realized something. This is the last weekend of the Renaissance Festival for this year. Just like the mythical Scottish town of Brigadoon, which sprang to life for only one day each century before vanishing into the highland mists for another hundred years (you Broadway queens out there know what I'm talking about here), the Renaissance Festival is gone after today until next year. And so is this Run. The Atons will have other runs, but there will never be another run quite like this 25th-anniversary run. It's about to disappear into the mists of history, and we'll only be able to call back our experiences of this weekend in our dreams and in our memories. All the while we've been celebrating 25 years of the Atons' history this weekend, we've been a part of making the history that our leather descendants—and some of us, I hope—will be remembering in 25 years at the Atons' 50-year anniversary run.

"I had another thought when I woke up this morning, and was thinking how magical this weekend has been. It's the same thought I have at the end of every leather event I attend, and I imagine some of you have had the same thought: I don't want this to end. Even for the Atons, who have been planning this for a year-and-a-half and are probably ready to have it end, I bet some of you are feeling the same thing I felt this morning: Life should always be like this. I want life always to be so magical. I want always to be surrounded by my tribe and feel the sense of camaraderie, caring and community I feel at events like this. I find myself, like Moses, wanting to live the rest of my life at the top of the mountain, in the presence of what I consider holy.

"But life isn't like that. We have to come down off our mountaintops. We have to go back out into that everyday 'normal' world that often doesn't understand us, doesn't always let us be who we truly are, and sometimes makes us feel out of place. Why do we have to live in a world where we feel marginalized, I was asking myself this morning. And the answer came back—because there are people out in that world who want what we have, who want what we have been enjoying this weekend—and who don't know how to find it. We have to go out there and let them know that they can be a part of this—they can be a part of us—if that's what they want. They won't be able to find it by themselves, and we won't be able to maintain it by ourselves. But by joining together with them and letting them join together with us—just as a bunch of guys joined together 25 years ago and created a club called the Atons—we'll ensure that our tribe continues and grows, and that for years to come we'll always have places and times like this weekend, when we can come together and be who we truly are, and celebrate."

Chapter 9

Sash Life
Leather contests, titles and titleholders

Leather Contests Explained
(and why they matter)

Published in *Lavender* #35 (September 27, 1996) and *Lavender* #69 (January 16, 1998)

The new International Mr. Fantasy was recently chosen in Omaha. In San Francisco this weekend the International Mr. Drummer contest takes place. Next weekend brings the Mr. Minnesota Leather '97 contest here in Minneapolis, the winner of which goes on to the International Mr. Leather (IML) contest in Chicago next May.

Where did all these contests (and all these titleholders) come from? What purpose do they serve for the leather community? And what difference do they make for anyone who's not into the leather Scene?

Where did they come from? The same impulse that in straight society finds expression in the Miss America Pageant find expression among members of the leather community in leather title contests. The drag/transgender community developed the Imperial Court system of royalty in response to the same impulses. As a psychologist would say: gay, straight, or whatever, we're all socialized the same. If the Imperial Court system produces the GLBT community's royalty (emperors, empresses and ladies-in-waiting), perhaps leather contests produce the members of the GLBT community's knighthood.

Both IML and Drummer started in 1979. "Beauty pageant winners" at first, the job of titleholder was transformed by the AIDS crisis — leather titleholders were among the first people to raise funds both for research and to benefit people living with AIDS, simply because they saw the need and were in a position to do something about it.

International Mr. Leather (IML) was started by Chuck Renslow, who thought that the leather community would enjoy the contest and would benefit from the leadership and positive role models such a contest would bring forward. International Mr. Drummer was started by *Drummer* Magazine for the same reasons, but also as a way of providing men for the cover and pages of the magazine. These two major men's leather titles coexisted quite nicely for years, with International Mr. Leather more political and International Mr. Drummer more sensual. In 1987, the women's leather community added the International Ms Leather (IMsL) title.

Then, a few years ago, rumors began to circulate that the Drummer title was going to end due to the financial problems that *Drummer* Magazine was experiencing at the time.* Perhaps coincidentally, or perhaps in response to these rumors, the International Mr. Fantasy title was created in Omaha, Nebraska, in 1995 by Dustin Logan and Bob Ewing. They had been producers of an annual event called "Fantasy" at which titleholders presented fantasies and other entertainment to raise money for charity. It has always been my personal feeling that this event became the International Mr. Fantasy contest to carry on the tradition and concept of the International Mr. Drummer title. It turned out that both *Drummer* Magazine and the Drummer title are still alive, however, and it is very much to the credit of International Mr. Fantasy's producers and titleholders that International Mr. Fantasy has become a credible title in its own right.†

At about the same time International Mr. Fantasy was being created, Dave Rhodes, publisher of *The Leather Journal,* created the Mr. and Ms Olympus Leather contest in conjunction with his "Pantheon of Leather" community-service awards held each year in New Orleans. The Olympus Leather contests differ from the other titles mentioned above by awarding both female and male titles and holding both competitions in the same event. In this way, neither

---

*Unfortunately, the rumors were true. See page 67.

†The International Mr. Fantasy contest lasted for only a few years after this was originally published.

sex is a guest at a contest for the other sex. (By the way, there is no connection between the Mr. and Ms Olympus Leather contests and similar-sounding men's bodybuilding titles.)

Why do all these leather contests exist? Certainly not because they're fantastic moneymaking opportunities. Winning a leather contest and holding a title is a difficult way to get rich and an easy way to become impoverished. The same generally goes for producing leather contests; they almost always have a raising-money-for-charity component, and any proceeds left over are generally kept as seed money for next year's contest. Cash cows they're not.

Leather contests exist because they offer something to the leather/ SM community. They're entertaining to watch. They're stimulating to enter. And they can be rewarding to produce. The leather impresario who gives time, effort and money to put on a contest knows that she or he is engaged in a very special form of community leadership and mentorship.

The contestants learn and grow by being in the contest, and their efforts at personal development reap benefits long after the competition is over. By standing on stage with pride before the community, the contestants become role models to the people in the audience. Entertainment, growth, personal development, leadership, mentorship, role models . . . all this and hot men and women on stage in leather, too. Need any more reasons?

What purpose do leather contests serve? A good leather contest is a challenge for the contestants and entertainment for the community. Watching a parade of beautiful bodies in full (or skimpy) leather and performing leather fantasies (erotic skits) makes for a pleasant evening for the audience. For the contestants and judges, of course, much more is involved.

The judges are as interested in the minds of the contestants as in their physical presence, which is why most contests include a private interview with the judges and a public speech before the audience. The judges are looking for the contestant who will be the community's best representative, both at local functions and in more advanced levels of competition.

Why would someone want to compete? There are many reasons. Some contestants don't care if they win or not; they compete for the chance to be in the spotlight for a few minutes. Others compete because they have something to prove, either to themselves or to others. At least a few international titleholders have entered a local contest on a dare. Then there are those contestants who earnestly want to win the contest and to have the experience of holding a leather title.

What's involved in being a leather titleholder? A certain amount of glamour and a lot of work—and the good feeling that comes from being able to give something back to the community. Besides going on to further levels of competition, titleholders raise funds for charities, educate, entertain, raise consciousness, and are community ambassadors—all things that make the leather community stronger.

How do leather contests and titleholders benefit the non-leather/ SM community? The most obvious benefit is fundraising: children's charities are a favorite benefactor, as are AIDS charities such as AmFAR, who sponsored Joe Gallagher, IML '96 and Andy Borden, 3rd runner-up for IML '95. But leather contests and titleholders serve another, perhaps less-obvious, purpose both for the leather community and for the GLBT community at large. The contests, and especially the fantasies, are positive, affirming celebrations of alternative sexuality. Leather titleholders promote that same sex-positive message to society at large—the idea that enjoyable, life-affirming, healthy sexuality isn't limited to the heterosexual missionary-position flavor. They are sexual freedom fighters working not just for the rights of the leather/ SM community, but for all sexual minorities.

What Are Fantasies? Leather Theater
Including "Fantasy Production 101"
Published in *Lavender* #113 (September 24, 1999) and *Lavender* #240 (August 6, 2004)

Regular readers of this column have often seen the words "fantasy" or "fantasy presentation" used in connection with leather contests or events. If you've ever wondered "What the heck is a fantasy?"—wonder no more.

A psychologist friend of mine is fond of pointing out that whatever our differences, and no matter what community (or communities) we belong to, "we're all socialized the same." Hence, the Miss America Pageant has the talent competition, drag queens have drag shows—

and the leather community has fantasy presentations. (The only major leather contest that does not feature fantasy presentations is International Mr. Leather.)

A leather fantasy is a skit built around leather/BDSM themes that is usually, but not always, performed as part of a leather contest. Fantasies are the leather/BDSM community's form of theatrical expression. If you have ever been onstage as part of a fantasy, you can legitimately impress people by telling them you have done performance art. Over the years certain fantasy performances have become legendary—for instance, anyone who ever saw one of Joey Kraly's Bugs Bunny/Looney Tunes fantasies will never forget it.

Like all theater, there are certain basic, practical rules of stagecraft that can make or break a fantasy presentation. I have seen some fantasies that were splendid, many that fell short of the mark, and more than a few that were utterly embarrassing. Generally, what made them embarrassing was that they were done with no regard for basic acting, stagecraft and storytelling practices.

My colleague, Robert Davolt,* recently wrote an essay (Myth #48 in his "Myths & Mysteries of Leather" series) that was critical of the entire concept of fantasies.† While I can't argue with what he wrote (Argue with Robert Davolt? Are you kidding?), I submit that a little community education could go a long way toward raising the entertainment level of leather fantasies. With that in mind, here are some helpful tips for those contemplating the presentation of a fantasy.

A good fantasy has honesty and authenticity going for it. If I'm not into flogging, but I decide to present a flogging fantasy because that's what I think my audience will like, it probably won't work. If I'm really into flogging, on the other hand, I can present a fantasy that communicates my passion to the audience even if not every member of the audience is into flogging.

---

*See footnote, page 8.

† Unfortunately, this essay was not included in Davolt's book and appears to be no longer available on the Internet. If memory serves, Davolt wrote that fantasies evolved as a low-budget way of entertaining the audience at leather contests. It was cheaper to press the contestants into service than to hire performers, but this often led to less-than-stellar entertainment.

Remember, this is theater. Now is the time to dust off your high school, college or community theater knowledge. You didn't get the theater gene? Then get someone who's theatrically literate to help you. You need to know at least the elementary rules of stagecraft to present a fantasy that works.

This time it's all about you. Think about who is the "hero," or most important character, in the fantasy. Structure and stage the fantasy to keep the focus on that hero—you, the contestant. Especially in a contest setting, the contestant should be the one to shine onstage, yet I've seen fantasies where the contestant simply lies there while various accomplices perform all the action and get all the attention. I once saw a fantasy in which a gentleman was escorted to a barber's chair where his body disappeared under a barber's cape and his face disappeared under lather. Then the barber exhibited his shaving, bondage and flogging skills. If I were judging I would have given the barber high marks—but it wasn't his fantasy. The contestant was the invisible guy in the chair who didn't really do anything. Moral: Keep the best lines for yourself.

Faces are more interesting than backs. There are few fantasies worse than five minutes of uninterrupted flogging during which nothing else happens. The only way to make a more deadly fantasy is to have both flogger and floggee keep their backs to the audience for the entire five minutes—which I have seen more than once. If you must do a flogging fantasy, consider positioning yourself and your co-stars in such a way that the audience can see your faces and your facial expressions.

It's supposed to be entertaining. Five minutes of unremitting flogging is not entertaining. Think of television—quick cuts for attention-span-challenged viewers. On stage it isn't possible to be quite that manic, but one rule of thumb I've heard (thank you, J.D. Laufman) is this: Something—the music, the lighting, an entrance, an exit, a prop—should change every fifteen seconds.

Say it with music. Use music to support and enhance the fantasy's action. Consider changing or varying the music throughout the fantasy rather than having one song or one droning rhythm soundtrack the whole time you're onstage. And please, please be sure the soundtrack tape or CD is of good recording quality and has smooth edits and transitions between selections. If you don't know how to make a good audio mix, find someone who does and let them help you.

Try not to say it with words. Microphones for spoken dialogue during fantasies can be a production headache, and voiceovers on the music tape or CD often turn into indecipherable mush. And what about those in the audience who are hearing-challenged or non-English-speakers? If no one can understand what is being said, the point of the fantasy can be lost. Consider instead telling the story without words. If you absolutely must use words, do the necessary planning and testing to make sure they will be understood. (See one contestant's success story below.)

The biggest prop wins... Just as Broadway has been overtaken with the spectacle of life-size helicopters on stage and crystal chandeliers that crash to the floor nightly, fantasies in recent years have fallen victim to what I call the "Biggest Prop Wins" phenomenon. I have seen it time and again—the elegant minimalist fantasy loses out to the one that includes a 10-foot rope spider web, a 12-foot condom or a 15-foot gallows. This is known in the trade as a "wow factor."

... or maybe not. Big props have to be designed, constructed and transported to the theater or bar where the fantasy is being performed. They cause all kinds of headaches for the contest production staff who have to move them onstage for the fantasy and offstage again afterward. Contestants who have to ship big props for long distances are at a disadvantage compared to contestants who are relatively close to where the contest is being held. Consider building props that look big but are lightweight, collapsible and portable.

Or **consider using other "wow factors" like good storytelling and presentation.** At the 2004 Mr./Ms Olympus Leather contest, contestant and writer Toni Pizanie's fantasy consisted of standing on stage and reading a piece she had written—the story of how she came to be on that stage that evening. No big props, no throbbing music, nothing changing every fifteen seconds. Just words—but she was charming, spoke clearly and had a good story to tell. And she had that audience in the palm of her hand. (It helped that she also had a good sound system at her disposal.)

I've seen other fantasies that connected with the audience while using almost no props. Personally, I think that's a greater (and rarer) accomplishment. And it certainly makes it easier to take the show on the road.

Use simple lighting. Find out what kind of stage lighting flexibility will be available—you may be limited to "on" or "off." If you're lucky you'll have a spotlight to work with. The time to discover this information is while you're planning your fantasy, not when you get to the theater or bar to present it.

The contest production staffers are your friends. Treat them nicely—their efforts are going to make you look good onstage (or not). Make their job as easy as possible, and your job will be easier too.

Rehearse, rehearse, rehearse. Rehearse before you get to the venue and, if possible, rehearse on the stage where you will be performing the fantasy. Don't think that not rehearsing will make the fantasy look spontaneous—not rehearsing will more than likely make it look amateurish.

Prepare for the unexpected. No lights? No sound? Missed entrance? The show must go on, so make contingency plans. This also applies to other people appearing in the fantasy who become ill, props that are lost in shipping, soundtrack tapes that are mysteriously erased— have understudies and alternative props available and carry duplicates of soundtrack tapes or CDs. If you ship props or costumes, plan ahead so you ship them with plenty of time to spare.

It's not a scene, it's a fantasy. Yes, as I mentioned above, you want to showcase something you're passionate about. But your fantasy is not about you getting off onstage, it's about you entertaining the audience (and if you're lucky, getting *them* off). Keep your priorities in perspective here.

Finally, **know what reaction you're trying to inspire.** International Ms Leather 1995 Pat Baillie once explained to me the effects a good fantasy can have on an audience: it can "make 'em hard" (or based on gender, "wet"), "make 'em laugh, or make 'em think." You get extra points for doing two of the above; come up with a fantasy that does all three and you stand a good chance of winning the fantasy category—and maybe the contest, too.

Inside IML
A judge's notebook
Published in *Lavender* #185 (June 28, 2002—printed here is the special extended Web version)

Wednesday, 8 A.M.: The train pulls out of St. Paul bound for Chicago and the International Mr. Leather (IML) 2002 contest weekend. The host hotel this year is the Hyatt Regency Chicago, the largest property in the Hyatt Hotel chain. I have been at the contest every year since 1994, but this year I will be seeing it from a very different and somewhat exclusive angle: In addition to my press badge, I will be wearing a badge identifying me as one of the weekend's judges.

Packed in my carry-on bag is a document I have been thinking about and constructing for the last three weeks: a five-page description of all the qualities I feel the man selected to be IML 2002 must possess.* My theory: if I have a very specific image of the man I'm looking for, I will recognize him when I see him; if, on the other hand, I don't know what I'm looking for, I'll probably wind up with something else.

Wednesday, 9:30 P.M.: This is surreal. Stefan Mueller, the outgoing IML 2001, has invited everyone to kick off the weekend at, of all things, a roller skating party (proceeds benefit the Leather Archives & Museum). I haven't roller-skated since high school. But I skate most of the evening and have a good time: I only fall down once, and I am able to avoid getting blisters on my feet. It's an odd but effective way to meet and interact with some of the contestants I'll be judging this weekend.

Thursday noon: At the Judges' orientation session I meet my fellow judges and we all meet Billy Lane, who competed in IML in 1998. He has been one of the judge handlers ever since, although this is his first year as Judges' Coordinator. We also meet his two assistants, John Brook and Bruce Saari, who promise to assist us in any way possible this weekend so we can concentrate on judging.

In addition to outgoing IML Stefan Mueller, my fellow judges are Jerry Acosta, American Leatherboy 1999, from San Francisco; Pat Baillie, International Ms Leather 1995, from Albuquerque, N.M.; Hervé Bernard, International Mr. Drummer 1998, from Paris, France;

---

*That document appears in this book following this write-up of IML 2002.

Patti Brown, general manager of The Leather Rack in Washington, D.C.; Brian Dawson, International Mr. Drummer 1989, from Los Angeles; Wayne Nesbitt, Mr. DC Eagle 1998, from Washington, D.C.; and Judge Emeritus (and fellow leather columnist) Marcus Hernandez, a/k/a Mister Marcus, of San Francisco.*

This is the first year of a new, revamped judging process for IML, and we're the guinea pigs. For the last several years a chief judge (Thom Dombkowski) has run the judging proceedings and provided continuity by returning year after year. But no longer—this is the first year of IML's new "no repeat judges" policy. IML has given us only a few basic judging ground rules and is trusting us as a group to come up with a judging process. We have the option of choosing a chief judge. We decide not to, although Brian, as the "point person," is always the first to speak to the contestants when they enter and Stefan usually asks each contestant their final question.

In previous years the tallymasters have been in the judging room to act as timekeepers, but this also has changed. It is up to us, the judges, to choose a method of timekeeping. Three judges volunteer to share those duties, but Jerry will end up being the sole timekeeper for the weekend's interviews—using the countdown timer on his cell phone.

Dividing the time available for interviews by the number of contestants leaves us with eight minutes per contestant. That hardly seems like enough, but if we exceed that time limit we not only increase our own workload, we also throw off contestant and staff schedules for meals, rehearsals and photo sessions. We decide we'll just have to make it work.

Thursday, 1:30 P.M.: The judges are officially introduced to the IML contestants at the contestants' orientation meeting. There is some social time and I speak to a few of them, but not as many as I expected. I am making mental notes of who takes the trouble to introduce themselves to me and who doesn't—some of the contestants seem to look right through me.

---

*Another sad update: Marcus passed away in 2009. His weekly column of "leather and dish" in San Francisco's *Bay Area Reporter* started in 1971 and ran for 38 years. He was my mentor, colleague and friend. I remember him fondly.

Thursday, 9 P.M.: Opening ceremonies. This isn't an official judging event, but I still take notes on how all the contestants present themselves and compile my eye candy list. (So do several of the other judges.)

As in other years, all the contestants get at least a polite response from the audience, while several contestants are obvious audience favorites and have larger cheering sections. The purpose of the evening is to draw contestant numbers to determine the order of competition for the rest of the week. Contestants are introduced in alphabetical order; each draws an envelope and gives it to Tom Stice, the weekend's emcee who holds the titles of Southeast Drummer 1998 and International Slave 1995. While Stice opens it (I notice they use really good glue on those envelopes), the contestant states his name, title and the city/club/sponsor he is representing. Stice then announces the contestant's number and is then supposed to hand the number to the contestant. Unfortunately, quite a few of them walk offstage without taking their number, making Stice run after them to give it to them. This happens every year—opening night jitters, I suppose.

Friday, 8 A.M.: The judges gather and prepare for the first day of contestant interviews. Continental breakfast is served. The contestants have been divided up into groups of nine or ten; the first group of contestants is ushered in promptly at 8:30 A.M.

Friday, 9:15 P.M.: Over thirteen hours later, I turn in my score sheets for the first day of interviews. We have talked to 38 out of 66 contestants. To the amazement of the IML staff, we have actually finished each group ahead of schedule—this is the first time anyone can remember that happening.

Looking back on the day, I am grateful that all the judges seem to be on the same wavelength and that we work together very well. With only eight minutes per contestant we are resigned to the fact that not every judge will get to ask a question of every contestant. But we pretty much hold to the eight-minute-per-contestant time limit, and none of the judges seems to feel he or she is not getting enough information.

Along with questions tailored to each contestant based on his entry form, certain questions have been asked of almost everyone. Surprisingly, Marcus Hernandez found very few contestants able to talk knowledgeably about ENDA (the Employment Non-Discrimination Act) and NCSF (the National Coalition for Sexual Freedom). Patti Brown found no one who knew what important and ubiquitous symbol the late Frank Moore designed (the red AIDS ribbon). Wayne Nesbitt stumped many contestants with his question about the only biological brother-and-sister team to hold the International Mr. Leather and International Ms Leather titles (Ron Moore, IML 1984 and Genelle Moore, IMsL 1997).

As a group I am very impressed with today's contestants. The old cliche about "There's only one IML, but all of you contestants are winners" never seemed more true. Several of them could be strong contenders for the IML title, but no one has distinguished himself as being head and shoulders above all others. Actually, that's good. It means it's shaping up to be a close contest, which is always more interesting than when someone walks away with the title.

Of course, that could change. We still have 28 more contestants to interview tomorrow.

But for now, it's time to drop in on some parties at the hotel: the traditional roast for outgoing IML Stefan, the bootblack party, the Canada party, the Texas party. It's a dirty job, but someone has to do it.

Saturday, 6:15 P.M.: The end of day two of interviews (only ten hours today). Again, I'm the last one to turn in my score sheets. (Memo to self: I won't be able to take so much time at the contest on Sunday night—things will be moving too quickly.)

Today we've seen the judging process evolve in subtle ways. Yesterday the contestants came in as a group and were introduced, and then all but the first contestant to be interviewed left the room. After we had spoken to each contestant individually, the entire group was again brought back into the room for one last look—but no more questions.

By contrast, when today's contestant groups were brought back into the room, the conversation continued: Was there anything they didn't get a chance to say during the interview that they would like to say now? What were they afraid we would ask that we didn't ask? What made them most uncomfortable during the interview? It evolved spontaneously, and it seemed to work very well.

Based on the interviews I don't have any inkling who will be chosen IML 2002. There are several contestants whom I believe would fill the role very well. But that's getting ahead of things—the more immediate parlor game is trying to guess who will or who won't make it into the ranks of the top 20 semifinalists, also known as "making the cut."

Okay, here's the Price Waterhouse moment: All 66 contestants are judged on both the interview (which contributes 70% of the preliminary score) and the Saturday night physique/personality pre-judging (which contributes 30% of the preliminary score). The contestants having the 20 highest scores are announced at Sunday night's contest and show, and go on to compete in the semifinalist speech and physique segments. These men start competition as equals, because no scores are carried forward from the prejudging rounds into the semifinalist competition. Olympic scoring is used throughout, which means that each contestant's high and low scores for each round are discarded before the scores are added up. (Games judges play: In both the prejudging rounds, where the scoring range is from 0 to 100, I never award anyone more than 90 points on the theory that fewer of my scores will be thrown out. But I wonder how many of the other judges are doing the same thing.)

What do all these judging mechanics mean in the real world? It means, as Billy Lane tells me: "All these men you've just finished interviewing? Two out of three of them will be disappointed tomorrow when they don't make the cut." That's sobering. And I realize I will be disappointed too, because there are at least 45 of them I would like to see make the top 20. There are 25 speeches I won't get to hear and 25 men strutting their stuff onstage I won't get to see. But that's the agonizing, excruciating part of judging this contest. In the candy shop that is IML, how on earth can anyone choose only twenty? How on earth can anyone choose only one?

Saturday, 9 P.M.: The Physique Prejudging, also known as "Pecs and Personality," begins. The contestants, who are wearing as little as they dare, walk the stage and let the audience admire them. They are then asked a question based on the information on their contestant application forms; their response will ideally be as witty, entertaining and seductive as possible. Some contestants look hot but don't do so well answering their question, while others who might not have the best physique get a tremendous audience response because they give the perfect answer to their question. Things move at a good pace and the evening goes by rather quickly. (But next time, IML, please give the guys some background music to strut to—after the applause stops, it's hard for anybody to be sexy against an aural backdrop of utter silence.)

Sunday morning: Free time—what a concept. Other than a group photo shoot at noon, the judges have nothing official to do until we board a bus at 5:30 P.M. for the contest and show at the Congress Theater. I finally get a chance to wander the Leather Market (116 vendors, something for everyone) and have my boots shined by one of the fourteen contestants in the International Mr. Bootblack contest, occurring concurrently this weekend with IML. But that's another column.

Sunday, 6:30 P.M.: The contest gets underway. There's a prison motif going on this year, with the contestants being presented as prisoners in a line-up. The jockstrap review contest segment is supposed to happen in the prison's shower room, but due to a problem with the showerhead scenery the audience only gets to see the towels (and very large jockstraps) hanging on the wall. That is still enough to set the scene, however.

Later: The top 20 are announced. Fourteen of them are on my personal top 20 list. Some of the other judges have a higher batting average, picking seventeen or eighteen out of twenty.

We hear the first ten contestants give their speeches and see the second ten strut their stuff. There is an intermission, then the second ten contestants speak and the first ten strut. It all seems to be happening extremely fast—I try to pay attention to what they're saying or what they look like, scribble a few notes, and calculate a score for them in comparison with all the other semifinalists.

The contestants are not making it easy for us judges. They're all good. They're all excellent. It's a twenty-way tie. I am convinced that IML Executive Producer Chuck Renslow and Coordinator Bill Stadt are sadists, gleefully watching the judges in agony. I'm not the only one who is feeling this way: Brian Dawson, who is seated next to me, at one point pounds his fist on the table in frustration and says something on the order of, "They're all too good! How can we choose?"

I jettison all thoughts of Olympic scoring and trying not to have my scores thrown out. If the content of someone's speech is amazing and the delivery is flawless, they get the highest score I can give. Ditto if their leather image, personality and attitude make me think, "It doesn't get better than this."

9:45 P.M.: Stefan Mueller is in the middle of giving his farewell, "step-aside" speech. I, however, don't have the luxury of listening to it right now because I am feverishly trying to get my score sheets done and handed in. (I'm tape-recording the speech, though, so I will be able to listen to it later.)

I hand the scores to Billy Lane, and then it hits me. It's over. I'm done. Mission accomplished. The adrenalin, which has been pumping continuously for three days, shuts off. In clinical terms I think this would be called a "delayed stress reaction." It is now safe to let the enormity of the weekend's undertaking come to the surface and overwhelm me.

The rest of the evening is a blur. Stefan finishes his step-aside speech by serenading the audience with charming renditions of "Wind Beneath My Wings" and "When Will I See You Again."* Then, while tallymasters Craig Beardsley and Jim Raymond busily punch numbers into their adding machines, diva extraordinaire CeCe Peniston entertains the crowd and calls Stefan to the stage for a brief duet.

10:30 P.M.: The winners are announced: 2nd runner-up Herb Kaylor, Mr. DC Eagle 2002; 1st runner-up Borisz Mos, Mr. Leather Holland 2002; and the new International Mr. Leather is Stephen Weber, Mr. Texas Leather 2002 from Dallas.

I think to myself: I'm very happy with the outcome, proud to think that I helped achieve it, and profoundly grateful for being given the chance to judge. Then I mentally remove my judge's hat, shift back into columnist mode, and rush the stage with the rest of the press.

Postscript: It's late Monday morning, Memorial Day, at a restaurant just down the street from the Hyatt where some friends and I are

---

*Well, I thought his singing was charming, but I may have been one of the few who found it so. Some people still talk about Stefan's singing stepdown, and not charitably.

having brunch. As I walk up to the buffet line I see Stephen Weber and his partner Blaine standing by the door. Stephen sees me and flashes me a big smile, and I walk over to talk to them. It turns out this is a reality check: Last night Stephen was celebrated all over town as the new International Mr. Leather, but that makes no difference this morning—the restaurant has stopped seating people for brunch, so he and Blaine will have to go elsewhere. After the whirlwind of the previous evening one would think they would have to be hungry and exhausted, but they handle the situation well. The irony of the situation doesn't seem to dawn on either of them. Good for them— I hope they handle the rest of the year's inevitable misfires and disappointments with such grace.

My Perfect IML

Published in Lavender #207 (May 2, 2003)

Last year at about this time I was contemplating my duties and responsibilities as a judge at the 2002 International Mr. Leather (IML) contest. At that time I had the idea that it might be easier to make an informed and sound choice of the next IML if I had a very clear understanding and image of the qualities I felt an IML titleholder must possess. After careful consideration I made a list of those qualities. Then I tried to distill them all down into one word.

Here's my list, presented as a thought-provoker and discussion-starter. This list is mine—yours might be different, so feel free to agree or disagree.

Profile of My Perfect IML*

1. Physical/Material Attributes

A. Looks: Attractive is a must. Beauty is nice, and built and buffed is nice, but sometimes those qualities can actually work against attractiveness. Attractive means approachable, not intimidating, so attitude is not what we're looking for here. Nice eyes, good grooming and a winning, genuine smile contribute to attractiveness.

*The eight categories are taken from a list of the ways in which people relate contained in *If the Buddha Dated: A Handbook for Finding Love on a Spiritual Path* by Charlotte Kasl (New York: Penguin, 1999)—one of the best books on human relationships I have ever come across. Highly recommended.

B. Age: Immaterial. IML can be 25 or 65. While age is immaterial, maturity is very definitely a necessity. IML should be old enough to be mature and young enough to have the stamina to do the job.

C. Education: A plus. But intelligence is more important. (See #2 below.)

D. Money: At the very least IML must possess the Basic 5 to which Guy Baldwin alluded in his speech at the 2002 Leather Leadership Conference: job, home, car, telephone, and enough disposable income. Looking at the reality of holding a title, the amount of disposable income needed is a significant consideration, along with the willingness to spend it on being IML. Holding a title should not be an honor that bankrupts the titleholder.

E. Status/Prestige/Social Position: Nice as long as they don't interfere with attractiveness and approachability, but not essential.

2. Intellect

A. Level: My preference is higher as opposed to lower. More intellectual horsepower means a better representative for the community, one who is more able to deal appropriately with people, situations and ideas.

B. Use: There's book-learning and there's street smarts. IML probably needs more of the latter than the former.

C. Wisdom: This is really what we're looking for. Wisdom is intelligence used in the service of spirit or principles; this makes ideas a means to an end. The opposite of wisdom is intelligence used in the service of the ego, in which case ideas are used to measure self-worth and to impress others; the ideas become ends in themselves.

3. Interests

A. Hobbies: IML should be someone who is really into leather. That should go without saying, but some IML contestants are still new to the scene and inexperienced. While they probably won't win the IML title, the experience of competing in IML can still be a priceless learning and growth opportunity for these contestants.

B. Work: IML needs an adequately paying job (see #1D above). But to be able to fulfill his obligations he also needs schedule flexibility and enough time off. IML should be "out" at work and have an employer who supports his holding the title.

C. Leisure time: IML should have lots, and be willing to give it up for a year. He should really enjoy being IML and thrive on it.

4. Values/Way of Life

A. Religion: Open to any or none.

B. Spirituality: An understanding of and interest in the spiritual aspects of leather would be an asset (see #7, below).

C. Ethics/Morals: An understanding of, respect for, and commitment to the leather community's code of ethics and sense of morality are essential. Again, this should go without saying, but unfortunately the judges can't necessarily count on it being present in every contestant.

D. Way of Life: Respect for the leather way of life is essential—except how do we define it? Who gets to define it? For example, does IML have to be a heavy player? Not necessarily, but he must be comfortable with and knowledgeable about that scene, since he will be a spokesman for its devotees. IML must be able to represent all aspects of our way of life effectively and believably, even though he may not partake of all of them.

5. Psychological/Emotional Attributes

A. Capacity for intimacy: Essential. He must have the ability to be open and to share himself with others.

B. Emotional maturity and balance: The counterpart of the above. IML must have a well-developed sense of decorum, appropriateness and boundaries, so as neither to take advantage of others nor to be taken advantage of by them. In other words, for just one example, the position shouldn't go to his head—he shouldn't become a sex addict just because he can have his pick of the bar, and he shouldn't feel he must sleep with everyone out of titular obligation. He must be comfortable with himself, self-assured, honest and kind.

6. Creativity/Passion

These would be definite assets, obviously. IML must be able to be new, interesting, fresh, exciting and novel.

A. Playfulness: IML must have the ability to laugh at himself and not take either himself or the title too seriously, at least not all the time. He will be the butt of many jokes during his title year and must be able to accept ribbing graciously.

B. Talents: He must be outgoing, able to meet people and schmooze comfortably, able to be "on" when necessary, comfortable on stage and in front of large and small groups, able to be the center of attention, to work a room, and to command and hold a crowd's attention.

C. Level of energy and joy: Must be high and boundless.

7. Spirituality

IML must possess a commitment to leather ethics and principles as well as to a path of truth, integrity and service. He should treat the title and the community with gratitude, realizing he has been given an extraordinary opportunity to play an important role in the community's life.

8. Essence

IML doesn't have to try too hard. He makes it look easy to be IML —and for him, it is. Former IML chief judge Thom Dombkowski has spoken about the King Arthur legend, the one knight who easily pulls the sword from the rock after all others have been unable to do so no matter how hard they tug.* The selection of the new IML may seem similarly preordained, perhaps because on some level it is. It's just up to the judges to recognize him when he shows up.

One word to describe My Perfect IML

Actually, I have two. As I made my list I decided the one word to describe IML was "ambassador." After last year's IML judging process was over I decided that I needed to add another one-word description that I learned from my fellow judges: "leader."

Life After the Leather Contest

Published in *Lavender* #238 (July 9, 2004)

Every year there are over 50 contestants for the International Mr. Leather contest on Memorial Day weekend in Chicago. One of those contestants is chosen as the new IML. Many of the other contestants go home from the weekend asking themselves varying versions of the same questions: Why didn't I win? What did I do wrong? What could I have done better? What could I do better next time?

Actually, these questions are part of the aftermath of every leather contest everywhere, all through the year. The person asking them could be either the winner of a local or regional contest who is considering what is necessary to get ready for the next level of competition, or one

---

*See "The Church of the Holy Circuit," page 270.

of the contestants who didn't win and is wondering why.

There are many who are only too willing to step into the void created by these questions and dispense advice either to someone who has lost a leather contest or to someone who just won one and is advancing to the next level of competition. Usually the advice they dispense is on the order of "You're perfect, now just change everything about yourself and you'll be even more perfect." They then proceed to tell the person to "go on a diet, change your hairstyle, buy all new leather, spend 60 hours a week at the gym, take steroids, get plastic surgery, and get rid of your partner because you'll be more tempting if it's known you are single, and therefore available." Incredible as it may sound, I am not exaggerating here.

The point of preparing for a leather contest is not to find a Henry Higgins top so that one can play an Eliza Doolittle bottom. A contest can be the occasion for "Extreme Leather Makeover," but only if that's what the contestant wants to do. On the other hand, I have known people (including myself) who have felt they wanted to make some more moderate changes, and entering a contest or winning a contest and advancing in competition was as good an excuse as any to make them. With motivation like that, there's a good chance positive changes will occur, and the changes will last even after the competition is over.

If you absolutely insist on asking someone for a critique of your performance during a contest and for suggestions for possible improvements—ask the judges. For two reasons, they are in the best position to give you realistic feedback about how you did: 1) They're the ones who scored you, and 2) they were there during the whole contest, including any private interviews. Anyone who was not a judge and therefore was not present during all segments of the contest can only guess at the thought processes the judges went through to arrive at their scores. Be aware that the judges aren't obligated to provide this service, but if you ask nicely they may. Be grateful for any feedback they offer, and thank them for taking the time to offer it.

Instead of, or in addition to, asking someone else what improvements could be made to become a stronger competitor, I challenge people to spend some time looking back at their contest experience and think about questions like these: When, during the contest weekend, did I feel most comfortable? What during the weekend made me feel uncomfortable or unsure of myself? What do I think I did really well? What do I think I could have done better? Which of the other contestants impressed me—made me think to myself, "That was really good. I wish I could do that. I want what they have."?

Don't just think about these questions—write them down, and then write down your answers to them. Those answers will point out to you both your strengths and the areas in which you want to improve. Take pride in your strengths, make plans for making the improvements you want to make—and then follow these plans.

Perhaps you know you will be advancing in competition, perhaps you're just thinking about entering another contest sometime, or perhaps you'll never compete again. It doesn't matter—you can still benefit from the insight gained by the above exercise.

Now, about that issue of competing in the future: IML competitors have already won titles in other contests; now that the IML competition is over they can turn their attentions to serving their communities until it's time for them to step aside and turn the title over to their successors.

But what about people who, although they have competed, have never won a contest and therefore have no title? During your contest preparation you probably did some thinking about what you would do with a title if you won. Would you have volunteered for a cause you believe is important? Would you have raised money for charity, helped to plan leather events, started a leather-related website? Whatever it might have been, you are hereby cordially invited to do it anyway.

If you want to, you can find ways to contribute to your community whether you have a title or not. Don't wait for a title to supposedly confer legitimacy and credibility on your efforts—get involved now. Your community will be a better place, and you'll feel good because you're helping to make it that way.

As a bonus: if you compete in some future leather contest, anything you do now will certainly look good on your application. Or you might find, as did your humble columnist, that you become so involved in serving the community that you never get around to entering another contest.

Disclaimer: The following column was written with tongue very firmly planted in cheek.

Humor: The Mr. Leather International Contest
Published in *Lavender* #131 (June 2, 2000)

I just got back from the Mr. Leather International (MLI) contest, that perennial leather-community springtime institution. The contest is presented each year over Memorial Day weekend in beautiful Atlantic City, New Jersey (the garden spot of the Garden State). Every year the sight of a bevy of leather Adonises in Speedos (black, of course) strutting their stuff on the Boardwalk never fails to inspire me. In keeping with the clean and wholesome image of this contest and title, all the competitors are certified steroid-free.

But it wasn't just the contestants who were interesting — this year's physique pre-judging on the Boardwalk attracted some notable celebrities. I spotted Al and Tipper Gore there with Hillary Clinton. I also saw George W. Bush taking in all the action and shaking hands; when asked how long he'd been interested in leather, he answered, "Oh, about fifteen minutes."

This was the 80th year for the contest, started in 1921, and the 47th time it's been on television (it's always a ratings winner for its time slot). After having been on all three major networks through the years, it was fitting that this year's contest was broadcast on Fox, the good-taste network. The MLI organization always prides itself on choosing the hottest names in entertainment for hosting duties — last year's emcees were Donnie and Marie Osmond. This year the emcee duties were handled by that dynamic duo of daytime TV, Regis Philbin and Kathie Lee Gifford.

The show, which was jointly sponsored by Miller Brewing Co. and lube manufacturer Wet International, opened with the requisite huge production number: Kathie Lee and 65 leathermen from around the world sang, danced and paraded to "Beautiful Men," a reworking of "Beautiful Girls" from Stephen Sondheim's musical *Follies,* featuring lyrics rewritten for the occasion by Sondheim himself. Then Regis introduced and chatted with each and every contestant in the spokesmodel part of the competition. Based on the spokesmodel scores, the field of 65 contestants was narrowed down to twenty lucky semifinalists.

Those twenty lucky semifinalists did another production number, "We're Here, We're *Cuir*," penned especially for the show by Elton John. The Evening Wear (leather tuxedo) and Swimsuit segments of the competition were next; both swimsuits and tuxedos were designed for the contest by Bob Mackie. The Talent segment of the judging was next, and it was a good chance for the contestants to differentiate themselves from the rest of the competitors. Todd Olansky of Winnipeg, Manitoba, Canada, did quite a mean fire-eating-and-breathing number, while Jason Jackson of Tupelo, Mississippi, combined a submissive, a flogger, an accordion and roller skates in a scene the likes of which I've never seen before and don't expect I'll ever see again. From tiny Luxembourg, Georg Hanfelmann's duct-tape-bondage-on-the-flying-trapeze number went slightly awry, but tragedy was averted by a well-placed safety net.

The crowd reserved their biggest oohs and aahs, however, for Jack Hendries of Cocoa Beach, Florida. Dressed head-to-toe in leather and backed by a chorus line composed of the entire membership of the Cocoa Beach Astronauts (truly a fun leather club if ever there was one), Hendries and company tap-danced their way through a reworking of Marlene Dietrich's classic "See What the Boys in the Back Room are Having." Hendries changed the lyric to "See What the Boys in the Back Room are Doing," and by the time the number was through most of the leather had been stripped off and it was pretty obvious what the boys in the back room were doing.

After a commercial break, it was time to narrow the field again, this time to ten lucky finalists, who went through the final judging event: the Pop Question. Philbin asked each lucky finalist the same question: "If you are selected as this year's Mr. Leather International, what will you do to unify the leather community?" The finalist then had 15 seconds in which to give his answer before the microphone was turned off. (The other finalists were kept in an on-stage glass isolation booth so they couldn't hear each others' answers.) After each contestant had spoken, Philbin repeated his catch phrase, "Is that your *final* answer?"—and the crowd went wild.

While the judges were deliberating, Kathie Lee entertained the audience with selections from her new CD, *Born For You* (fourteen ballads, both old and new, in stores now). Finally, it was time to announce the winners. The second runner-up, winner of a $5,000 scholarship, was Jason Jackson. Todd Olansky took first runner-up honors and won a $10,000 scholarship. And then, the evening's winner was announced—pandemonium broke out as Jack Hendries was awarded the MLI 2000 title! He goes home with a $15,000 scholarship and a new Daimler-Chrysler PT Cruiser! As a finale, Regis and Kathie Lee invited all 65 contestants back to the stage for a rousing rendition of Jerry Herman's "The Best Of Times Is Now."

International Mr. Leather Contest, Chicago

Since I planned to be in Atlantic City for the MLI contest, I sent aspiring leather journalist Steve Harrington to Chicago to cover the International Mr. Leather contest, which was happening the same weekend. (That Johnny-come-lately contest has only been going on for 21 years, but I guess it's newsworthy too.) Well, the funniest thing happened—he was so taken with the contest he decided to enter it right then and there, and he wound up winning the title! And I haven't heard a word from him since. But I'm sure he'll have all the details of the IML contest next issue.

The preceding column was published in 2000, and the contestant names I mentioned in the piece were a complete fabrication. (The Cocoa Beach Astronauts leather club doesn't really exist, either.)

Four years later, a gentleman named Jason Hendrix was chosen as International Mr. Leather 2004. Jason Hendrix. "Jack Hendries." Coincidence?

IML vs. IMsL
A handy comparison chart
First publication; intended for *Lavender* #110 (August 13, 1999) but not used

This chart compares the 1999 International Mr. Leather (IML) and International Ms Leather (IMsL) contests. Both of these contests have been around long enough to develop their own distinctive personality and traditions. Let's see what's the same and what's different:

	International Mr. Leather Contest	International Ms Leather Contest
Host city	Chicago (always)	Las Vegas (this year)
Producer	Chuck Renslow	Amy Marie Meek*
Preferred host hotel hangout	Lobby	Pool
Favorite smoke	Big, nasty cigars	Big, nasty cigars
Local water feature	Buckingham Fountain (as seen on the opening of "Married With Children")	Bellagio Hotel Fountain (direct descendant of Liberace's "Dancing Waters")
Places to go	Bars	Casinos
Contest entertainment	Erin Hamilton, dance-music diva for gay boys	Cafe Tormento, lesbian accordion/vocal duo specializing in tangos
Contest winner	IML 1999 Bruce Chopnik, event planner	IMsL 1999 Pam Meyer, construction foreman
Weekend fetishwear	Jockstraps	Strap-ons

---

*In 2006 Meek passed the IMsL producer torch to Glenda Rider.

Chapter 10

Proud Life

The Secrets We Keep
Why I came out—twice
Published in *Lavender* #166 (October 5, 2001)

I came out as a gay man at the age of 19, and had my second coming-out as a leatherman at age 37. Although certain aspects of the two experiences were the same, there were some significant differences.

First, some history: In homosexual culture at the dawn of the twentieth century, the words "coming out" were not automatically followed by "of the closet." The notion of the closet did not yet exist, and "coming out" was used to connote initiation and celebration as one embraced one's homosexual aspects and the homosexual community. Just as debutantes of the era were introduced to high society at coming-out balls, so too young men of a certain bent were mentored by their "aunties"* before "coming out" at extravagant drag balls.

Somewhere in the middle of the twentieth century, the notion of the closet was born as society told homosexual men and women in no uncertain terms that their sexuality was not okay and would not be tolerated. By the time of Stonewall in 1969, coming out of the closet had become more of a political statement, an act seen more as courageous and defiant than as joyous and celebratory.

---

*Aunties: Archaic term for older homosexual men who mentored younger homosexual men in the ways of gay society and culture.

Today the significant rite of passage and the claiming of one's place in the GLBT community is more likely to happen at a March On Washington or a Human Rights Campaign (HRC) dinner than at a drag ball—celebratory, yes, but also very political. I'm not saying this is necessarily bad, I'm just commenting on how things have changed over the course of a century.

By contrast, a modern-day leather coming-out is less political and still retains some sense of celebration and initiation, perhaps partly due to the more tribal and less political structure of the leather/SM community. People are in a dungeon or playspace to enjoy themselves and each other, and therefore tend to check their politics at the door. Another contrast: I see much more mentoring going on in the leather/SM community than I do in the wider GLBT community.

What did my two coming-out experiences have in common? Before each of them I had to deal with the same issues. Before I came out at age 19, I had to deal with feelings of shame, guilt and embarrassment, and fears of ridicule, non-acceptance, disapproval and violence. I knew society wasn't terribly accepting of homosexuals back then, but what would my family think? If I actually did come out, what kind of a life would I have? Why would I want to identify as part of this hated minority?

In spite of my doubts, fears and trepidations, I came out anyway—because I had to. The alternative was to live a life of dishonesty with myself and others about who I was. I would be sentencing myself to a life of just existing, a joyless life of continual fear, shame and worrying about being found out. A line from Clare Boothe Luce's play *The Women* describes it perfectly: "the seasonless world; where you shall laugh, but not all of your laughter, and weep, but not all of your tears."*

Before I came out as a leatherman at age 37, I had to deal with the exact same feelings and fears. I knew that society—including parts of the GLBT community to which I comfortably felt I belonged—weren't terribly accepting of the leather community. Why would I want to identify with this less-than-popular minority within a minority? I have heard the same worries expressed by others contemplating a

---

*Clare Boothe Luce was quoting Kahlil Gibran.

leather coming-out: What will people think? What will they say? What kind of a life will I have?

Again, for me, the answer was clear: I had ignored this part of myself for too long; I wanted to experience it. And I didn't want to experience it skulking around in guilty shadows. It's hard to enjoy something fully (and, from a practical standpoint, it's hard to be safe) when you're constantly looking over your shoulder because you're afraid someone might see you.

There's a saying that's popular with the twelve-step recovery community: "It's the secrets we keep that get us in trouble." The converse is also true: living without secrets is living free.

What's in a (Scene) Name?

Published in *Lavender* #226 (January 23, 2004)

Hi, I'm Steve Lenius. Pleased to meet you.

For pretty much my whole life I've been known by that name. When I was very young I was called "Stevie," but as soon as I was able to express a preference and make it stick I put a stop to that. When I started writing I decided that I would refer to myself in print as "Stephen A. Lenius," but such a formal byline just didn't seem to work at the beginning of a leather column. So here I am— your humble columnist, Steve Lenius.

Even in the world of the Internet, I've pretty much had one online handle since I first started my online life. That handle, "slenius"— eminently practical if unimaginative—has lasted me through, at last count, four different Internet service providers.

Contrast that to the experience of noted playwright/lyricist/ screenwriter/performer Betty Comden. She devotes the first chapter of her autobiography, *Off Stage*,* to the succession of names by which she has been known over the course of her lifetime. She makes the point that "one's name is, after all, the label by which one identifies oneself. If it keeps changing, perhaps one's sense of identity keeps shifting about also."

In light of this point, consider the use of names as they relate to the leather/BDSM milieu. It has been my observation that if you are

*New York: Simon & Schuster, 1995.

in a leather bar and introduce yourself to a gay leatherman, he will most likely introduce himself using the name with which he was born. Occasionally he will introduce himself using a nickname, and this nickname will be the name by which everyone else in the bar knows him, and perhaps even everyone else outside the bar. That's just the name he goes by. The same can be said of the vast majority of leather lesbians I have known over the years.

The issue of names is handled somewhat differently in pan-sexual/heterosexual BDSM circles. Here people who identify themselves by their birth name seem to be the exception; the norm is to identify oneself by one's "scene name" or "handle," which is a pseudonym either that an individual has chosen or that has been bestowed on them by someone else. A scene name is usually chosen for its uniqueness, at least within a given community—although as the Twin Cities pansexual community grows I am increasingly seeing confusion arising from two or more people sharing similar or identical scene names. And some people use one scene name in person but have a different online handle, which can make things even more confusing.

Hearing people's scene names can be interesting and even titillating. A scene name is useful in that it often tells you something about the person's interests or preferences, and for added spice the name often contains an element of fantasy/mysticism/sexiness. Especially in chatrooms and other online parts of the leather/BDSM community, a scene name can be evocative, and it can also be a good conversation-starter—I have seen fascinating online discussions about the derivation of people's scene names. Seeing a scene name online, and reading what the owner of the name has written, has often made me curious enough to want to meet the person and to seek them out at a munch. A scene name represents an identity tailor-made for the BDSM world, and the conglomeration of all the scene names in a room or a chatroom is an integral part of defining that scene.

But unaccustomed as I am to being referred to by multiple names, sometimes I have to wonder about the practice. If I had a scene name, would I feel like Sybil, of multiple-personality-disorder fame? Would it be hard for me to remember who I was and what personality I was manifesting at any given moment? Would I be segmenting the BDSM part of my life and my personality and keeping it somehow removed from the rest of my life?

Another thing I've noticed about scene names: While they can be practical in some ways, they are very impractical in others. The fact that I know someone only by their scene name effectively limits the ways in which I can interact with them. I can't look up their scene name in the phonebook if I want to call them, and I can't find their address if I want to send them a card. Scene names can enhance safety, but at the cost of reducing intimacy.

Pseudonyms can be a way of hiding one's identity. And, now that I think of it, at one point in my life I did create an alternate identity. When my mother, Mary Borhek, wrote her book about coming to terms with having a gay son—me—she used her own name on the cover of the book. But every other character in the story was allowed to select their "nom de book," as we referred to it. I chose "Eric Borhek," and the book therefore became *My Son Eric.** (I thought the title had a nice ring to it.) That was in 1979, and none of us knew what would happen when the book was published. If she were writing it today, I wouldn't feel it was necessary to hide behind a pseudonym.

Sometimes it seems to me that the use of scene names is a response to oppression. It is an instance of taking a problem, such as the necessity for secrecy about one's activities, and turning it into an asset by eroticizing it. My intent here is not to make accusations or to cast blame. For the vast majority of people I know in the pansexual/heterosexual BDSM scene, the necessity for secrecy about one's activities is not because of guilt or shame on the part of the participants. It is because so much of the rest of society does not look kindly on those activities and stands ready to punish people who engage in them—perhaps by the loss of a spouse, children or job.

There was a time, not so long ago, when GLBT folks had to keep their activities and major parts of their personalities hidden for exactly the same reasons. Life today, several decades after Stonewall, is much freer for gay leathermen and leather lesbians. I can only hope that the pansexual/heterosexual BDSM community has its

---

*New York: The Pilgrim Press, 1979.

own Stonewall and reaches the point where a scene name is a choice, not a necessity.

Kinksters and Pervs
The words we use and the messages we send
Published in *Lavender* #154 (April 20, 2001)

Words are powerful things. The words we use to refer to ourselves and our community send strong and sometimes unintentional messages about how we see ourselves. And, in addition to sending those messages to everyone else, we're reinforcing them in ourselves.

With that in mind, here's a quick word-association test. You don't need to grab a pencil and you don't need to write anything down. Just look at the list below and mentally note the first word, image or feeling that comes to mind:

1. Leather
2. Rubber
3. Uniforms
4. SM
5. Bondage
6. Kink
7. Fetish
8. Pervert
9. Queer

This test is my own creation and is based on no scientific underpinning whatsoever. Your results may be different, but to me the first five words, which describe areas of community interest, are fundamentally different from the last four words, which can entail value judgments.

Who is my audience for this column? Do we call our community "leather," "leather/SM" or "leather/BDSM"? These are simple statements of what we're attracted to or what we like to do. Or do we refer to our community as the "kink" or "fetish" community and to ourselves, with a wink and a nod, as "kinksters" and "perverts"? These are "loaded" terms implying that there's something wrong with what we're attracted to, and therefore there's something wrong with us.

Here's how the Merriam-Webster Collegiate® Dictionary defines "kinky" (definition #2): "relating to, having, or appealing to unconventional tastes, especially in sex; also: sexually deviant." Here's the sole dictionary entry for "perversion": "an aberrant sexual practice, especially when habitual and preferred to normal coitus." Nowadays the only place you're likely to see the word "coitus" is in a dictionary (unless it's immediately followed by the word "interruptus"), so here's the definition of "coitus": "physical union of male and female genitalia accompanied by rhythmic movements usually leading to the ejaculation of semen from the penis into the female reproductive tract; also: INTERCOURSE" (definition #3) "—compare ORGASM."

Dictionaries are such stimulating reading, don't you think? These definitions seem so matter-of-fact on the page. But in real life things can grow ugly; being labeled a "sexual deviant" often brings intense disapproval from society, and some people believe "perverts" deserve to be hated, demonized, harassed, bashed and killed.

I realize that bringing up this line of discussion risks wading into the same territory that the final word in my little quiz, "queer," brings up. (Ethnic minorities can also have these kinds of discussions around various racial slurs that have been used against them over the years.) For years words like "queer" and "faggot" were slams and insults; they were yelled in anger and their intention was to hurt. But when we consciously use these words to describe ourselves (seen on a t-shirt: "That's MISTER Faggot to you"), the words supposedly lose their power to hurt—"Yeah, you're right, I'm queer, so what?" The fact that I personally still don't feel comfortable describing myself as "queer" (I prefer to call myself a gay man) tells you that I don't entirely buy that argument. (Since this seems to some extent to be a generational thing, it also tells you I'm over 40.*)

In much the same way, even if I use the terms "kinky" or "pervert" ironically or sarcastically—or even if I only use them when I'm with other like-minded community members—I'm still using someone else's value judgments, instead of my own, to define myself. If I don't agree with the value judgments, why should I first call attention to them before saying I don't agree with them? Why should I even let them occupy valuable real estate in my mind?

Words like "queer" or "kinky" or "perverted" simply don't resonate with me. Being sexually attracted to another man comes as naturally

---

*Yeah—way over.

to me as breathing—there's nothing "queer" to me about it. I like the look of black leather or a nice, masculine uniform on a man; to me that's natural and normal, not a "fetish." To me it's not kinky, it's just the way it is. For me to engage in what Merriam-Webster defines as "normal coitus"—now that would be strange.

I've heard things like this from other people, too: "Oh, you write that leather column? Well, I'm not into leather" (or "I'm not kinky"), "*but* . . . ." And then they reveal they like getting their nipples played with, or their ass paddled, or that handcuffs excite them. But to them it's not kinky, it's just the way it is.

One important feature of the leather/BDSM community's code of ethics is being non-judgmental of other people's interests and attractions. Stop and think about the hankie code, and what a wonderful social institution it is: different colored hankies stand for different sexual appetites, and no judgment of the rightness or wrongness of those activities is necessary. You can flag whatever color you want, and even if that's not the color I'm looking for, I will still defend your right to flag it. The community takes non-judgmentalism so seriously that it has evolved an acronym for the act of being judgmental: YKINOK, which stands for "Your Kink Is Not OK." This is not something of which one wants to be found guilty in leather/BDSM circles; instead of making the value judgment of "Your Kink Is Not OK," it is more proper to express "Your Kink Is Not My Kink"—we don't all have to agree, and to each his or her own.

Gee, I wish the rest of the world were more like that.

By the way, in the above example you may have noticed I'm still using the word "kink." Henceforth, when I talk about "kink" I will not focus on Merriam-Webster's definition #2 (quoted above), but will instead focus on definition #3: "a clever, unusual way of doing something."

Symbols of Pride
Published in *Lavender* #80 (June 19, 1998)

As a way of exploring both gay pride and leather pride, here's a look at the icons and symbols of the gay and leather communities. (Logos and other identity symbols happen to be one of my special interests, as well as one of the primary parts of my career as a graphic designer.)

Green and Yellow: Color has always played an important part in enabling gay people to identify each other. In Victorian England, the color green was associated with homosexuality. In the early part of the twentieth century, homosexuals identified themselves to each other by wearing green and yellow. What are the initials for "green and yellow"? G-A-Y. That's one explanation for how the word "gay" came to be identified with homosexuality.

Triangles—Pink, Black, etc.: Over time other colors, such as lavender and pink, became associated with homosexuality. One of the most prevalent gay symbols, the pink triangle, has its roots in Nazi concentration camps, where prisoners had to wear armbands emblazoned with colored inverted triangles to designate their crime. The most famous of these armband insignia are two yellow triangles overlapping to form a Star of David, which identified the prisoner as a Jew. Green triangles were for common criminals, and red triangles were for political prisoners. Lower on the totem pole, the pink triangle was for homosexual men. A yellow Star of David with a pink triangle superimposed on top identified the lowest of the low: a gay Jew.

Pink-triangle prisoners often were given the worst labor assignments, and were subject to a disproportionate number of attacks by guards and sometimes by other prisoners. Even after the war was over, many homosexuals remained prisoners, because the German laws making homosexuality illegal (which predated Hitler, incidentally, although he made them much tougher) weren't repealed until 1969(!).

In the 1970s, Gay Liberation groups adopted the pink triangle as a symbol of the gay rights movement. It reminds us of the oppression and persecution we suffered then and still sometimes suffer today; among other things, it is the gay community's version of the Jewish Holocaust vow: "Never Again." The triangle is usually seen inverted (pointing down). But in the 1980s, ACT-UP (a group of radical AIDS activists) started to use the triangle pointing up to symbolize an active fight against oppression rather than a passive resignation to fate. If you've ever seen a "Silence=Death" bumper sticker, you'll notice that the triangle is pointing up. That's why.

Some prisoners in the Nazi concentration camps wore black triangles. This is not because they were lesbians—lesbianism wasn't included in the German laws against homosexuality, because evidently it was not as threatening as homosexuality among males. No, black-triangle prisoners were those who exhibited antisocial behaviors. But in a Nazi society where women were expected to be good wives and mothers, lesbians certainly qualified as "antisocial," as did prostitutes and women who refused to bear children. Today, the black triangle has been reclaimed by lesbians and feminists in much the same way as the pink triangle has been reclaimed by gay men and the gay community in general.

Bisexuals have their own version of the pink triangle. It's really two overlapping triangles, one pink and the other purple or lavender. As far as I know, this is a modern adaptation and was not used in the concentration camps.

One final note on triangles: There have been apocryphal reports that burgundy triangles were used in the Nazi camps to identify trans-gendered prisoners, but this has never been definitively substantiated.

Rainbow flag: Some people don't like the idea of the pink triangle as a gay symbol. They object to its Nazi origins and its focus on oppression. They prefer a more positive and uplifting symbol: the rainbow flag.

Rainbows have been connected with issues of gender and sexuality in Greek, Native American, African, and other cultures throughout history. In modern times, rainbows have served symbolic purposes for causes as diverse as Jesse Jackson's Rainbow Coalition and Eva (Evita) Peron's Rainbow Tour. But it was in 1978 that San Francisco artist Gilbert Baker made the rainbow a gay symbol when he created the first rainbow flag.

Baker came up with the flag in response to a local activist's call for a gay community symbol that could be used year after year. The first rainbow flag had eight stripes: hot pink (which Baker felt repre-sented sexuality), red (life), orange (healing), yellow (sun), green (nature), turquoise (art/magic), indigo (harmony), and violet (spirit). Baker and thirty volunteers hand-dyed and hand-sewed the first two flags, which appeared in the 1978 San Francisco Gay and Lesbian Freedom Day Parade. Subsequently, the 1979 San Francisco Gay Pride Parade Committee decided to use Baker's flag in the 1979 parade. However, some changes had to be made. When Baker asked the Paramount Flag Company in San Francisco to mass-produce rainbow flags for the parade, he was told that "hot pink" was not a commercially available color in flag material. The flag was now down to seven stripes. Then the parade committee decided to make the flag six colors by eliminating the indigo stripe—that way the colors could be evenly divided along the parade route, with three colors on one side and three on the other. Royal Blue was substituted for turquoise, and the rainbow flag assumed the form in which it primarily is known today.

From San Francisco in 1979, the rainbow flag has spread around the world. (Imagine my surprise when I stopped recently at a factory outlet mall off a freeway in the middle of nowhere and was greeted by the sight of rainbow flags hanging from the rafters as part of the decor. Was that just coincidence, or was the display person at that mall showing his or her "true colors"?) Rainbow flags appear on car windows and bumpers everywhere, and the six colors of the flag have been used in "freedom rings" and countless other products and fashion accessories.

You occasionally will see variations on the rainbow flag, including a rainbow flag/pink triangle combination and a U.S.A. rainbow flag with a field of blue and 50 stars in the upper left-hand corner. And there is the "Victory Over AIDS" rainbow flag where the purple stripe on the bottom has been replaced with a black stripe to commemorate those who have been lost to AIDS. One of those we've lost is Sergeant Leonard Matlovich, a gay Vietnam veteran whose tombstone in Arlington National Cemetery reads, "When I was in the military, they gave me a medal for killing two men, and a discharge for loving one." Before he died, he suggested that when a cure for AIDS is found, the black stripes should be removed from all the flags and ceremoniously burned in Washington, D.C.

Normally, the rainbow flag is displayed with the red bar at the top and the violet bar at the bottom. Occasionally, however, you will see an upside-down rainbow flag, and it's probably an intentional upside-down placement by a gay person who is also into new-age spirituality. I have been told that when the rainbow flag is inverted, the colors correspond to the first six of the body's chakras (in eastern and new-age spirituality, the chakras are the body's energy centers). The color belonging to the seventh chakra (the crown, at the top of the head) is white, and white light is a combination of all the other colors of the rainbow.

Leather pride flag: This flag was designed by Anthony F. DeBlase, and was first displayed at the International Mr. Leather contest in the spring of 1989. DeBlase was a noted artist, writer, editor and publisher who was involved with many leather/SM publications over the years, including *Drummer* Magazine. Even though it's called a "leather pride" flag, it encompasses leather, levi, SM, BD, uniforms, cowboys, latex, and every other fetish that is identified as part of the leather/SM community. And just as the leather community includes all genders and sexual orientations, so the leather pride flag is not an exclusively gay symbol.

The common symbolism attached to the leather pride flag is this: the black is for black leather, the blue is for blue denim, the white stripe in the middle is for integrity, and the heart is love. Nice symbolism—but unlike Gilbert Baker, who knew the meaning of each of the colors of the rainbow flag, DeBlase has said he had no specific symbolism in mind when he designed the leather pride flag.

Some people outside the leather/SM community erroneously assume that the black and blue colors are derived from the phrase "beating someone until they're black and blue"; let me repeat that this is a mistaken assumption.

Bear pride flags: The Bear community, composed of men who are sometimes large and always furry, has gotten large enough in the last few years that the idea of a bear pride flag seems a natural. But many competing flag designs are currently in circulation, vying for adoption as the "official" bear pride flag.

Since this column was first published, more flags have come along: a leatherboy flag, a leathergirl flag, and even a leather puppy flag for devotees of puppy play.

GLBT Pride, Leather Pride
Not yet obsolete
Published in *Lavender* #132 (June 16, 2000)

Because GLBT Pride is celebrated in the Twin Cities at the same time as Minnesota's Leather Pride celebration, the end of June is the time of year when I can be doubly proud—or maybe it's Pride to the second power. But where did these pride celebrations come from, why are they necessary, and where are they going? Have they served their purpose? Is Pride becoming obsolete?

One thing that tends to make members of a minority band together as a group and feel pride in that group identity is the experience of being faced with oppression. History is filled with examples: The ancient Egyptians enslaved and oppressed the Jews, and before long—Exodus, Moses parting the Red Sea and leading the children of Israel to freedom. Early Christians were oppressed by both the Jews and the Romans. In more modern times, the Nazis hated the Jews so much that they tried to completely eradicate them.

Every American immigrant group in the late nineteenth and early twentieth century—Irish, Germans, Scandinavians, Jews, Italians, Poles, Chinese, and so on—experienced some measure of oppression from the mostly WASP society of the time. Blacks were freed from slavery after the Civil War but still found themselves victims of massive oppression, which led to the civil rights movement of the 1960s (out of which came the Gay Liberation movement of the 1970s).

What happened to all these groups and movements? Christians went from being a hated minority to the (sometimes hateful) majority, in much of the world anyway. The experience of the Jews in the Nazi concentration camps led to Zionism and a new Jewish identity, along with a determination to never forget what happened and to never let it happen again.

The Ellis Island immigrant groups of yesteryear have pretty much assimilated into the fabric of American society and have become today's white Europeans at the top of the food chain. They occasionally are proud (as in "On St. Patrick's Day, everybody's Irish") and, for the most part, are not too oppressed, unless one counts their fear of losing their dominant status to today's immigrant groups—Hmong, Hispanics, East Indians, and people from the Middle East, to name a few.

The civil rights movement of the 1960s brought major positive changes for African-Americans, or at least for some of them. But much still needs to be done to improve their lot, and they'll still be celebrating Juneteenth this year.

Whatever happened to Gay Liberation? The movement broadened to include bisexuals and transgendered people along with gay men and lesbians and became the GLBT movement. At the same time, a gay men's leather/SM community started coalescing; this community later broadened to include kinky lesbians, kinky bisexuals, kinky transgendered people, and even kinky heterosexuals.

Neither GLBT people nor kinky people are geographic or ethnic nations—they are (sometimes overlapping) minority subsets of every society that has ever existed, and probably that ever will exist. But both communities, and the members of these communities, have experienced and continue to experience the same processes of oppression and liberation as the ethnic groups described earlier.

Oppression results from being hated, either by others or by oneself. To the extent I feel hated by others for being my kinky GLBT self, I am oppressed by them. To the extent I let them teach me to hate myself, what I am and what I stand for, I oppress myself. Pride can be the first step out of such oppression, either for an individual or for a group. But this first step can be derailed by anger and hatred and a wish for vengeance against one's oppressors. This is one of the justifications people use for fighting wars. It's also why some gay people call heterosexuals "breeders." These are both examples of how anger prolongs and intensifies oppression.

But, if we are able to forgive those who formerly oppressed us, we no longer have to hate them. We focus instead on our gains—we make the mental shifts from victims of oppression to survivors of oppression to victors over oppression. We are proud of our victory and we savor it for a while. Then life moves on, and our victory becomes a part of us—but only a part, a memory.

If part of my self-identity has been as part of an oppressed minority and I no longer feel oppressed, do I still feel like I belong to that group? If an entire group is so successful fighting oppression that none of the group feels oppressed, what's left to unite the group? Does pride in belonging to that group become obsolete? Maybe— but I don't believe that either the GLBT community or the leather/ SM community has reached that point yet. Both GLBT Pride and Leather Pride exist right now because enough people see a need for them and are willing to support, plan and participate in them.

Yes, the nature of Pride celebrations is changing. The children of the immigrants who came through Ellis Island tended to be more assimilated into the dominant culture and therefore identified less as an oppressed group; the same thing is happening today with the children of Hmong and Hispanic immigrants. And so it is with the GLBT community; younger people who are coming out now weren't even alive when the Stonewall riots happened — it's history-book stuff to them. They have come of age in a time when there has been more openness and less oppression. Likewise, people who live in large urban areas, where life is good and there's an atmosphere of acceptance, tend to forget that there are plenty of small towns where life is not like that.

For all these reasons it makes sense that Pride celebrations have evolved from political demonstrations into "the gay State Fair." Some people have lost touch almost entirely with the notion of oppression. They won't be at Pride, or at least not this year — not until another Matthew Shepard or Billy Jack Gaither* touches their lives. Then they'll understand that, as long as there are hate crimes, there will be a need for public statements of pride.

As we continue to fight oppression we also must take care not to blindly oppress others, either in our own community or in other communities. Some gay people find drag kings and queens and those in the leather/SM community an embarrassment and an inconvenience. They're trying to fit in with the mainline, majority heterosexual community. Their argument is, "We're just like you." And then here come the drag kings and queens and the leather contingent in the Pride Parade, the Moral Majority's cameras spring into action, and acceptance/assimilation is set back another few notches. Darn those people anyway.

Or maybe it's leathermen (who constitute the vast majority of the GLBT leather/SM community) being insensitive to leatherwomen, leather trans people or heterosexuals. Maybe it's kinky heterosexuals being uncomfortable with gay men. Or maybe it's the gay men, lesbians and heterosexuals not knowing what to do with those bisexual boundary-crossers.

We still need pride. But we don't need the kind of pride that fosters an attitude of superiority, which leads to rudeness, inconsiderateness,

---

*Don't know who they are? Look them up using your favorite Web browser and search engine.

anger or hate. How much better to feel the kind of pride that unites us—the kind we want to share and to pass on to others as a gift, so they also can be proud of who they are.

Three Kinds of Pride

Published in *Lavender* #55 (July 4, 1997)

In the Twin Cities, both the GLBT Pride and Leather Pride celebrations are the weekend before Independence Day, so I've come to think of the Fourth of July as "U.S.A. Pride." This is when the (non-GLBT) rest of the country finally gets to engage in the kind of celebratory activity that we GLBT and leather types recently have been enjoying. And isn't it grand that we get to enjoy the fireworks right along with them? We are, after all, just as much a part of this country as anyone else. And although our country, our politics and our society are far from perfect, I feel proud and privileged to be a citizen of the U.S.A.

Many people today see patriotism and civic pride as maudlin anachronisms. Many others see them as the property of the religious right, and therefore want nothing to do with them. We in the leather community, on the other hand, have our own style of patriotism and civic pride. We appreciate the good things about our society and this country. We also recognize our society's problems and are committed to making them better by getting involved. That fosters a realistic, practical patriotism, as opposed to a starry-eyed, my-country-right-or-wrong view of things. I have been at many runs, contests, award ceremonies, and other leather events that start with the singing of various national anthems. The assembled leather crowd's rendition of those anthems is always stirring, heartfelt and impressive.

So I have three flags on my figurative flagpole: the Stars & Stripes, the rainbow flag, and the leather pride flag. And I'm proud of all of them.

The Pink Triangle Project
A modest proposal

Published in *Lavender* #265 (July 22, 2005)

For some time now we've been hearing that the GLBT acronym has been widened to GLBTA: Gay, Lesbian, Bi, Trans and Allies.

That's the society we're trying to build—a society where every sexuality is accepted (not just tolerated, but actually accepted and honored) and no sexuality is discriminated against.

If you ask me, the leather/BDSM/fetish community could serve as a prototype, model and mentor to society at large, because we've already evolved into that kind of society. That idea brings up several points.

At a recent Twin Cities Gay Men's Chorus concert, the chorus sang a song called "Not In Our Town" about what happened in 1993 in Billings, Montana, when white supremacists started committing hate crimes against minorities there. There wasn't much reaction at first.

Then, one night during the holiday season, a cinder block was thrown through a window displaying a menorah. The town's residents responded by displaying paper menorahs in a window of almost every home, whether the people who lived there were Jewish or not.

The owner of a sporting-goods store posted a message outside his store that quickly became a rallying cry: "Not in Our Town. No Hate. No Violence. Peace on Earth."

That's what I call having allies.

I recently read that when the Nazis invaded Denmark and ordered the Jews there to identify themselves by wearing a yellow Star of David, the response of the Danish people was for everyone to start wearing the Star of David, whether or not they were Jewish.

It's good to have allies.

I recently heard Judy Shepard, Matthew's mom, talk to members of several GLBT employee groups in Minneapolis. She talked about the importance of coming out, and also of having everyone who knows us come out as having a lesbian daughter, gay uncle, transgender teacher, or whatever.

If the Danes could all wear Stars of David to protest the Nazis' discrimination and hate, and if the people of Billings, Montana, could photocopy, color and display thousands of menorahs, what would happen if large numbers of people everywhere—gays, lesbians, bisexuals, trans people and allies alike—all started wearing pink triangles?

Maybe armbands would be a bit much, but how about cloisonne pink-triangle lapel pins? Even if we ourselves don't happen to be gay, lesbian, bisexual or transgender, what would happen if we wore a pink triangle as a show of solidarity with and support for those who are?

Would that be like the menorahs in the windows of all those homes in Billings, Montana? It would.

Would that send the same message, that hate and discrimination are not wanted, not welcome and will not be tolerated coming from the mouths of our political leaders and our religious leaders? It would.

Would that mess with people's minds, when they see a happily married woman or man—whom they've known for years, with children at home, who ushers in church on Sundays—wearing a pink triangle? It would. And that would be good.

Would things change? I think they would.

So, I hereby call for the start of a movement—an ongoing, quiet demonstration. I think the leather/BDSM/fetish community should be among the leaders—or, if you will, the instigators.

Wear a pink triangle. Wear it all the time. Wear it proudly. When people look shocked and say, "I didn't know you were gay," either tell them, "Well, I am" or tell them, "Well, I'm not—but I have a lot of friends who are, and I don't like seeing them discriminated against."

Pink triangle pins are out there. Everybody doesn't have to wear the same one. But wear one. Be a proud GLBT person or become an honorary one. In the short run it might be uncomfortable. In the long run, it will be much more comfortable for everyone when society doesn't spend all that energy on hate and can use it for better things.

No hate. No violence. Not in our town. Not in our state. Not in our country. Not in our world.

Peace on Earth.*

---

*A movement began recently that is similar to the pink-triangle project proposed above. Called the White Knot for (Marriage) Equality movement, it involves wearing a strip of white ribbon, with a knot tied in its middle, to show support for the idea that "Everyone should have the right to tie the knot."

Chapter 11

Healthy Life

Safety and Sanity

Published in *Lavender* #8 (September 15, 1995)

One of the leather community's mottos is "safe, sane and consensual." Those are good words to live by, and not just within the confines of a scene. Let's ponder how we can apply them to life in general.

Safety can mean taking precautions so you don't get hurt and you don't hurt others. Sanity can refer to our community's high regard for personal integrity and honesty in ourselves and in others. Unfortunately, we sometimes find that even in the leather community people can be dishonest. What can we, as individuals and as a community, do about that?

I'm going to save the topics of consent and community safety for another column,* and write here about individual personal safety. While this certainly includes safe sex, it also includes much more. AIDS and other sexually transmitted diseases are good things to avoid, but I'm sure we would also like to avoid property theft, muggings, and other such unpleasantness. Unfortunately, the precautions given below can't guarantee totally smooth sailing. Whether it's a one-night trick, an occasional sex partner or a dating situation, there are risks involved. Short of becoming a hermit, those risks can't be completely eliminated, but here are some ways of reducing them.

---

*See "Trust, Intimacy, Consent—and Rape," page 209.

Our local leather community is a pretty tight group; to say that "everybody knows everybody" is an exaggeration, but not too far from the truth. Use this fact to your advantage! News travels fast, and if certain people have a tendency to act in a less-than-honorable fashion, they tend to develop a reputation. So . . . let's say you just saw someone across a crowded room and now your hormones are in a frenzy. You've never noticed them before, but right now you're not noticing much of anything else. First tip: Before you jump, check them out. Ask around and you'll probably find someone who knows them, or at least has seen them before. You don't have to let other people make your decisions for you, but it couldn't hurt to ask. When I was first getting into the leather scene, I only half-jokingly formulated a rule: "If you're going to play with me, you gotta have references."

Suppose you ask around and nobody raises any red flags. Assuming you are successful in setting up a rendezvous with the other person, here's tip #2: Introduce the other person to your friends. Make sure somebody knows where you will be, and with whom.

Tip #3: When you finally get physical, do it safely and sanely. Know the facts about what is considered safe and unsafe, and know what risks you are willing or unwilling to take—and stick by your decisions. If you see a rash or a sore that doesn't look right, don't be afraid to ask about it, and don't be afraid to bring the action to a halt if you think the situation demands it. You have the right to do that (that's what "consensual" is all about). And even if you see no obvious problems, don't assume it's okay to be unsafe "just this once" because the other person "looks okay." Being safe "some of the time" is another name for being unsafe.

One more way to keep yourself safe: keep your judgment un-clouded. It's difficult to make good determinations about a prospective partner's character when you're out of control because you're too drunk or high to care. If you have an alcohol or drug problem, the rest of the community may be more aware of it than you are; be honest with yourself and get the help you need.

I later incorporated some of the above ideas into a brief safety checklist:

Let's Be Careful Out There

Published in *Lavender* #43 (January 17, 1997), reprinted several times thereafter

- Get to know something about a prospective play partner. Check their references by asking friends about them.
- When it's time to leave the bar or party, let other people know where you're going and with whom.
- If you're not driving, be sure you have cab fare and change for phone calls.*
- Keep a clear head. It's difficult to watch out for your safety when you're under the influence of alcohol or drugs.
- Negotiate the scene beforehand. Use agreed-upon safewords to slow or stop the action if necessary.
- Remember: "Safe, sane, consensual." If you aren't familiar with all the things those three words entail, find out.
- Endure nothing. If you don't feel comfortable with the way things are going, do what you need to do to keep yourself safe. That may include either leaving or kicking someone out. (Sometimes these things happen.)

The leather/SM community's ideal is respect for every community member and for the rules of safety. Unfortunately, there are people who don't play by these rules; these are not people with whom you want to play. Following the suggestions above will lessen your likelihood of becoming their prey, or will help ensure your safety if you suddenly find yourself confronted with a dangerous situation.

Please, play safe and play smart.

Barebacking, BDSM, and Bicycle Helmets

Published in *Lavender* #245 (October 15, 2004)

There are so many things lately I don't understand.

I don't understand why anyone would want to see George Bush re-elected president.

I don't understand reality TV.

I don't understand rap music.

---

*This was written before cell phones became ubiquitous. Even so, cell phone batteries die and cellular service is sometimes spotty. So maybe it's still a good idea to carry change for a pay phone—assuming you can find one.

And I don't understand why anyone in their right mind would bareback.*

Please understand that your humble columnist is an excellent example of someone who in financial circles is known as "risk-averse." Given the choice between a high-risk mutual fund with the potential of big returns and a low-risk money market fund that pays a pittance, I'll take the money-market fund every time. (I drive my broker crazy.)

I always wear my seat belt when I drive.

I look both ways when crossing the street—even on one-way streets.

And I was using condoms even before they were fashionable, because even before AIDS there were plenty of other venereal diseases I didn't want to catch.

"So, Mr. Risk-Averse," I hear you saying, "How does that square with writing a leather column? Here you are, writing about high-risk activities like SM sex and riding motorcycles."

Yes, you're right. And the contradictions get worse: I don't ride a motorcycle, but I do ride a bicycle. And when I ride it, Mr. Risk-Averse doesn't wear a helmet.

And why don't I wear a helmet? Not because it's too hot or too uncomfortable—not even because it might mess my hair. I don't wear a bicycle helmet because I think bicycle helmets look dorky. I refuse to look like I'm wearing Darth Vader's facemask, upside down and backwards, on top of my head.

And when I get on my bike without a helmet, do I get a rebel thrill because I'm cheating death? No. On the contrary, I try not to think about the risk. When I'm on my bike I'm in denial.

Sound familiar? "I don't want to wear this condom. It's uncomfortable. It's confining. It interrupts the action while I put it on." Or "I don't want him to wear a condom. I don't want to feel latex, I want to feel the intimacy of his skin." How many people, all the while they're having unprotected sex, are in denial that they're doing anything risky?

Wearing a helmet, of course, has no effect on whether or not I will encounter an unsafe situation. I may encounter one or I may

---

*Barebacking: Fucking without a condom.

not. But if I do encounter an unsafe situation, I will be safer if I am wearing a helmet. Except for very rare, fluke occurrences, I will not be less safe with protection than without it.

There's more to safety than simply wearing a helmet, however. Whether for biking, motorcycling or SM, another big safety factor is education and training: knowing safe ways to operate a bike, a motorcycle or a flogger simultaneously increases enjoyment and reduces risk.

Unprotected sex, or barebacking, is different from these other activities. It is inherently risky, and no amount of education, training or technique can mitigate that risk. The best way to make it less risky is just the same as with bicycles and motorcycles: wear a helmet, so to speak.

But then, of course, it isn't barebacking anymore. Barebacking's aficionados would say that this advice is tantamount to saying the safest way to own a motorcycle is not to ride it.

There are only two circumstances of which I am aware in which barebacking can be considered to meet the definition of "safe" in the sense of the BDSM community's "safe, sane, consensual" mantra: a) two HIV-negative partners who are monogamous; or b) two HIV-positive partners who undergo medical testing, determine that they are both infected with the same strain of the HIV virus, and are thereafter monogamous.

Other than in these two rare and tenuous circumstances, barebacking is worse than riding without a helmet. It's skydiving without a parachute.

The ethic of the leather/BDSM community is that we all look out for, and take care of, each other. If an activity is not safe, sane and consensual, it is abusive and should not be tolerated. Even in a situation where barebacking might unfortunately and perversely meet the consensuality test, it still fails the test of safety and, I would argue, of sanity.

Why would anyone consent to an activity that has a high probability of being lethal, either quickly or slowly, or at the very least could make life much more complicated and much less pleasant?

I suppose there are as many reasons to bareback as there are barebackers. Some think it's romantic to be Mimi in *La Bohème*. Some think that becoming positive will bestow on them a life of sympathy and insurance benefits. Some think it's intimate and romantic to share the virus with the one you love or to have them share the virus with you. Some are angry at being infected and want to infect as many other people as they can before they check out.

Some are fatalistic and figure it will happen to them eventually, so they might as well get it over with. Some take the opposite tack — AIDS will never happen to them because they are somehow invulnerable. (I would note here that there's a great difference between saying, "It will never happen to me because I won't let it — I will take action, every time, to protect myself" and saying "It won't happen to me because I'm magically immune, and therefore I can do whatever I want and don't have to worry about protection." And yes, I know, that second instance is what I'm saying to myself as I ride my bike without a helmet.)

That's what some people who bareback may be thinking. But the reality is that once someone seroconverts, there's no going back. Life will either be very short or else will be filled with doctor visits, strict treatment schedules and an ongoing regimen of expensive drugs with major and unpleasant side effects.

There was a time when we didn't know what caused AIDS and didn't know how to stop it from spreading. An unconscionable number of people died as a result, and that was tragic. Now we know how to stop the spread of the virus, but in spite of this some people are intentionally helping to spread it. That's still tragic, but it's also perverse.

There are plenty of other, safer ways one can still enjoy sex — and perhaps even enjoy it more because one's horizons have been widened. Be adventurous! Try something new (and, incidentally, safer).

I have no illusions that I can singlehandedly stop people from barebacking, any more than anyone can make me wear a helmet when I ride my bike. But I can at least say, "Stop and think about what you're doing if you bareback. Realize the consequences."

It's all fun and games until someone gets infected.

Barebacking: Just Don't Do It.

Replacing Safe Sex with . . . Smart Sex!
Published in *Lavender* #304 (January 19, 2007)

Here's a New Year's resolution for you: Resolve to stop worrying about Safe Sex. Resolve instead to start having Smart Sex.

Smart Sex made its debut in 2006 in Issue #11 of *Instigator* Magazine and in palm cards handed out at the International Mr. Leather contest in Chicago. The advertising campaign promoting Smart Sex is a joint effort of *Instigator* and asspig.com.

The concept of Smart Sex is the long-overdue re-tooling of what has been known as Safe Sex or Safer Sex, a concept that was a prominent, if not always welcome, feature of the sexual landscape during the latter part of the twentieth century.

When AIDS first showed up no one knew what caused it or how to prevent its spread. But once the virus that caused AIDS was discovered and its transmission paths were identified, ways to prevent the spread of the virus started to be publicized.

At first these techniques were called "Safe Sex." The term was later changed to "Safer Sex" in recognition of the fact that, although these transmission-prevention techniques can reduce the risks associated with unprotected sex, they are not foolproof. Condoms, for example, sometimes break.

So, just to be clear, it's not called "Safer Sex" because it's safer than "Safe Sex"—it's called "Safer Sex" because it's safer than unsafe sex.

For a generation of gay men, Safe Sex was something to practice religiously, or to feel guilty about when they didn't. For awhile, thanks to a massive educational effort, many gay men changed the way they had sex much of the time.

As the years wore on, however, the sexual landscape changed. Battle fatigue set in, and it became harder for men to be vigilant for safe sex every time. Protease inhibitors and other antiretroviral drugs meant that AIDS was no longer necessarily an immediate death sentence, which led to "being safe each and every time" seeming less important.

A new generation of young gay men, who had never known sex without the baggage of HIV but who had also not lived through the nightmare of watching their friends die agonizing deaths, were blasé about AIDS. They didn't appreciate being told what to do, and especially what not to do, by older men and public health authorities.

And for men in the leather community, where danger and edginess are part of the thrill of leathersex, and where a rebel/outlaw mentality is often part of the mindset, Safe Sex equaled Boring Sex.

The old concept of Safe Sex appealed to fear, and it needed fear to be taken seriously. In a culture of young males, gay or straight, who pride themselves on fearing nothing (even to the point where "No Fear" has become a brand name), Safe Sex came to be viewed as lame and wimpy.

The genius of Smart Sex is that, instead of being built around fear, it is built around and reinforces a positive quality: intelligence. Most of us like to think of ourselves as smart people doing smart things and making smart choices. We normally don't take pride in being dumb and doing dumb things (the people in the "Jackass" movies being the exception).

Therefore, who would want to have Dumb Sex?

Safe Sex tends to assume the worst about people, possibly insulting their intelligence in the process (i.e., "your good sense goes out the window when you get horny, so you'd better listen to us"). Smart Sex assumes people are intelligent and encourages them to think about themselves that way.

Condom use, keeping toys and playspaces clean, and getting tested periodically are examples of smart things to do and smart choices to make—choices that are more likely to lead to a long, healthy, sexually fulfilling future. What's not to like about that?

If the concept of Smart Sex in itself represents a major paradigm shift, the advertising materials put together by *Instigator* and asspig.com are no less revolutionary. The language used in the campaign is refreshingly straightforward. Facts are presented simply, with no shaming, judging or moralizing. The overall attitude is one of care and concern—but in a brotherly voice, rather than from a parental or authority-figure viewpoint.

Art, photos and other graphics featured in the campaign are hard-hitting and explicit, which is perfectly appropriate to *Instigator*'s and asspig.com's audiences. Richard Smith, president of the company that owns asspig.com, was quoted in *Instigator* as saying, "Why can't we show hot men, having balls-to-the-wall sex without missing out on anything except maybe HIV and Hepatitis C" (or, I might add, syphilis, gonorrhea, hepatitis B, and a host of other problems).

It's interesting to note that this Smart Sex paradigm shift is not happening solely in the gay men's or leather/BDSM/fetish communities.

An Internet search for "Smart Sex" turned up approximately 30,000 hits and showed the words "Smart Sex" being used in the service of a wide variety of causes as varied as avoiding teen pregnancy, avoiding herpes and other sexually transmitted diseases, and "finding life-long love in a hookup world."

No one, it seems, wants to have Dumb Sex.

BDSM, Therapists and Sanity

Published in *Lavender* #130 (May 19, 2000)

Recently, I was invited to be a co-presenter speaking about leather and BDSM sex to a group of GLBT mental-health providers. The fact that mental health was the topic of the day fit in perfectly with the "sane" component of the community's "safe, sane, consensual" mantra.

A therapist needs to be able to judge if a client's behavior is sane or not. But if a therapist's shame, personal prejudice or ignorance about leather and BDSM interferes with that judgment, they may not be helping their client in the most effective way.

We talked about the leather community's view that leathersex done right, and for the right reasons, is heightened and healthy sexuality and also heightened and healthy intimacy. Done wrong, or for the wrong reasons, it's not healthy and it's not BDSM; it's abuse. How can a therapist tell which is which? How can their clients? How can you?

Here's one example from the seminar. One member of the group asked about knifeplay and cutting—how could that be considered sane? (The same question could be asked by the uninitiated about almost any common dungeon activity.) I answered that it's sometimes necessary to look at the motivation behind the action.

Some people are into cutting and scarification for ritual value in much the same way that other people get tattoos or piercings. The cutting, tattooing or piercing is the ritual that the person is using to mark an event in their lives, and the body jewelry, tattoo or scar is the lasting reminder of the ritual.

In this context, what's the difference between a nipple ring and a wedding ring? People might do body modification for healthy or unhealthy reasons, and people get married for healthy or unhealthy reasons. A little (or a lot) of investigative work will shed light on the reasons behind people's actions, and a therapist can then make an evaluation of whether the motivations are healthy or unhealthy. (Yes, I know, I'm making it sound a lot simpler than it usually is.)

Here's another cutting scenario that shows a completely different motivation: a teenage girl, alone in her room, takes a razor blade and slowly, deliberately, makes cuts in her arm. She watches, fascinated, as the blood trickles out of the cuts. This isn't the first time she's done this—it's becoming a habit, and her parents are worried. When the therapist asks her why she does it, her unemotional reply is simply this: "Because I feel the pain, and I see the blood flow, and I know I'm alive."

This is not BDSM. This is self-mutilation, and it's more common than you might think. This is the desperate cry of a tortured soul in real pain. The parents are right to be worried, and the patient and therapist have a lot of work ahead of them.

What's the difference between BDSM and abuse? Look at the motivations behind the actions, and the feelings that come from the actions. Here are some questions to ask about a situation to help clarify whether it's healthy or unhealthy.

How do you feel while it's happening? Whether topping or bottoming, BDSM sex will feel good; while engaging in it you may feel buoyant and exhilarated or you may feel relaxed, dreamy and euphoric. You should feel loved and respected. Abuse will not feel good; you may feel anywhere from slightly ridiculous to somewhat uneasy to terrified, panic-stricken and frightened. You may feel used and objectified. You may feel anger and rage. Honor your feelings and what they're telling you. If you feel a mixture of both good and bad, try to determine where the bad feelings are coming from—they're trying to tell you something important.

How do you feel after it's over? Warm, satisfied, giggly, contented, euphoric, glowing, cared for—in other words, happy? Has your life been enhanced? Or do you feel bad—hurt, used, angry, abandoned, sad, denigrated, disrespected? Do you feel like you've just been raped, punished, abused or violated? Do you want revenge? Are you feeling a mixture of good and bad feelings? Again, pay attention to what your feelings are telling you.

What feelings are your BDSM experiences reinforcing—good ones or bad ones? If your BDSM experiences enrich and enhance your life, don't feel you need to apologize to a therapist or anyone else for being kinky. But if you feel you need to be punished, beaten up or hurt—if your BDSM experiences are feeding feelings of self-hate or low self-esteem—that's not a healthy reason to engage in BDSM. Nor is it healthy if you feel a need to go out occasionally and find a willing punching bag on whom you can vent your frustrations. In either case, you are skating on the kind of thin ice where anger is in control and people get hurt as a result. That most definitely is neither safe nor sane. Run, do not walk, to your nearest GLBT-friendly and kink-friendly therapist (aren't we lucky there actually are such people?) and let them help you help yourself.

Trust, Consent, Intimacy—and Rape

Published in *Lavender* #127 (April 7, 2000)

Let's consider the third part of the "safe, sane, consensual" mantra—the dynamics of consensuality and nonconsensuality.*

Consent is not just for those in the SM community. All sex and all intimacy is based on consent, and that consent is based on trust. In an SM setting, if trust is violated and non-consensual things happen, it's no longer "safe, sane, consensual" SM—it crosses the line and becomes abuse, or even rape. Intimacy implies vulnerability, and SM is an experience of both hyper-intimacy and hyper-vulnerability. Abusers and rapists take advantage of that vulnerability.

Consent, Trust and Communication

Consent comes from trust, and trust is maintained through communication. Good communication is essential to any kind of scene or intimacy. Communication is necessary before the action starts—both to establish consent on the part of all participants, and to define everyone's boundaries. Communication also is necessary during the scene to keep it on track.

The leather/SM community has evolved a form of communication known as the "safeword"—when any participant in a scene speaks a safeword, the action instantly stops. Participants in a scene can agree on whatever safewords they want to use, but one of the

---

*See page 199 for a discussion of the first two parts of the mantra, safety and sanity.

most universal safeword schemes is modeled on traffic light colors: "green" means everything is okay, keep going; "yellow" means slow down a bit or lighten up; and "red" means stop everything right now. In addition, it's usually a good idea to keep in mind the ultimate safewords: "No" means NO, and "Stop" means STOP.

Safewords are one way of communicating during a scene, but they aren't the only way. Communication during a scene may take many forms: verbal, physical gestures, eye contact or body language, to name a few. Obviously, if a bottom is blindfolded and gagged, the top won't be able to get any information from their eyes and the bottom's voice won't be able to be used for much more than muffled moans. If the bottom is in bondage and completely immobilized, they can't gesture very effectively. Fit the safeword to the scene, remembering that it may not always be a spoken "word."

Once a safeword has been established, take it seriously. Don't use it if you don't mean it. Don't use it in a confusing manner—don't say "red" and giggle, for instance. If you hear your partner use a safeword, the safest thing to do is bring the action to a halt immediately. Then check in with your partner and see what's going on. Maybe the action will start up again, maybe it won't. But don't take chances.

Why does communication in a scene break down? Perhaps at least one person stops sending clear communications and instead starts sending confusing signals and mixed messages, or they may stop communicating altogether. Or, perhaps at least one person stops paying attention to the signals the other person is sending. Whether I am top or bottom in a scene, it behooves me to send clear communications and to pay close attention to what my partner is telling me. A breakdown in communication interferes with the safe, sane, consensual nature of a scene and opens the door to an abusive situation.

Staying Out of Trouble

Obviously, no one wants to find themselves in an abusive or rape situation, but it's not always possible to detect an abuser beforehand. They may wear leather and practice SM, or they may not. Abusers may be someone you've never met before but find very attractive, they may be someone you think you know well, or they may be a well-known community leader. They may be sweet—except when they're drunk or high. Or they may not need a chemical assist to bring out their abusive qualities. As I've said before, a jerk wearing leather is still a jerk. Trust your gut—if something doesn't feel right, don't do it.

Also as I've said before, it never hurts to check references. If you're considering doing something with someone, but you're a beginner and people tell you this person plays pretty hard, maybe it's not a good match. What seems like a hard blow to you may only be their warming-up strokes.

When Things Go Wrong

Okay, you've set up the scene beforehand—you've both agreed on what you expect, what your limits are, what each of you will and will not do. And then the scene starts, and something goes horribly wrong. You as bottom forbade the top to do something; now, in spite of your screams of protest, it's happening anyway. Rape, sexual assault, sexual abuse—call it what you will, it's happening to you. What do you do?

Or, say you're topping someone and suddenly they freak. Things they agreed to before are now not okay. They may become violent. They may turn on you and start attacking you.

What do you do? You do what's necessary to survive. Depending on the situation, you resist, you submit, you escape, you attract help, or you incapacitate your assailant. Follow your instincts, and know that if you survive, you made the right choice.

If you're the top, you have the power and also the responsibility to bring the scene to a grinding halt, and to do whatever is necessary for the physical and psychological well-being of the bottom—as long as doing so doesn't threaten your own physical and psychological well-being. If the bottom is attacking you, see the previous paragraph.

According to Scott Bartell, a Licensed Independent Clinical Social Worker with Family & Children's Service of Minneapolis, "Your physical and spiritual survival justifies doing whatever you need to do in a sexual-abuse situation. Your actions may need to be passive-aggressive, duplicitous or even violent. You need to get out of the situation, and then get professional help for trauma survival." Both your body and psyche have been assaulted and both need attention. Get medical care if necessary, and be honest with medical personnel about what happened and how it happened. And seek out a GLBT-

and kink-friendly counseling resource—you will need to do a lot of emotional processing to come to terms with what you've been through.

Leather Justice

Do you press charges? Do you name your abuser so they don't do this to someone else? These are tricky questions, fraught with all sorts of uncertainties. The community depends on checking references and self-policing because we know from past experience that police and the judicial system tend not to be terribly sympathetic or understanding toward SM-related issues. But even in the leather/SM community, sometimes it's the same as with heterosexual date-rape accusations: it's your word against theirs. Since smear campaigns and witch hunts are not unheard of, other people may take your accusations with a degree of skepticism until they've heard both sides of the argument.

Generally, though, when a community member doesn't play by the rules, the word gets around—but unfortunately it usually takes a few people getting hurt before the message hits home and sticks. In the case of serious accusations, impromptu leather/SM community "courts" have been convened to hear the complaints and decide what action should be taken, up to and including censure and banishment from the community. At the very least, someone who is accused of nonconsensual or abusive behavior will be under increased scrutiny by the rest of the community. They may eventually clear their name and reputation, or they may prove there were grounds for the original accusations. Or they may move, and the cycle may start all over again in another city's leather/SM community.

One final point: these problems are not by any means exclusive to the leather/SM community or to any geographical area. All the concepts discussed here can be applied to other communities as well. It is an unfortunate fact that assault, abuse and rape happen in all communities—and all communities, leather/SM included, firmly state that assault, abuse and rape are not acceptable behaviors.

Leather and Domestic Violence

Published in *Lavender* #19 and #20 (February 16 and March 1, 1996)

Domestic abuse has certainly gotten its share of attention in mainstream media, from O.J. and Nicole to various members of the

Minnesota Vikings football team to at least one Minnesota state politician. But almost all the mainstream publicity frames the problem as the man ("perpetrator" or villain) beating his wife (victim). This model doesn't really apply to either gay male or lesbian domestic violence. And we in the leather/SM community, being the creative tribe that we are, have invented flavors of domestic violence that would boggle the minds of "battered women" advocates. How does one explain a Mistress who abuses her boy? Or a slave who abuses his or her Master or Mistress and then says, "If you don't like it, you can take your frustration out on me in the dungeon"?

Whether anyone wants to admit it or not, domestic violence does happen among gays and lesbians and in the leather community. And it can be stopped. I'm living proof of both these statements. I was in an abusive relationship for eighteen years. With lots of help and lots of support, I was able to stop the abuse by getting out of that relationship.

What qualifies as abuse? An easy answer is when your partner hits you, but for people into SM that answer may not apply. Then again, it may—if what is going on is not safe, if it's not sane, or if it's not consensual, it qualifies as abuse.

Abuse can be physical, but it also can take other forms. Abuse is about one person trying to control another, and the abuser may use many control methods. There may be emotional or psychological abuse, preying on a victim's self-image to make him or her easier to control. The victim's property, pets or even children may be abused, the implied message being "If you don't toe the line, you're next." Sexual abuse can take many forms, including both enforced sex (rape) and withholding sex. Abuse can even be financial.

In abusive relationships, the perpetrator's objective is to maintain control over their victim. Paradoxically, they create in their victim the illusion that the victim is in control—and is therefore responsible for the fact they're being abused ("I wouldn't hit you if you didn't deserve it" or "Oh, you're really asking for it now, aren't you?") The victim thinks he or she provokes the abuse, and constantly "walks on eggshells" hoping—in vain—to avoid another blowup.

One other form of abuse needs to be mentioned here: chemical abuse, which often accompanies domestic abuse. It could be reasonable to expect that if a perpetrator abuses their partner they might also abuse chemicals. And victims often turn to alcohol or other substances to deaden their pain. Unfortunately, the effects of chemical abuse and domestic abuse tend to magnify each other, quickly making bad situations even worse.

Like chemical abuse, domestic abuse is progressive—it rarely gets better on its own, and almost always escalates. I'm lucky my abuser didn't kill me. And when I see news reports of victims who kill their abusers for reasons of self-preservation I realize that, had circumstances been just a little different, that could have been me.

So who exactly are these perpetrators of domestic violence? Who are their victims? You can't tell by looking at them. All abusers are not overbearing ogres; all victims are not spineless wimps. Abusers often are able to function normally in social situations, and even can be quite charming. They manage to hide their abusive tendencies from the rest of the world, reserving them exclusively for their victim(s).

Because abuse victims fear embarrassment (and retaliation from their abuser) if anyone else discovers they are being abused, they may present a calm, confident face to the rest of the world that belies the hell in which they're living.

Beneath the labels and the stereotypes, both abusers and victims are still people—people with a problem that needs to be dealt with. They're people who never thought they would resort to hitting someone they love, or who never thought they would stand for such treatment. They're people who may have thought they were immune to such things, and one day realize they're in the middle of an out-of-control situation.

One strategy that is probably not a good idea is couples counseling; in situations where abuse is present it is almost always counterproductive. Counseling only helps when counselor and clients deal with the truth. When their abuser is sitting right there in the counseling session, the victim can't be truthful about the abuse they are enduring for fear of retaliation from their abuser after the session is over.

Here are two books for further reading on this subject:

- *Men Who Beat The Men Who Love Them,** by Patrick Letellier and David Island, was the book that finally broke down my

---

*New York: Harrington Park Press, 1991.

denial and my defenses and convinced me I had to get away from my abuser. I can't recommend it highly enough.

- For women, there's *Naming the Violence—Speaking Out About Lesbian Battering,** edited by Kerry Lobel.

What To Do If the Authorities Show Up

Published in *Lavender* #195 (November 15, 2002)

Suppose you're attending a dungeon party. Suppose you're in the middle of heated action and there's a knock on the door. It's the police. What do you do?

Now suppose you're the host of said dungeon party. What do you do?

Or suppose the party is being hosted by an organization of which you are a member, or even of which you are the leader. What do you do?

In all three of the above scenarios, your preparations need to start long before the authorities ever arrive. Actually, there are steps that organizations, private hosts and partygoers can take that will minimize the possibility of the authorities showing up. If (in spite of everyone's best efforts) the police pay a call anyway, there are things that can be done that might defuse the situation before it spirals out of control.

This information comes to you from the National Coalition for Sexual Freedom (NCSF). Disclaimer: Neither NCSF nor your humble columnist is in the business of presenting legal advice. These are common-sense guidelines. Every situation is different. Your mileage may vary.

Whether hosting a party or attending one, one of the first things to consider is the question of how likely it is that this party will attract the attention of the authorities. What will be happening at the party? A grope/orgy room in the basement? BDSM activities in a dungeon? Is the BDSM "non-sexual" or might it include sex? Is the party all male, women only or mixed-gender? It is unfortunate but true that certain activities and certain groups of people are of less concern to the authorities than certain other activities and groups of people.

---

*Seattle: Seal Press, 1986.

Imagine you're a law enforcement officer. You know about as much as the average citizen about sex parties or BDSM activities. You have probably not been given training in these areas.

As an individual officer you might take action against activities you find at these types of events for any number of reasons: You might perceive the actions as illegal; there might be peer pressure from other officers; you may be afraid not to do something in the situation (CYA, in other words); or you just might not like someone's attitude and feel like teaching them a lesson. Your law enforcement agency might encourage or direct you to take action against these kinds of activities for all the above reasons and/or for the added reasons of politics (internal or external) and community pressure. That's some of what's motivating the officer who knocks on your door. Following are some ways to minimize the chance of that officer paying a visit.

Some things not to do: Perhaps no alcohol. Definitely no illegal substances. Definitely no minors. No money should change hands at the door — that looks too much like "sexual services" for compensation. Either let it be a free party, use a true donation system, or preregister attendees in advance.

There's a formidable amount of legal research that should be done beforehand, including applicable state and local laws, local permit rules, zoning ordinances and fire codes. Don't allow occupancy by more than the legal number and don't block fire exits. You might also want to consider the matter of insurance coverage for the event.

Don't draw unwanted attention. Advertising and invitations must be targeted and discreet. Respect the neighborhood: Partygoers should not park illegally, should be wearing street-legal attire to and from the party, should not litter and should obey all local smoking ordinances. Too much noise or any public displays of activities that the neighbors might find offensive are sure ways to get the authorities on your doorstep.

The entry to the party must be a defined area that is visually separated from the various activity areas, and there should be no sex, BDSM activities or socializing in the entry area. There should be designated door personnel who should admit only people who have been invited to the party. As guests arrive they should be asked to sign a "Waiver of Liability" or "Assignment of Risk." A sign in the entryway and a statement on the sign-in sheet should inform guests of the nature of the party; this demonstrates that all guests had "informed consent" as to just what kind of party this is.

These preparations will pay off if, in spite of all your precautions, the party is visited by law enforcement personnel. If that happens, one of the designated door attendants should go outside, close the door and ask if they can be of assistance. Try to resolve the issue there. If a law enforcement officer wants to gain entry, the door attendant should politely advise them that they do not have the authority to grant entry and that they will go get a person who does. They should then *leave the officer outside* while getting the host or other person in charge of the event, or the property owner or other person in charge of the property. That person should then go outside and talk to the officer, again trying to resolve the matter there.

All this time, of course, word should be spread to the rest of the party so guests can compose themselves. Stop the action, clean up and get dressed as soon as possible.

You do not have to allow a "consent search" or a "voluntary entry." However, if the officer does not want to wait and decides to enter without permission, do not block the officer's entry. That would be called "obstruction of justice." Voice your objection and stand aside.

The following tips are taken from a "Pocket Reference" card provided by the NCSF. They are important for anyone to remember, and not just at parties:

In dealing with law enforcement officers:
• DO stay calm.
• DO be respectful, polite and courteous.
• DO use your common sense.
• DON'T have a "bad attitude."

In connection with statements and communication:
• You have the right not to make statements.
• You have the right not to incriminate yourself.
• Be honest in whatever you decide to say.
• Use simple language, clear and easy to understand. (You don't want to come across as speaking down to anyone.)

In general:

- In cases of interrupted BDSM play where a law enforcement officer suspects abuse, volunteer to have your partner talk with them to reinforce the consensual nature of the action.
- Transport toys in a secure container, and in the trunk of the vehicle. Do not consent to a search.
- Keep in mind the things which demonstrate that consensual SM is different from abuse.

And finally, although I sincerely hope you never need to use this piece of advice—if you are arrested, DO NOT make any statements, and DO ask for an attorney.

NCSF has much more information available on this topic—contact them about their Law Enforcement Outreach Program.

Scarfing: Not Safe and Not Sane

Published in *Lavender* #31 (August 2, 1996)

A leatherman who was prominent in a certain East Coast leather community was recently found dead in his basement—hanging by his belt from an overhead pipe. The community was stunned. Was it suicide? Or was it foul play?

I later heard the death had been ruled accidental. My friend had evidently been "scarfing"—choking off his oxygen supply to intensify sexual feeling. Obviously, this is a very dangerous thing to do and falls well outside the boundaries of "safe, sane and consensual." Please, I implore you—don't even think about doing this.

In early 1994 a high official of the British government died the same way, and the British tabloids had a field day with it. It even was written up in *Newsweek,* where I read about it. I briefly thought to myself, "What a stupid thing to do!" before turning the page.

About a week later, I got a letter from my mother. In it was a copy of that same *Newsweek* article and a note: "I know, I know—you're a big boy now and don't need your mother clucking in the background. However, when I read the enclosed article I couldn't help thinking . . . . Sexual highs are one thing, and I know you pursue them. Just don't cross the safety line. Know that I send this because I love you, because I care. Enough said. Much love, Mom."

Thanks, Mom. My sentiments exactly. (Have I got a great mom, or what?)*

Electricity: Please Don't "DieHard"

Published in *Lavender* #63 (October 24, 1997)

To anyone out there who is considering exploring electricity from an SM perspective, a request: Learn about Mr. Kilowatt before you play with him. There's a lot to learn—much more than this column can go into, so I'll only touch on a few of the basics here.

For SM purposes, there are two kinds of electricity: electricity that moves along the surface of human tissue, and electricity that penetrates human tissue and moves through it. Violet wands are of the former type; most other electrical toys are of the latter.

Violet wands were originally sold as medical devices but now are widely recognized as medically worthless. In SM situations, however, they provide both an interesting tactile sensation and an impressive visual image. (However, I don't play with them because my instincts tell me that they burn holes in one's aura. Your instincts may tell you something else, and that's fine.)†

Now, as to the other kind of electricity: Think of the various kinds of interactions between electrical current and the human body in non-SM situations. Downed power lines can be lethal. Hairdryers in bathtubs can be lethal. Electric chairs are designed to be lethal. Some non-lethal uses of electricity applied to the human body include torturing political prisoners and using "stun guns" to subdue attackers. And there's the legendary convention-time prank involving male conventioneers using cattle prods on female showgirls—all in good fun, of course (or so the men think).

---

*Scarfing is just one type of breathplay, and it's especially dangerous because it's often done in solitude and in secret—when something goes wrong there's no one there who can help. Other scene-based types of breathplay involve one person controlling another's air supply. I know many people who engage in activities of this sort, and so far none of them have been struck by tragedy. But still, to me, it seems like a very high-risk activity. Now, in the words of my mother, "Enough said."

†When this column was originally published, this statement raised eyebrows and caused comment. Nevertheless, I am including it in this book because my instincts haven't changed. One rule regarding violet wands that everyone agrees on is that they should not be used around the eyes.

Medical science uses electricity with somewhat loftier intentions. Electricity to the head (electroshock therapy) has been used for decades to treat mental illness and depression, but even after all these years there are still some major side effects to deal with. And in emergency rooms, electric paddles are used on the chest to jump-start a heart that has stopped beating. If you've ever watched "St. Elsewhere" or "ER," you know the strength of the jolt the paddles deliver.

Conversely, an electric shock can stop a beating heart. Years ago I learned from a TV repairman that when he was messing around inside a TV set he always kept one hand in his pocket. That way if he got a shock it would only go up one finger and down the other; if he had both hands inside the TV the shock could go up one arm, through the heart, and out the other arm—possibly killing him in the process.

So, since we don't want electricity around the heart or the brain, the mantra for everyone involved in electrical play is (repeat after me): "Never above the waist." One major manufacturer of electrical toys for SM play feels this is such an important rule that they've incorporated that slogan into their logo.

If the idea of electrical play intrigues you, don't just buy a cattle prod at Fleet Farm and start experimenting, and don't try to see what else you can do with a car battery and jumper cables. Before you actually do anything with electricity, learn about electrical play by reading about it and/or by talking with others who have some experience in this field.*

---

*This column inspired letters to *Lavender* saying your humble columnist should not be writing about matters about which he knows nothing. This was in the relatively early days of the column, and one of the writers accused me of writing about SM in an effort to "boost my readership." In my response to those letters, published in the December 5, 1997 issue of *Lavender*, I responded:

I don't choose topics for the "Leather Life" column to "boost my readership"; I choose them based on questions and comments I hear from the community. I try to include things the community either wants or needs to know. Here's what sparked (excuse the pun) the electricity column: I was talking with a gentleman at a party, and the topic of conversation turned to electrical play. I mentioned the "never above the waist" rule—a rule with which this gentleman was unacquainted. His response was that gee, it sure was a good thing we talked about this because he had been considering experimenting with a car battery

Poppers: What You Need To Know About the Little Brown Bottle

Published in *Lavender* #128 (April 21, 2000)

This edition of this column is not just for the leather/SM community, and it's not just for guys. It's for anyone—of any gender—who uses poppers. For the uninitiated, the name "poppers" refers to any of several nitrite chemicals that cause a "rush" when inhaled. Amyl nitrate is the oldest, and was first developed for relief from angina (heart pain). It is a clear golden liquid usually sold in a cloth-covered glass capsule; when the capsule is crushed (or popped, which is where the term "poppers" comes from), the liquid soaks into the cloth and the vapors are inhaled. Since 1979, amyl nitrate has been legally available only with a doctor's prescription.

Why do poppers do what they do? They're vasodilators, which means they cause blood vessels to enlarge and make the heart beat faster, sending large amounts of blood and oxygen rushing through the heart and brain. That euphoric "rush" feeling comes on quickly and only lasts a few minutes. Poppers also relax smooth muscle tissue, and some people use them during anal sex to relax their anal sphincter.

---

and jumper cables—one clamp to one nipple, one clamp to the other. I told him that was not a safe thing to do, and thought to myself, "Well, there's a column that needs to be written."

I have always tried to make "Leather Life" sex- and SM-positive, within the bounds of intelligence, common sense and good taste. The message of the electricity column was not "Don't play with electricity," it was "Don't kill yourself or someone else while you're doing it." In this context, I considered descriptions of other electrical phenomena involving the human body relevant in establishing a healthy respect for electricity and illustrating the importance of approaching electrical play in an intelligent manner.

When "Leather Life" started two-and-a-half years ago, it was decided that it would not be a "how-to" column, since that information is available elsewhere. Coverage of SM in this column has been concerned with reinforcing awareness of the community's "safe, sane, consensual" motto or has been targeted to those who are new to the community and have questions. The intent of this particular article was not to set myself up as a master "electrician," but to emphasize the importance of seeking out those who are experts at electrical play and learning from them.

When amyl nitrate became a controlled substance, recreational users switched to butyl nitrate or one of several other related nitrite chemicals. These chemicals are often sold in small brown glass bottles, and their manufacturers get around controlled-substances laws by clever labeling—you're not buying an inhaled stimulant, you're buying something else like "liquid incense," a "room odorizer," "video head cleaner," or the latest ruse: "polish remover." That allows the product to be sold even though both buyer and seller know that it won't be used as an Airwick substitute and that you haven't had polish on your nails since Halloween in 1987.

But "room odorizers" don't require, and therefore don't get, the kind of warning labels that would have to be attached if everyone could be upfront about what was being sold, and the way in which it was being used. This column does not advocate drug abuse, but it also doesn't advocate ignorance, so here's what those warning labels would say if they could:

"Contents are highly flammable. Do not use around open flame." Movie buffs may remember that movie film was originally nitrate-based and had a penchant for bursting into flames for no apparent reason. Nitrates are also used in dynamite and other explosives. Poppers, which are also nitrates, evaporate very quickly and the vapors are very flammable. So if you're using poppers, don't have candles or incense burning at the same time, no matter how romantic it is. Don't use poppers in a basement dungeon that's right next to the furnace or water heater. Don't smoke tobacco, marijuana, or anything else while you're using poppers. And, for heaven's sake, don't use them during a fireplay or hot-wax scene.

"Do not allow contact with skin. If contact occurs, wash off immediately. Do not swallow or inject." Most people uncap the bottle of poppers and put it up to their nose to inhale the vapors, while other people inhale the vapors through their mouth. Either way, be careful not to spill the liquid or let it splash out of the bottle—it can cause a nasty chemical burn on skin and can do even worse damage on mucous membranes like the inside of your nose or mouth. It's very toxic, so if it gets in your mouth, don't swallow it, and don't use it as an injectable drug.

"May cause headache, flushing of the face, decreased blood pressure, increased pulse rate, dizziness, lightheadedness, nausea, vomiting, fainting, slowed perception of time, coldness of the skin and swelling of the nasal passages. Long-term effects may include a rash around the nose, mouth or cheeks. Discontinue use if any of these symptoms occur.

"Also discontinue use if the desired results are not achieved. Tolerance may build up over time, with heavy use putting a strain on the heart, possibly leading to circulatory collapse and death.

"Poppers increase pressure within the eyeball and therefore should not be used by anyone with glaucoma. Do not use poppers if you suffer from heart problems, high or low blood pressure, anemia, or breathing problems. There are some indications that poppers inhibit the immune system and should not be used by people with suppressed immune systems, but this has not been conclusively demonstrated.

"Do not use Viagra* in combination with poppers (or with other prescription nitrate-based heart drugs such as nitroglycerin). The combination can cause a fatal drop in blood pressure." On the Web I found a letter to physicians from Pfizer, the makers of Viagra, discussing this issue. Here's what it says: "Although we have not specifically studied this, we believe that nitrates that are inhaled for recreational use (including amyl nitrate/nitrite or 'poppers' and others) will have the same effect [as has been observed with prescription nitrite drugs] when combined with Viagra." And this warning doesn't apply only to men—the letter goes on to say "In addition, although Viagra is only FDA approved for the treatment of male erectile dysfunction, we are aware that women have started taking it, either on their own or via an off-label prescription from a physician. Therefore, although the scenarios described above would be more likely to occur in men, if such off-label use continues, they could also occur in women." To summarize, if you decide to try Viagra, lock up the poppers. If you just can't have sex without poppers, don't experiment with Viagra. (And remember, Viagra is a prescription drug. If you think it's for you, talk to your doctor about it first.)

Finally, here's what the 1999 Minnesota Statutes say about poppers (chapter 609.684): In Subdivision 1 both amyl nitrate and butyl nitrate are defined as "toxic substances," and Subdivision 3 says "A

---

*This applies to Levitra and Cialis as well.

person is guilty of a misdemeanor who uses or possesses any toxic substance with the intent of inducing intoxication, excitement, or stupefaction of the central nervous system, except under the direction and supervision of a medical doctor. A person is guilty of a misdemeanor who intentionally aids another in violation of this subdivision." So in case the dungeon is ever raided, just remember this alibi: "But Officer, I was only doing my nails!"

Leather/SM and Drug Usage
Published in *Lavender* #75 (April 10, 1998)

The leather/SM experience, for many people, includes the use of drugs. Alcohol is the most obvious because it's legal; some members of the community also use illicit drugs such as marijuana, cocaine and crystal meth. Some people would add poppers to this list; others don't consider them drugs. And very few would add steroids to this list, since no one takes steroids to get high. Yet the fact remains that steroids are illicit substances that are used (and sometimes abused) for reasons that are often questionable, and often with undesirable side effects.

Before I continue, a disclaimer: I am *not* speaking from experience here. My firsthand experience with drugs has been almost nonexistent. I drink only occasionally; poppers give me a headache, so I avoid them. I've never even experimented with any other drugs. But lest you think I sound too much like Nancy "Just Say No" Reagan, let me say that the message of this column is *not* that drug use is always bad, and it is *not* that no one should ever use them. I would urge, instead, responsible usage. I simply and respectfully ask that you consider these points about drugs and their relation to leather/SM sex and the community:

- There is nothing magical about leather or SM that makes drugs more acceptable or less potentially damaging or addictive than they would be in any other setting.
- Remember "safe, sane, consensual" applies to drugs. Playing under the influence of excessive drug usage is neither safe nor sane. Drug usage can impair judgment; as a result of that impaired judgment an SM scene may go too far, resulting in someone getting hurt.

- Tops/Daddies/Masters: You are responsible for your own drug use, but you are responsible for your bottom's/boy's/slave's drug use as well. If you give them any substance as part of a scene, you are responsible for knowing exactly what it is, how to use it and how much of it to give. Any substance use during a scene must be by the consent of all parties involved.

- Bottoms/boys/slaves: You are responsible for your own drug use. You have the right to say no to anything in a scene that makes you uncomfortable, including drugs. If you choose to use drugs before or during a scene, it should be with the consent of your Top/Daddy/Master. At the very least, if you are using a substance, your Top/Daddy/Master needs to know about it for the sake of your safety and his.

- Leather/SM sex is not a competitive event. The use of drugs to allow yourself to "take more punishment," thereby impressing your Top or the crowd around you, is misguided. This isn't the Olympics; no one is keeping score. You won't impress other people, and you run the risk of being injured by trying to take more than your body can stand.

- The Leather/SM community values authenticity and reality; drugs are artificial. Whether it's the artifice of a steroid-bulked body, or the ephemeral high of crack, drug usage can represent either a counterfeit experience or a retreat from reality. The genuine high that comes from a chemical-free SM experience is something that is at best only dimly approached by chemical substitutes; at worst the chemicals interfere with the SM high and degrade it. SM is about being in tune and connected with your body, and savoring every sensation that the SM experience provides. Drugs can get in the way—they can put you out of touch with what's really happening and substitute their own sensations. One common-sense way to evaluate drug usage in connection with leather/SM sex is this: Do the drugs enhance the experience? Or do they detract from it? Are they a substitute for the real thing?

- If you think you might have a drug problem, you owe it to yourself to deal with it. If you need help, get it; many kinds of help are available.

Where Leather and Sobriety Intersect

Published in *Lavender* #44 (January 31, 1997)

Leather/SM prides itself on its diversity and its inclusiveness. We, as a community, try to welcome everyone with an interest in our many and varied forms of alternative sexuality. We include women and men; young, old and everything in between; gay, bisexual, queer, pansexual and even straight (but not narrow); all colors and ethnic backgrounds; and people living with AIDS and other physical challenges. Unfortunately, there's one group of people in our community that sometimes doesn't get the respect it deserves.

Here in Minnesota, the land of treatment centers and twelve-step groups, many members of our leather community are in recovery from alcoholism or other substance abuse. Some grew up here; others came to Minnesota to go through alcohol or drug abuse treatment and have decided to stay. Other community members may not be in recovery but still choose not to use alcohol or drugs.

Many leatherfolk who go through treatment ask the same question: "Now that I'm in recovery, do I have to give up leather?" It's not a frivolous question. How do they fit into a community that sometimes seems to revolve around the use of mind-altering substances? Throughout history, leatherfolk have met and cruised at bars, and many of those bar names are now part of our folklore. Today, almost every leather event, party, fundraiser or contest is held at a bar—and free tap beer or drink specials are advertised as an inducement to attend. Illicit drug usage is sometimes a feature of heavy-duty SM and fisting scenes. The unspoken but implicit message often seems to be that drinking and drugs are integral parts of the scene, necessary elements of machismo; if you don't partake, maybe you're not a *real* leatherman or leatherwoman.

Some of us manage to deal with situations like these. We attend the events and enjoy the fellowship, but we drink soft drinks instead of beer. (When soft drinks are included in the price of admission, we bless the event planner's inclusiveness; when the beer is flowing freely but soft drinks aren't, we feel we've been dissed.)

Some of us find that for the sake of our sanity we have to avoid bars, so we look for other, safer meeting places. Some of us are lucky enough to become part of a clean-and-sober family of leather brothers and sisters. But many of us still feel isolated from the rest of the leather community—and, therefore, from a significant part of our sexuality.

Once in a while we see signs of awareness and acceptance. San Francisco's Sober Defenders is a clean-and-sober leather club. There is a sober leather/SM twelve-step meeting in Greenwich Village in New York. Chicago's International Mr. Leather contest has a highly visible recovery component including meetings, a recovery hospitality suite and badges for staff members in recovery. And everywhere, the community's mantra of "safe, safe and consensual" serves as a reminder that playing under the influence of too much alcohol or drugs is neither safe nor sane.

Those are encouraging trends, but more can be done both locally and nationally. Perhaps it would be helpful to have some way for chemical-free leatherfolk to recognize each other. I have seen many lists of hankie colors and what they stand for, and it amazes and saddens me to report that nowhere, even on the most comprehensive lists, is there a color that stands for "clean and sober" or for "drug-free play."

Actually, it doesn't matter if the symbol for clean-and-sober leather is a hankie color, a club pin, a dog tag, or something else. It would just be helpful if there were something that allowed us to recognize each other, and that was recognized and honored by the rest of the leather community as well. For those already in the leather community and for those interested in joining it, such a symbol would affirm that it's possible to be in leather and in recovery at the same time.

Since the above column was published in 1997, some things have changed. The gay male leather community is still bar-centered, but now there are more non-bar social alternatives than there were in 1997. The pansexual community has evolved such that their social events, in my experience, tend to revolve more around food and less around alcohol, and many pansexual play parties are no-alcohol events. But some things have not changed: for example, there still is, to my knowledge, no hankie code for clean and sober or drug-free play.

No More Toxic Toys

Published in *Lavender* #311 (April 27, 2007)

The Coalition Against Toxic Toys (CATT) wants you to know that toys can be hazardous to your health.

And they aren't talking about the kind of toys that come in a Happy Meal.

Based in Minneapolis, CATT is a nonprofit consumer advocacy and education organization dedicated to ending the manufacture, distribution and retail sale of toxic sex toys. The coalition is allied with Smitten Kitten, a retailer of sex-related goods that prides itself on not selling toys that are toxic to people or to the environment.

Far from being the small, fringe industry of yesteryear, adult sex toys today are a $500,000 industry in the United States alone. The largest market for them is middle-class couples, 35 and older, in a committed relationship.

But this huge market is for the most part unregulated. Medical devices, teething rings for baby and even your dog's chew toy are regulated by the U.S. Consumer Products Safety Commission. These products can be made only from materials that are certified as safe and pose no health threats.

But dildos, vibrators, cock rings and other adult sexual paraphernalia receive almost no regulation or oversight at all. No government agency is responsible for ensuring that the toys in the drawer of your bedside table are safe and don't contain hazardous materials. Adult toys avoid regulation by being labeled "for novelty use only." (Translation: these are gag gifts to be giggled at, not to be put to any actual use. You want to do what with it? Oh, we won't take any responsibility if you do that.)

What kind of hazards are we talking about? Independent testing has revealed that many toys contain a variety of toxic compounds including cadmium, lead and toluene. Some toys (and some lubes as well) contain ingredients that can irritate sensitive tissue. Some plastics leak hazardous compounds. Toys made of porous materials can never be adequately cleaned or sterilized. And then there's the more global issue of environmental consequences from the manufacture of certain materials.

One of the plastics often used for adult toys is PVC (polyvinyl chloride), a material that is cheap and easy to work with but that has long been decried as unfriendly to the environment during both manufacture and disposal.

PVC used in sex toys is often laced (or loaded) with phthalates, which can create an invitingly soft and flesh-like surface. Some toys are flesh-colored, while "jelly" toys are often brightly colored and stretchy.

The PVC/phthalate combination is not chemically stable, which means the phthalates leach out of the plastic over time. When that happens the toys change color, texture and smell. Some users of these products have reported irritation after using them.

But even if no contact irritation occurs, there might be more serious problems down the road. Phthalate-exposure studies in mice and rats have linked the chemicals to reproductive organ damage, liver damage and liver cancer. Four studies have linked high phthalate exposure to a variety of human health problems. However, most of the research on humans and phthalates has involved skin or oral exposure to the chemicals. Very little, if any, research has been done concerning phthalate exposure through sensitive human genital or rectal tissues.

Based on the research that has been done, the United States, Japan, Canada and the European Union restrict the use of certain phthalates in children's toys. But no such restrictions exist for adult toys. In this instance, at least, our sex-negative government is staying out of our bedrooms—with unhealthy and hazardous results. Right now users of adult toys are, in effect, the government's guinea pigs. If problems develop and a negative public-health trend emerges, maybe then the government will take action—as it finally did with asbestos and PCBs, substances once thought safe.

In addition to containing toxic chemicals, the plastic used for cheap toys is porous and can never be adequately cleaned or sanitized. Because the pores in the plastic can harbor bacteria, viruses and fungi, toys made with porous plastic can spread disease if shared.

The good news is that you can buy toys that are safe. Toys made out of materials like high-quality glass, medical-grade silicone, high-quality stainless steel, hard acrylic plastics and polished non-porous stone will last almost indefinitely and can be cleaned and sterilized.

The bad news is that good toys will probably cost more than cheap, inferior toys.

Not all plastic toys are toxic (although they still may be porous, and thus impossible to clean). Responding to market pressures, many toys are now being marketed as phthalate-free. But remember, this is for all intents and purposes an unregulated industry, and no watchdog is making sure that the claims on product packages are truthful. So don't blindly trust packaging claims.

When shopping for toys, CATT recommends using the "smell test": If an item smells perfumey, or like a new shower curtain, it's giving off chemicals. Medical-grade silicone, glass, stainless steel and stone have no odor because they are not emitting chemicals. A toy should also be considered suspect if it looks shiny or feels greasy.

You can find much more about this subject at CATT's website.

Chapter 12

Political Life

Sex and Politics

Published in *Lavender* #335 (March 28, 2008)

This edition of this column was inspired by, and is dedicated to, Eliot Spitzer.

What, you may ask, is the former governor of New York doing in a leather column? He's serving as a good example of a bad example. The leather/BDSM/fetish community can learn much from his recent misadventures. We ignore these lessons at our own peril.

It was dizzying to watch how quickly Spitzer went from being spoken of as a possible presidential contender in a few years to being spoken of as Client 9. Eliot Spitzer now joins Larry Craig, David Vitter, Rudy Giuliani, James McGreevy, Mark Foley, Bill Clinton, Gary Condit, Gary Hart, and many other powerful male politicians (yes, so far they've all been male) who have been the subject of sex scandals.

Our society is obsessed with the combination of sex and politics, and also with the combination of sex and religion (as with Ted Haggard, Jimmy Swaggart and Jim Bakker). When something goes wrong with either combination it can create scandal—and we as a society are so absolutely, totally disgusted by sex scandals that we absolutely, totally can't get enough of them. Since scandal sells newspapers and grabs television-viewing eyeballs, the media are only too happy to cater to our loathing.

What is there about sex and politics, or sex and religion, that's such a hook for so many people? Whether politics or religion, the people at the center of sex scandals are always powerful people. Wait a minute—sex and power . . . playing with sex and power . . . does that sound like anyone we might know? Like, maybe, us? The National Coalition for Sexual Freedom (NCSF) conducts a "Sex and Politics" workshop and has even gone so far as to produce a very attractive t-shirt emblazoned with "Sex and Politics" (along with the NCSF logo).

NCSF, the Woodhull Freedom Foundation and other leather/BDSM/fetish community organizations and think tanks spend a lot of time contemplating sex and politics, and how to make things better for our community. Along these lines, one long-term goal that has been identified, and is now starting to be acted upon, is the decriminalization of BDSM activity. But as we craft our strategies to achieve this and other community goals, it might be instructive for us to look especially closely at the somewhat frenzied nature of the current sociopolitical climate—the ocean in which we, along with the rest of society, are all swimming.

For example, instead of merely garden-variety Internet prostitution, what if the governor had been caught being involved with, say, a pro domme (professional dominatrix)? Or even a pro dom—another male? Would he still be governor? Would the shame have been less? Or would it have been even worse?

All we as a community can do with the above questions is to speculate, of course, because we all know how unlikely it is that any of our elected representatives in Washington or elsewhere would do anything so depraved as to utilize the services of a pro domme. Certainly none of our elected representatives or officials are involved in BDSM, are they?

All kidding aside, I expect one day we'll find out how the above hypothetical situation plays out for real, when a congressman or senator is caught *in flagrante dungeon*. We have already seen what happened when *The Washington Post* outed one of the UN weapons inspectors in Iraq as being a member of the BDSM community. If there can be that much of a media firestorm for someone who wasn't an elected official . . . .

On the other hand, what if someone who was a proud member of the leather/BDSM/fetish community were to run for public office and win—and then be popular enough to be re-elected? That kind of popularity has happened for several openly gay politicians, including Representatives Barney Frank, Gerry Studds and Tammy Baldwin. Both Frank and Studds even survived their own political scandals. The man who led the charge in 1990 to expel Frank from Congress was, incredibly enough, Larry Craig.

Maybe it all comes down to shame and secrecy. Right now, in the public mind leather/BDSM/fetish sexuality is in the same category as prostitution and other scandalous things—in much the same way Trent Lott once put gay people in the same category as kleptomaniacs. That was in 1998, and Lott discovered a large segment of the population did not agree with his comparison, because by that time many people had decided that being gay, lesbian, bisexual or transgender was nothing to be ashamed of.

In much the same way, I think the day is coming when leather/BDSM/fetish sexuality will be nothing to be ashamed of. If part of what gets us there is working to decriminalize BDSM, we have our work cut out for us—but we need to do it. Both our community and society at large will be better for it, because so many members of our community have so much to offer the wider society. If politicians professing to be God-fearing Christians have made such a mess of things over the last few decades, it might take a bunch of people formerly known as "pervs" to make things better.

An Open Letter to Senator Larry Craig
Published in *Lavender* #322 (September 28, 2007)

Dear Senator Craig:

You've been having a bit of a rough patch lately, haven't you? My condolences. I, for one, believe you when you say you're not gay, and I applaud your decision to fight to clear your name.

It's all so ironic, though, isn't it? You, a stalwart spokesman for traditional family and moral values and against sexual lewdness and perversion, get very publicly trapped in a men's room sting operation at the Minneapolis airport. If President Clinton and Monica Lewinsky caused eight-year-olds to ask questions about oral sex, you now have introduced them to the subject of tearoom trade. And all because of a perfect storm of misunderstanding.

That men's room was known, in certain circles, to be cruisy. But, since you're not gay, you wouldn't know that. So you walked, blithely unaware, into this den of iniquity. You just needed to relieve yourself—and not in the sexual sense. Although, heaven knows, flying is so stressful nowadays it's not inconceivable that a man might need a little stress relief once he gets off a plane.

You saw a stall, but the door was closed. You really wanted to use that one, though, and it might have been vacant. It couldn't hurt to see if it happened to be empty.

You peered through the crack between the door and the partition. You peered for several minutes. Maybe you were waiting for the other guy to finish.

Finally you gave up, went into the adjacent stall, and sat down. You put your suitcase in front of you in the stall, because where else were you going to put it? Sadly, you didn't know how incriminating a place that was to put a suitcase.

You had just heard a rather catchy melody over the airport's background-music system, one of those melodies you just can't get out of your head. You unconsciously started to tap your toe to it.

As you have stated, you are a big guy and have a rather wide stance. And, like airplane seats, those stalls seem to get narrower and narrower. You inadvertently touched the foot of the gentleman in the next stall. You probably didn't even notice.

Then, all of a sudden, your reverie was interrupted when you spied a renegade piece of paper on the floor. You didn't put it there, and technically it may not even have been in your stall. But you knew the world would be a better, neater place if you picked it up.

So you put your hand down to pick it up. You put your hand down several times—you haven't explained whether there were several pieces of paper or whether you repeatedly missed picking it up. Perhaps you couldn't reach it because it was too far into the other stall.

Your heart must have sunk when the policeman showed you his badge. What was happening? What do you mean, I'm under arrest? Soliciting? For what? Officer, this is all a horrible misunderstanding. I'm not gay. I don't do that sort of thing.

A brief aside, Senator: I'm gay, and I don't do "that sort of thing." I'm attracted to black leather, not white porcelain.

But "that sort of thing" works for many men because it's the only outlet available to them as they anxiously live their double lives — straight, but occasionally needing a little covert man-to-man action. But since you "don't do that sort of thing," you wouldn't know what that kind of desperation feels like.

Perhaps, however, you are beginning to understand the agony these men go through when they're finally found out.

Maybe, Senator, some good can yet come of this. As I said, I hope you clear your name. But I also hope that, whether in the Senate or out of it, through this experience you will have gained some sympathy and compassion for men trying to tamp down secret desires, and occasionally failing.

Perhaps in the future you will be less quick to criticize gay men now that you've been misidentified as one of them. Now that you've tasted anti-gay harassment, maybe you'll be moved to help put a stop to it. For years men have been having sexual encounters in men's rooms. For years police have been trying to stop it. Lives have been ruined in the process.

If you, Senator, really want to make a difference, introduce legislation to make sex clubs legal. That way, men who crave anonymous sex with other men will have a controlled, safe place in which to play, and the nation's public restrooms can be returned to their original purpose. That would be a win for everyone.

Now, Senator, one last thing. If this were anyone else, I would urge them to get tested for AIDS and other sexually transmitted diseases. Sadly, men who engage in covert sex tend to be less informed about the health risks involved, and hence often don't take proper safety precautions. One of the things that might lead to their cover being blown is when they pick something up — anything from crabs to AIDS — and pass it on to their wives. I'm sure this doesn't apply to you, though, so never mind.

In closing, good luck in the battles ahead, Senator.

Sincerely,

Your humble columnist

An Election-Year Fantasy

Published in *Lavender* #133 (June 30, 2000)

"The reason we have [the International Mr. Leather] contest is not to establish a national leader. It's not about choosing Bill Clinton— it's about choosing Vanna White."—Tony Mills, International Mr. Leather 1998, as quoted in *POZ* Magazine

Fair enough, Mr. Mills—although:

If we chose International Mr. Leather (IML) like we choose the President of the United States:

- *The Leather Journal* would have more than enough advertising revenue from all the political ads. They could go back to being a magazine—a four-color glossy magazine. And they could publish weekly. (Are we as a community ready for a magazine called *Leatherweek*?)
- Some of that advertising revenue would probably spill over to local publications as well. (What am I bid for the page opposite my column? I know the strings to pull to make sure you get it.)
- There would be only two candidates for International Mr. Leather, from the two major political parties: the Old Guard and the New Guard.
- Each leather voter would register to vote at their local leather bar, which would also be the polling place.
- International Mr. Leather would not be elected on a strict majority vote. The majority winner at each leather bar would get all of that bar's electoral votes; some bars would be worth more than others. Each bar would then send a representative to the Leather Leadership Conference to formally cast that bar's electoral votes and determine the new International Mr. Leather.

On the other hand, if we chose the President of the United States like we choose IML:

- It would be called the American Mr. President (AMP) contest. In spite of the efforts of Geraldine Ferraro and Liddy Dole,* there would probably be no corresponding Ms title.

---

*And Hillary Clinton.

- There would be no more four-year terms. The American Mr. President winner would be in office for only a year, and there would be no repeat titleholders. If he had something he wanted to accomplish, he would have to be snappy about it.
- There would be more than two candidates from which to choose. Bored with Gore? Don't like Dubya? AMP would have room for Ralph Nader, Pat Buchanan, Ross Perot, Bill Bradley, John McCain . . . and even Jesse Ventura. Guaranteed variety— something for everyone's taste.
- American Mr. President would be chosen each year in Chicago by a panel of judges. The American Mr. President contest (except for the interviews with the judges) would be televised on all the major networks so that all Americans could be inspired and entertained by the event, which is all it seems the majority of today's American public wants. They would no longer be able to vote for the president, but many if not most Americans don't vote now.* At least the American Mr. President contest would be televised—this year the major networks aren't even bothering to televise the Republican and Democratic conventions. Instead they are leaving that chore to CNN.
- The American Mr. President judging panel, nine wise elders of the community (otherwise known as the Supreme Court), would be entrusted with the task of choosing the man to lead the nation for the next year. The Supreme Court would be chosen every year as well, with no repeat judges. (Who would choose the Supreme Court each year? Well, whoever chooses the judges for IML seems to be doing a good job; let's leave it to them.)
- The fact that the selection of American Mr. President would rest with only nine people would mean that polls and focus groups would be unnecessary, and there would be no huge expenditures for advertising. Which would mean no huge advertising budgets. Which would mean no fundraising, no fundraising scandals, no

---

*A hopeful sign that this might be changing for the better: U.S. voter turnout in the 2008 elections, expressed as a percentage of eligible voters, was the highest in 40 years.

PACs or lobbyists. The American Mr. President candidates would be judged not by how much money they raised, or whether they said what they thought people wanted to hear. They would instead be judged on their character and record of service to their community.

- The position of Vice President would be replaced by the position of President's boy. He would be responsible for presiding over the Senate as well as White House bootblacking and other duties.
- During the contest each candidate would take a question at random from the audience and would have 90 seconds to answer the question before the microphone was turned off. Think about that while you're watching the summer's presidential debates.
- The winner of the American Mr. President contest would receive no compensation, only a travel fund. His reward for being American Mr. President would be the places he'd go, the people he'd meet and the knowledge that he was able to be of service to his country.
- There would be one slight difference between International Mr. Leather and American Mr. President: IML's "physique" segment (also known as the "jock walk") would have to be replaced with something else (a leather jock would not be flattering attire for most presidential candidates). And the American people know just what to replace it with, too. Since nowadays the #1-rated cable television shows all feature wrestling, that's obviously what the public wants. Why not replace the jock walk with a presidential-candidate wrestling match? (The fact that Minnesota governor Jesse Ventura would be a shoo-in for this category has absolutely nothing to do with this suggestion.)

Now, on a serious note: This is an election year, and it's an important one. Here's what IML Founder and Executive Producer Chuck Renslow said from the stage of the recent International Mr. Leather contest:

"The next political party [in power] will most likely appoint judges to our Supreme Court. We must use our power to make sure that the next court is attuned to our needs." Renslow expanded further on this theme the next day: "Right now I believe there are 23 federal judge vacancies open . . . I'm just worried that if we get an extremely conservative Congress, or a president who's from the religious right, they're going to appoint judges to that court—and I don't mean just the Supreme Court, I mean district courts and any federal court— and the religious right is out, as I said last night, to annihilate us. . . . They've tried it in Washington, they've tried it in other places, and it hasn't worked because they don't have the power behind them. But if they ever get the power behind them, they will succeed. And I think it's up to us to make damn sure that they don't succeed."

How do we do that? We vote. We vote intelligently. We pay attention to the candidates. We support candidates who support us, and we don't support candidates who don't support us. And we mobilize others to vote intelligently, too.

At times it's tempting to say that none of it matters anyway because it's "only politics" and tune it out. But we as a community can't afford to do that this year.

The above was printed before the Bush vs. Gore presidential election in 2000. As the summer wore on, I had some further thoughts:

A Leatherman Looks at the Presidential Race
Published in *Lavender* #137 (August 25, 2000)

Recently I wrote a column comparing the way we select the President of the United States with the way we select International Mr. Leather. On further observation I'm beginning to think this year's presidential election has more in common with a local leather contest—one of those contests where the promoters have been able to come up with only two contestants, and as you watch them onstage you wonder if either of them will be able to serve the title properly. Forgive me for delving into political waters again, but it is, after all, an election year. This is what one leatherman thinks about the presidential race so far.

First of all, neither of the major candidates has said anything about being kink-friendly. In this post-Monica age (have you forgotten about Monica? The folks in Washington, D.C. haven't), where Altoids and cigars are considered kinky and where the pendulum continues to swing further toward "traditional family values," I think it will be quite awhile before a presidential candidate courts the kink vote. So we shall have to judge them on other criteria.

By almost any criteria (on second thought, delete that "almost"), I don't like Bush and don't want to see him in the White House. It's appropriate that I live in Minnesota; according to *Newsweek,* Minnesota is the only state that's more or less a sure thing for Al Gore.

So I guess that means I cast a vote for Gore as my "George W. Bush over my dead body" vote. But I'm not all that excited about Gore, either, because he hasn't given me much to get excited about. Aside from the legendarily wooden way he presents himself (which I guarantee you would not score big points in a leather contest), he hasn't really said much of anything about anything. So far, he's a blank. His wife, Tipper, seems to have taken firmer stands on more issues than he has. I sincerely hope he is able to better define himself before the election in November.

The news media are constantly pointing out that this is the first presidential race where both candidates are of the boomer generation. Is this really the best my generation can do? Are we boomers really that lightweight? Eight years ago I thought Clinton, also a boomer, was lightweight—now, compared to Gore and Bush, he seems like a brilliant statesman.

If this were a leather contest and I were judging, I would watch the proceedings and I would mark my score sheet. And I would do so secure in the knowledge that most leather contests are set up so that if none of the contestants receives a certain minimum number of points (usually 70% of the maximum number of points possible), the title will not be awarded. This is another instance where the leather/BDSM community has come up with a way of doing things that society in general might do well to follow.

Contrast this with the way a presidential election works: No matter how turned-off the electorate becomes, no matter how many voters stay home, each state's electoral votes will go to one candidate or the other (barring a third-party-candidate upset). Theoretically a president could be picked by only 10% of the country's eligible voters, even if the other 90% were so disgusted with both the candidates that they decided to stay home on election day.

In this country there's no such thing as a presidential no-confidence vote. You can vote for a third-party candidate as a way of saying you don't like either of the two major-party candidates, but that's usually called "throwing away your vote." I say "usually" because when Jesse Ventura won the Minnesota governor's race in 1998, he proved that if enough people feel enough disenchantment with the two major parties, a third-party candidate can win. Will Nader or (perish the thought) Buchanan pull off a Ventura-style upset nationally? Wait and see.

I suppose we can take some comfort from history. Just as the leather nation has survived the occasional lackluster titleholder, the United States has survived the occasional lackluster president. Even so, whether we're talking about a Hobson's choice between leather title contestants or one between presidential candidates, the lesser of two evils is a better choice than the greater of two evils.

One final thought: Al Gore made history by selecting as his running mate Joseph Lieberman, the first Jewish candidate on a major-party presidential ticket. That started me thinking about other presidential barriers that have been broken, such as John F. Kennedy in 1960 being elected the first Roman Catholic president, and vice-presidential candidate Geraldine Ferraro in 1984 being the first woman on a major-party presidential ticket (chosen as Walter Mondale's vice-presidential candidate, she and Mondale lost).*

How long will it be before we have a self-proclaimed member of the GLBT community as a presidential or vice-presidential candidate on a major-party ticket? Or the first openly kinky candidate? Or maybe even both at once? It could happen one day, and that day might be sooner than you or I expect. But it won't happen through apathy and hiding. It will happen through involvement and pride. Be proud enough this year to get involved in the political process — even if that involvement is "only" paying attention and voting intelligently, and encouraging others to do the same. I said it before and I'll say it again: This election is too important to tune out.

We all know how the 2000 election turned out. To my surprise and chagrin, I was almost clairvoyant, as I pointed out in my final column of 2000:

---

*If I were writing this column today I would add Barack Obama to this list.

Election Fantasy? Election Nightmare

Published in *Lavender* #146 (December 29, 2000)

In the June 30 issue ("An Election-Year Fantasy") I wrote what I thought was a satirical piece, fantasizing about what would happen if the country chose the President of the United States in the same way the leather community chooses International Mr. Leather (IML). The contest would be called the American Mr. President contest, and the titleholder would be chosen "every year in Chicago by a panel of judges," as International Mr. Leather is chosen. I wrote that the judging panel, "nine wise elders of the community (otherwise known as the Supreme Court) would be entrusted with the task of choosing the man to lead the nation for the next year."

Aided by masterful election engineering by those wonderful folks in Florida who brought you Anita Bryant, this election came down to the Supreme Court effectively awarding the "American Mr. President" title to George W. Bush.

In some ways the analogy between presidential election and leather contest was not followed. Allow me to again compare the presidential race to IML and other leather contests: Normally the winner of a leather contest is not announced until the tallymasters have completed their counting and, we hope, rechecked their figures. Better to make sure the figures are correct before announcing them than to risk an error, a challenge and subsequent embarrassment. But I guess they don't feel that way in Florida or Washington, D.C.

Of course, at a leather contest there's an entertainer, usually a fabulous diva, on hand to keep the audience amused while the tally-masters total up the scores. If the contest entertainer has finished their set and the tallymasters still haven't finished their tally, the audience waits and the entertainer does an encore. By contrast, the presidential election-night coverage was followed by a seemingly endless parade of politicians, lawyers and court cases. That's entertainment? It seemed to enthrall much of the nation, or at least the media, in the same fashion as the O.J., Princess Diana and Monicagate stories. But for many it was simply the latest in a long series of media-hyped train wrecks, and they tuned it out. Maybe if Babs or Cher or Donna Summer had provided post-election entertainment, the recounts could have continued. Oh, well—I guess we'll never know.

Several groups and organizations have expressed interest in doing an after-the-fact count of the Florida ballots under the provisions of Florida's Sunshine Law. What happens if that recount shows that Al Gore actually won the popular vote in Florida, as he won the nation-wide popular vote? Well, in the leather community anyway, that calls for stripping someone of their title and awarding it to the person who should rightfully have it.

Unfortunately, nobody stripped W of his title, and the nation endured eight long years (how were we myopic enough to re-elect him?) of the Bush/ Cheney administration, with all its attendant disasters.

I must say that when I wrote this I was probably too hard on Al Gore, and that in the ensuing years my estimation of him has risen tremendously.

Chapter 13

Eclectic Life
Creative writing

Here are a few eccentric columns that don't fit into standard categories. They were fun to write, though, and I hope you find them amusing.

Hey, Mr. Producer!
I'm talking to you, *Sir!*
Published in *Lavender* #241 (August 20, 2004)

What do you get when you cross a leatherman and a show-tune queen? You get your humble columnist. Sometimes I view the world through leather-colored glasses and sometimes through the lens of musical theater. When I combine these two ways of seeing the world, things can get interesting.

I've seen (or been part of) some really good leather fantasies over the years. (Just to remind you, the word "fantasy" in a leather context connotes an erotic skit).* But I'd like to see the concept taken to the next level. I'm talking about more than skits here—I'm talking about a full-blown leather musical revue.

This stage production I'm proposing was inspired by "Fantasy," the Omaha-based festival of fantasies that was created and produced for several years by Dustin Logan and Bob Ewing. "Fantasy" was a revolutionary idea for its time: an evening of fantasy performances for the sole purpose of entertainment, not as part of a competition.

---

*See page 159.

"Fantasy" was thoroughly enjoyable, and I miss it. Hence the desire to not only bring it back, but to take the concept and make it big—and accessible to a broader audience as well. I have had this idea for a long time. For now it's just a closet (you should pardon the expression) musical revue, but I dream that one day I'll actually see it on stage. Read, and fantasize along with me.

The show starts with a big opening number in which the cast of characters invites the audience into their somewhat dark but fascinating world. What follows touches on as many different fetishes and scenes as can be crammed into an evening in the theater.

After the opening the show dives right into "It's Raining Men," a watersports number for the yellow-hankie crowd—simulated, of course (wink wink).

"Electrician Blues," performed to the classic naughty blues song of the same name, includes both TENS-unit and violet-wand play (on a dim or dark stage to enhance the spectacle). The same performer later sings "Dentist Blues," as made famous by Bette Midler: "You thrill me/When you drill me/And I don't need no Novocain today!"

"The Teddy Bear Picnic" is sung and danced sweetly and innocently by a stage full of hunky, furry bears. Here's a sample of the lyric: "Beneath the trees where nobody sees/They'll hide and seek as long as they please/'Cause that's the way the teddy bears have their picnic."

A tango number: A spotlight shines on the bare back of a man wearing black leather pants and a harness. He starts to slowly revolve to face the audience, and we see that it's Dan Chouinard, an accomplished accordion player and all-around musician from Minneapolis. His accordion is attached to the harness. Chouinard plays "Kiss of Fire" (including the lyrics "If I'm a slave, then it's a slave I want to be!") while a couple performs a combination of tango and fireplay. Chouinard and the dancers are brought back later for Tom Lehrer's "The Masochism Tango."

A comic number: "I Want To Be Happy (But I Won't Be Happy/ 'Til I Make You Happy Too)," from *No, No, Nanette,* sung by an eager-to-please top to a jaded bottom. Following this is a non-comic dance interlude to the same song, featuring something I've always wanted to see onstage: an all-male synchronized dance line in full black leather and boots with taps on them. (Which leather company will get all the publicity that will come from supplying the leathers for the dance line?)

Whipmaster Robert Dante shows off his amazing whipping skill and technique, including his famous black-light whipping.

"Treat Me Rough," originally a madcap comic number from *Girl Crazy* by the Gershwins, is reworked with slight changes to the lyrics to be a sensual, sultry number in the style of 1930s Berlin.

A gay-male version of the 1964 hit by the Shangri-Las, "Leader of the Pack," is sung and dramatized by a male doo-wop group in black leather.

Another amazing dance number: synchronized flogging, combining flogging with tap dancing or Irish or American clog dancing (clogging while flogging!). Then the lights go down for something I recently saw at a run: flaming floggers, a combination of flogging and fireplay.

No revue is complete without a tearjerker. In this case it's Al Jolson's classic "Sonny Boy," reworked for the continuing age of AIDS (including a safe-sex message, of course).

Sung by either a boy or a slave, Cole Porter's "My Heart Belongs to Daddy" includes the formerly censored lines following "My Daddy, he treats it so well": "He treats it, and treats it, and then he repeats it."

And finally, the big finish (known in the trade as the "eleven-o'clock number"): "Leatherella," in which our hero wants to go to the run but is forced by his Wicked Daddy and Stepbrothers to stay at home—after polishing all their leathers and boots. Fairy GodDaddy appears and produces a complete leather outfit and a Harley to go to the run. After meeting the Handsome Titleholder, Leatherella is forced to make a quick getaway on the Harley, which at the stroke of midnight turns into a unicycle (or a Segway—whichever would get more laughs). Next day the Handsome Titleholder comes calling with the boot that Leatherella left behind. You can figure out the rest.

Where to find the people to make this dream a reality? To quote a Stephen Sondheim lyric from *Follies* (with added leather emphasis): "Hey, Mr. Producer/I'm talking to you, SIR!" You don't suppose there are any theater producers in the leather community, do you? Or directors, choreographers, actors, dancers, technicians, set designers, costume designers, etc.? Or any angels/backers out there to finance it?

I can see it now — it opens in the Twin Cities and goes on to play Chicago (with an excerpt as the opening number at IML), Los Angeles, San Francisco and New York before becoming a Las Vegas perennial at the newly opened Caesar's Dungeon (built just for the show).

For now, it's just my fantasy. Could it be a reality someday? To paraphrase Bloody Mary in Rodgers and Hammerstein's *South Pacific*: "You got to have a fantasy/If you no have a fantasy/How you gonna have a fantasy come true?"

Torture TV
Referring to the audience, of course
Published in *Lavender* #175 (February 8, 2002)

The latest proof that America's television networks are both desperate and clueless comes in the form of two new shows, Fox's "The Chamber" and ABC's "The Chair." Some point to these shows as evidence of the continuing mainstreaming of BDSM. I say they appropriate BDSM imagery and misrepresent it, and I can only hope that by the time you read this both these shows will have been yanked from their respective networks' schedules.

I must confess that I watch very little television these days. Somewhere in the mid-1990s so much of television became so stupid that I just couldn't stomach it anymore. So I was somewhat hesitant when *Lavender* editor Tim Lee* invited me to watch "The Chamber," but when he listed the various traditional BDSM-community practices that were being put on display in prime time (fireplay, electrical play and psychological torture, to name but a few), I thought I would at least have to see if he was telling the truth.

The two shows are similar in many ways — so similar that "The Chair" is suing "The Chamber" for stealing their idea. ("The Chamber" has filed a countersuit.) They are extreme versions of one of the oldest television programming concepts, the quiz show. But both shows up

---

*Again I must add "the late" in front of someone's name. Tim disappeared in October, 2002; his body was pulled from the Mississippi River the following March. Prior to his disappearance, he had been hospitalized for depression. He was only 34. I miss him very much and remember him fondly.

the ante by strapping the contestants into a chair and putting them in extremely stressful situations while the emcee asks them questions. Contestants are penalized if they get too excited (as measured by a stress-monitoring device to which they've been attached).

On "The Chair" a stressful situation is having a live alligator, lowered from the ceiling in a harness, dangling inches from your face. But that's wimpy compared to "The Chamber," where the chair containing the contestant is drawn into a see-through torture chamber which subjects the contestant to increasing degrees of extreme heat or extreme cold, flamethrowers or high-pressure water jets, earthquake simulations, muscle spasms induced by electric shocks and reduced oxygen levels—all while being asked, for example, where former president Bill Clinton is building his presidential library. The shivering contestant's guess: "Washington, D.C.?" Wrong—the correct answer is Little Rock, Ark. But how clearly would you be thinking if there was frost forming in your hair?

Is this the next wave of BDSM? Will leather contests start incorporating torture events as part of the proceedings? Instead of fantasy presentations, will we have flog-a-thons while we ask the contestants leather trivia questions? THWACK! "Who was International Mr. Leather in 1988?!" THUD! "Coral hankie, right pocket! What does it mean?!" On second thought, maybe this should be incorporated into the interviews with the judges.

No, I don't think this is the next wave of BDSM. I think these shows exist because it's no longer acceptable to entertain ourselves by throwing Christians to the lions or by having gladiators fight to the death, and this is as close as we can come. It's interesting to note that the rest of the world has been seeing stuff like this on their televisions for years (the idea for "The Chair" originated in New Zealand). The American networks used to have broadcasting standards and practices that prevented them from lowering themselves to this level, but evidently those days are long gone.

I can't sound my familiar protest that "This isn't BDSM because it's not safe/sane/consensual." These shows go to great lengths to be safe (when was the last time you saw a heart monitor in a dungeon?), although one female contestant allegedly burned herself getting out of the chamber on "The Chamber." There are doctors supervising the proceedings, and supposedly in the name of safety they stop the action if the person becomes too stressed—although that's equivalent to failing, wimping out, losing the game. It could be argued that the action on these shows is consensual, although the lure of Winning Fabulous Prizes might cloud some people's judgment. I wouldn't call it sane, but very little on network TV these days is sane.

I can and do protest, however, that this is sending a bogus message to viewers. BDSM is not about seeing how much you can endure to impress other people, and it's certainly not about seeing how much you can endure in order to Win Fabulous Prizes. And just as I don't want non-leather types gawking at the perverts in a leather bar, I don't really want people getting their vicarious thrills watching other people get tortured. Blood lust is not what the scene is supposed to be about.

As I watched "The Chamber" it dawned on me that the contestants aren't the only people being tortured here. I felt tortured just watching it. I did, however, find myself being drawn into the spirit of things: in the name of art and intellect and research and impressing my readers, how much of this torture can I stand?

I must confess that I wimped out—I couldn't make it through the whole show. In this instance, the safeword was the off button on the TV remote.

Dispatches from the Future
The leather summer of 2028
Published in *Lavender* #165 (September 21, 2001)

With autumn fast approaching, it's time for a look back at some of this summer's leather activities. And what a summer it's been! But how could the season not be fabulous with a kick-off event like the 50th International Mr. Leather (IML) contest? The event was held over Memorial Day weekend, as always. And for that weekend, Chicago's McCormick Place became the world's largest leather bar— filled to capacity with leatherfolk of all genders, ages and descriptions.

A capacity crowd jammed the McCormick Place auditorium to watch the contest, and estimates placed the number of viewers who watched the contest via the Internet in the millions. The evening's most unforgettable moment: first-ever IML titleholder David Kloss (all these years and he still looks good!) received a standing ovation from the crowd after reading the list of next year's judges. New IML Lik Tinghe (from Antarctica—it's only the second year they've sent a contestant) won't be spending much time at home this year as he fulfills his titleholder duties.

In contrast to IML, which is firmly rooted in Chicago, the International Ms Leather (IMsL) contest in recent years has never been in the same city twice in a row. This year they returned to Las Vegas, Nevada, where Mary Kay Khali, Ms Leather Dakota, was chosen from a field of 64 contestants as the new International Ms Leather. The last time they were in Las Vegas was back in 1999, and what a difference the intervening years have made! This year's host resort was Las Vegas' newest and kinkiest showplace, The Charenton. Named for the insane asylum where the Marquis de Sade spent his last years, it was a perfect backdrop for the weekend's activities. Imagine—a hotel where every one of the 5,000 rooms is a fully equipped dungeon. Only in Vegas, folks.

The excitement of IMsL had barely subsided when it was time for another competition of a different sort: the Summer Olympics, this year returning to Greece. Several new competitive events have been added this year; after much campaigning and lobbying by members of the leather community we will finally get to witness both Tag Team Fisting and Competitive Bullwhip. Tag Team Fisting was first proposed as an Olympic event by a contestant in International Mr. Leather 2001—that's how long it has taken to get that event added to the Olympic lineup.

The leather/SM community also continued to influence the world of entertainment. Last year's Broadway smash *Fantasy: The Musical,* an all-singing, all-dancing revue of breathtaking leather fantasy performances, is still packing them in—you'll be lucky if you can get tickets for 2031. Building on the success of the musical, *Fantasy On Ice* has been touring major metropolitan ice arenas this summer, and from the crowds lining up at box offices across the land it looks like Disney has another winner. (But how they can skate and flog at the same time is beyond me—after the show in Minneapolis one of the cast members got me on the ice and I tried it, but even with his coaching I just couldn't make it work.) By the way, plans are in the works to make *Fantasy: The Musical* the permanent show at The Charenton in Las Vegas.

And now, a look ahead: The Leather Summer of '28 will officially close with another milestone, the 50th annual International Mr. Drummer contest. This year it finally returns to San Francisco (as the song says, right back where it started from) to be held in conjunction with the Folsom Street Fair—which outgrew Folsom Street years ago and now stretches along Market Street from downtown to the reclaimed and revitalized Castro. Drummer and Folsom in the same city on the same weekend—all's right with the world again.

And now, here's the strangest Leather Life column ever (so far, anyway). This was written for a "Lavender Lampoon" (April Fool's) issue, and the idea was that my fellow columnist, off-the-wall humorist Julie Dafydd, and I would switch places. Julie wrote a leather column about a geriatric leather contest in Sun City, Arizona. Julie's column is called "Consider the Source," and she ends each column with "Bye for now, Kiss Kiss." I wrote the following, trying to match her writing style as best I could. When the column originally appeared in Lavender, *it was shortened; it is printed here, for the first time, as it was originally written.*

Lint Life (A *Lavender* Lampoon Special)
by Steve Lenius posing as Julie Dafydd
Published in *Lavender* #178 (March 22, 2002)

Some people have big mouths. Or big noses or big feet or big hands or big—well, you get the idea. But I don't think I've ever heard anyone talk about having a big navel. So I guess I'll have to talk about it.

I didn't used to think my navel was anything special or out-of-the-ordinary. It wasn't until I was an adult that I realized that not everybody had a navel that could hold a Volkswagen. I am the world's biggest "innie." I used to be glad I wasn't an "outie," because I thought they looked funny. But now I'm not so sure, because "outies" probably don't have to deal with navel lint.

Let me tell you about navel lint.

I'm not talking about the lint that you get on your tongue when you unbutton all fifteen buttons on a sailor's pants with your teeth (yes, there really are fifteen buttons, although for some reason the

Navy only officially recognizes thirteen of them). What I'm talking about is also known as belly button lint, belly button fuzz or navel fuzz—as opposed to a Fuzzy Navel, which is peach schnapps and orange juice over ice, which you probably already knew. But I digress.

When I was a kid, I didn't understand it when people talked about lint in their belly buttons. How could a belly button collect lint, I wondered? Mine never seemed to. Why in the world would it want to?

Then suddenly one day, about ten years ago, I was drying off after my bath and realized there was this dark-colored something poking out of my navel. Well, of course I was concerned. Was my life turning into a B-movie? Had my body been taken over by an alien creature growing in my stomach, now fully developed and about to burst forth? I tried (unsuccessfully) to remain calm, and got a tweezers to try to gingerly extract whatever this thing was.

Unbeknownst to me, for all the preceding years my belly button had been collecting lint. Talk about a navel reserve! And it was so navel-retentive it hadn't even had the decency to tell me.

You know how lint is—it doesn't hold together very well. When I tugged with the tweezers at what was sticking out of my belly button, it just separated from the rest of the lint that remained comfortably lodged. I stuck the tweezers into my navel and pulled out a few more shreds of lint, and then a few more and yet a few more. I finally lost the tweezers.

I tried fishing around for the tweezers with a Q-tip and lost that, too. Things were not going well. I had visions of my gluttonous belly button swallowing the towel, the bathroom, and finally the whole world, myself included. And then where would I be? Up a creek without a paddle, up a tree without a ladder, up an asshole without a rubber glove. But I digress.

Somehow I became obsessed with the idea my belly button was rebelling (rebellying?) because I hadn't kept it clean, and that if I got all the lint out of it the universe would be safe again. Here, in order, are the methods I tried: a) a vacuum cleaner; b) Drano; c) dynamite. It was the first time my trusty Electrolux ever failed me, and the Drano also wimped out. But the dynamite actually helped. My navel wasn't really clear, though, until I called the friendly Roto-Rooter man. When he left, my navel was clean as a whistle, and when I bent down and hollered into it I could hear an echo. I thought that was a good sign.

Since then I have tried to maintain scrupulous navel cleanliness. I thought about calling a well-drilling company and having it capped, but reconsidered when I realized that all that cement might be kind of heavy and therefore tiring to lug around all day.

Having a navel as deep as the Homestake Mine makes for some interesting situations. Shortly after I got it cleaned out I found myself in an intimate situation with a very handsome gentleman who offered to introduce me to the esoteric and obscure practice of navel fisting. He gazed longingly at my navel and said, "You could make me and about a hundred other guys happy, all at the same time."

The prospect of hosting my very own navel invasion was intriguing, but ultimately I decided against letting the fleet sail in. I told him I was greatly flattered and thanked him but demurred, because at that time I was not yet into all the kinky stuff I'm into now (and some of you out there reading this know just exactly what I'm talking about, and quit smirking). But I digress.

Some of you may know that I'm writing a book. (Some of you may not know that fact, although now you do.) And some of you may know that I'm a bit of a pack rat. I save everything, on the theory that I'll eventually find a use for it. Well, here's my plan: I will become a Famous Minnesota Author, and the folks at the Minnesota Center for the Book Arts will put out an exquisite limited edition of one of my books. It will be hand-printed from hand-carved, handset type on handmade paper and each copy will be hand-bound (leather binding, of course).

That's why I saved all the lint—I figure it should make enough handmade paper for a limited run of at least 15,000 books. So when you're standing in line at the autograph party clutching your copy of my book for which you've just paid $250, think about the paper it's printed on and Consider the Source.

Bye for now,

Fist Fist

Chapter 14

Holiday Life

Every columnist who is fortunate enough to have their column run for more than a few issues eventually has to decide what to do about holidays. Do they even acknowledge them in their column? What can they say about them that hasn't been said before? What can they say about them that will resonate with their readers? Here are some holiday columns: a column on holidays in general, followed by two columns about Valentine's Day, one about Halloween and two about Christmas as seen through leather/BDSM/ fetish eyes.

High Holy Days
A multicultural odyssey
Published in *Lavender* #158 (June 15, 2001)

As I write this I have just returned from the International Mr. Leather (IML) contest in Chicago. Last year, contest founder Chuck Renslow called IML "the High Holy Days of the leather community." I am now looking forward to two more High Holy Day-type events, the Twin Cities GLBT Festival of Pride and Minnesota Leather Pride.

I recently saw a poster called the "2001 Chronology of World Cultural Events" that currently is on employee bulletin boards at many of Minnesota's best-known corporate offices. Produced by the Minnesota Cultural Diversity Center, this worldwide listing of celebrations and festivals is culturally diverse enough to include the fact that June is Gay Pride Month in the U.S.A.

Every culture has High Holy Days. For instance, Jews observe Passover to remember and celebrate their escape from the oppression of slavery in ancient Egypt. For Christians, Easter takes the Passover metaphor and extends it to humankind's emancipation from the oppression of sin and death, as symbolized by Jesus' resurrection.

Although the word "holy" connotes religion, even cultures that don't revolve around an organized religion have some form of High Holy Days. American blacks remember and celebrate their emancipation from slavery during Juneteenth. Americans celebrate the anniversary of their independence from England on July 4. Mexican Independence Day is Cinco de Mayo (May 5). And gay pride festivals everywhere commemorate 1969's Stonewall Rebellion and the birth of the modern GLBT-rights movement. One might say Stonewall was the start of the GLBT community's own exodus out of the oppression of the closet.

Other holidays (a word derived from "holy days") commemorate leaders and heroes. Christmas is a commemoration by Christians of the birth of Christ. The birthdays of great civic leaders—Washington, Lincoln and Martin Luther King, Jr.—are commemorated by U.S. government holidays. St. Patrick's Day began as a Catholic feast day for the patron saint of Ireland (although nowadays it might as well be called Irish Pride Day). And the International Mr. Leather contest is about selecting a leather community leader and spokesman for the next year.

It's interesting to note that the International Mr. Leather contest always takes place on Memorial Day weekend. Memorial Day (originally Decoration Day) is the U.S. holiday set aside for remembering and honoring soldiers who have died in war. But the day takes on added significance for the leather community as we remember all the community members we've lost to AIDS—especially this year, as the community mourned the passing of one of its giants, Tony DeBlase. A signboard on a restaurant across the street from this year's IML host hotel proclaimed, "Remember our fallen heroes!" Wow, I thought to myself, it's great that they put that sign up for all of us attending IML. Then I realized that they were talking about America's fallen war heroes, not about the leather community.

Although we sometimes don't want to admit it, we humans are more alike than different. Humans of all cultures have the same needs and impulses, which are expressed in ways that are often remarkably similar (see table, "Handy Multicultural Guide to High Holy Days," following this column).

What do we do on High Holy Days? We remember our struggles and sacrifices, and we celebrate our victories. We celebrate in every way possible, because every culture appreciates a good excuse for a party. We don our most festive clothes. We prepare special foods. We make pilgrimages. We have parades. We make speeches. We have special entertainment. We greet each other with special greetings of the day. We reaffirm and reinforce our values. We expend time and effort beforehand planning and preparing; afterwards we feel gratified, ready to let our regular, "normal" life continue.

And always, as the Thanksgiving hymn goes, we gather together. Sometimes we travel great distances to be with our family or our tribe. We see people whom we may not see any other time of year, whether that means running into someone in Loring Park* at Pride, getting reacquainted with someone from another city at IML, or shaking hands with someone who only attends church services on Christmas and Easter.

All cultures and communities have High Holy Days because all cultures and communities need them.

---

*A park in downtown Minneapolis where the Twin Cities Pride Festival is held each year.

Handy Multicultural Guide to High Holy Days

First publication; intended for *Lavender* #158 (June 15, 2001) but not used

Festival:	Passover	Easter	Christmas	St. Patrick's Day	Fourth of July	GLBT Pride, Minneapolis	IML
Event celebrates:	Exodus from Egypt	Christ's resurrection	Christ's birth	Irish patron saint	U.S. independence from England	Stonewall Rebellion, 1969	Select new tribal spokesman
Parade:	—	Easter Parade	Macy's Parade (actually Thanksgiving, but Christmas theme)	Absolutely	Yes, plus fireworks	Pride Parade	Parade of leathermen across stage
Festive dress:	—	Easter bonnet	Santa hat	Anything green	Anything red, white & blue	Anything with rainbows	Leather/ Levi/Latex/ Uniform
Festive food:	Kosher for Passover	Lamb	Goose, plum pudding, fruitcake	Everything green, including beer	Hot dogs & burgers	Hot dogs & burgers ($10 each)*	Ann Sather's cinnamon rolls
Commerce bonanza:	Kosher for Passover	Easter basket candy	The perfect Christmas gift	Anything green, including beer	Anything red, white & blue	Hot dogs & burgers ($10 each)*	IML Leather Marketplace
Travel:	—	—	Home for the Holidays	Downtown to see the parade	Anywhere to see the fireworks	Loring Park	Chicago
Saying:	Next year in Jerusalem	He is risen	Merry Christmas	Erin go bragh	Ooh! Aah! (referring to the fireworks)	Happy Pride	Thank you, sir! May I have another?

---

*Okay, I'm exaggerating. But for many years, the high prices for food and refreshments at concession booths during the Twin Cities Festival of Pride have drawn complaints. However, income from these concession booths constitutes a major source of funding for the festival—and it should be noted that the Twin Cities Festival of Pride has no gates and no admission charge, while every other GLBT pride festival of similar size or larger now has an (often substantial) admission charge.

Love, Leather-Style

Published in *Lavender* #253 (February 4, 2005)

After Christmas, the next holiday on the calendar of the nation's retailers is Valentine's Day. February 14 soon will be upon us, which means it's time to talk about love, sweet love. It's time for romance, hearts and flowers, and candy—lots of candy. Especially chocolate, which famously contains the "love chemical" phenylethylamine and several other mood-enhancing substances.

Leathersex aficionados certainly enjoy Valentine's Day as much as anyone else. Of course we love to celebrate love—why else would a red heart be part of the leather pride flag? But is the concept of "love" in a leather context different from "love" anyplace else?

Being a preacher's kid, I remember hearing my father preach many sermons on love. I guess the fact that I still remember them this many years later shows they were good sermons. Usually he talked about the fact that the English language has only one word for love, and that one word has to cover many bases.

But the Greek language (you will recall, I'm sure, that Western civilization is based heavily on thought and philosophical systems of the ancient Greeks) has different words for different kinds of love, four of which are eros, philia, storge and agape.

While the popular public perception of the leather community may be that it revolves around eros, I think leather culture has a lot to teach the rest of the culture about all four of these words.

Eros is the Greek word for physical love, i.e. sex. Eros was the Greek god of love, passion and desire (Cupid was his Roman equivalent). Both are commonly pictured with a bow and arrow, and it was thought that when Cupid's (or Eros') gold-tipped arrow hit someone, they were inflamed with love, passion and desire. It's interesting to note that to the Greeks these passions were sometimes enjoyable but were sometimes considered a torment, a burning itch that simply had to be scratched no matter what the cost.

Today eros sometimes is translated erroneously as "romance." The Greeks didn't have a word for romance because romance had not yet been invented. The concept of courtly love, and the necessity of a man winning a woman's admiration and adoration through heroic feats, would have been meaningless to them considering the extreme subordination of women in Greek society.

The English word "erotic" is derived from eros. Sometimes Eros was worshipped as the plural Erotes. The pluralization symbolized all the various kinds of attractions Eros inspired—including both heterosexual and homosexual ones. The Greeks thought of eros as strictly a physical, biological urge.

Eros and the erotic have for a long time had a bad reputation, at least in sex-negative circles, as dirty, shameful and immoral. Leather, on the other hand, proudly and joyfully celebrates sex. Entered into with the proper mindset, many people feel that sex is for adults what play is for kids—it's a fun, enjoyable activity that can lead to personal growth and to bonding with and closeness to other people. In other words, eros can lead to philia.

Philia is the Greek word for friendship. Modern-day Americans will recognize the word in Philadelphia, the "city of brotherly love." I think it's telling, however, that in the English language "philia" has become a suffix for words denoting feelings that generally are considered far from noble, and even far from normal; pedophilia, necrophilia, and other assorted paraphilias (sexualization of things "normal" people don't sexualize) are examples. In some circles almost everything in leather culture is considered a paraphilia, starting with the leather itself. Many kink-friendly psychologists and other mental-health professionals have spent many years trying to change this situation.

In my opinion, though, the noble aspect of the original Greek usage of philia is evident at leather gatherings everywhere. "Friendship" seems too pale a word for the sense of bonding and community that goes with leather. The sense of brotherhood and sisterhood often seems almost familial—which brings us to storge.

Storge is the Greek word for familial love, as in the love of parent for child. It may be trite to say "In leather we are family," but there's a lot of truth in that statement nonetheless. For some people who have been cut off from their biological family because of their leather proclivities, their leather family is their only family. And how much more familial can we get than daddy/boy or daddy/boi* relationships? Is that storge or what?

---

*boi: This term (always with a lowercase "b") has different meanings in different communities. For our purposes here, it means a biological female who thinks and acts as a leatherboy except, in one boi's words, "without the boy parts."

Agape is the Greek word for selfless love and caring for humanity. Unlike the other types of love discussed above, which are conditional, agape is unconditional. I very rarely hear this word outside of conservative Christian circles, whose members seem to have claimed it for their own.

But the principle of agape, if not the word, is well known in leather culture, as demonstrated by the amount of money raised by the community and the volunteer hours donated by community members. I also see the principles of agape in one of leather's most basic principles: respect for oneself and for others.

So there they are: four kinds of love, all intensely—and, to a great extent, intentionally—present in leather, there for the rest of the world to see if it cares to look. If one thinks about it, this way of loving should come as no surprise—leather's intense sexuality needs to be practiced with intense love, caring and respect. Selfishness in vanilla sexual relationships leads to emotional pain and unfulfilling relationships (and more material for stand-up comics, TV sitcoms and country-western songs). Selfishness in leather relationships can lead to physical injury.

Selfishness run rampant would lead to the end of leather. This is why it is not well tolerated by the community—and why people who value leather tend to cultivate values, attitudes and practices that build up the culture and the community rather than tear it down.

Here's one more Greek word for one more kind of love: mania, which literally translated means "madness." Mania is the over-the-top, out-of-control love that made teenage girls scream when the Beatles appeared on the Ed Sullivan show. Mania is what made grown women throw their panties or hotel-room keys at performers like Tom Jones and Engelbert Humperdinck.

For some reason, leather culture has never developed a good sense of mania. It's not that we don't try, of course; the concepts of leather contests and titleholders have been in the community for years. But whenever a leather contest reaches its peak and the new titleholder is sashed, the only people who rush the stage are the press. I have yet to see a single leather jock or hotel-room key thrown onstage. We, as a community, will have to work on that one.

Or maybe not.

Piercings by Cupid

Published in *Lavender* #201 (February 7, 2003)

Valentine's Day and leather go very well together. In fact, the combination is a better fit than you may have realized. Think of all the symbolism that Valentine's Day involves.

First there's Cupid, a master piercer if ever there was one. Cupid, the Roman god of love, was the son of Venus, the Roman goddess of love and beauty. Venus was the Roman version of the Greek goddess Aphrodite—that's where the word "aphrodisiac" comes from. In the same fashion, Cupid was the Roman version of the Greek god Eros, from whose name comes the word "erotic"—and for whom the Atons of Minneapolis have named their annual springtime "Eros" parties.

Next: The symbol of love that's on every Valentine card—a heart—is also a prominent part of the leather pride flag. There are very few other flags in the world that incorporate a heart. How few, you ask? I recently visited a website called Flags of the World, which is paradise to anyone into vexillology.* A search of 32,000 images of flags reveals a mere 23 that have the keyword "heart" associated with them. On further investigation, the heart-shaped thing on several of the flags is really a leaf or a lily pad. Many of the other flags that include a heart in the design use it as a representation of being "at the heart of" something, the center or crossroads of a geographical region. (Example: The Canadian city of Chilliwack has a flag with four green hearts representing that Chilliwack is "the green heart of British Columbia.") Disqualify the historical flags that are no longer used, and the leather pride flag emerges as the most widely flown modern-day flag incorporating a heart. Of all those 32,000 flags, the leather pride flag's use of a big, bold, unabashed red heart pretty much stands alone.

Now, what about the man who gave the day its name? According to various legends, Saint Valentine was a physician/healer and also a (reputedly chaste) Christian priest who was executed on February 14, 269 A.D. Emperor Claudius II was the leader of the Roman Empire at the time and was having trouble getting Roman men to join his army. He reasoned that they didn't want to leave their wives and families;

---

*Vexillology: the study of flags.

therefore, he canceled all marriages and engagements. Valentine, however, continued to marry couples in secret, for which he was jailed and ultimately martyred.

More legend: Valentine was put in prison while he awaited execution. His jailer had a blind daughter whose sight was restored by Valentine. They became friends, and when Valentine was executed he left a note to the jailer's daughter thanking her for her friendship and support. He signed it, "From your Valentine."

That note signed "From your Valentine" might have remained obscure were it not for what happened 200 years later. The custom of the Roman empire at the time was to start the Feast of Lupercalia honoring Juno, the goddess of "feverish" (*febris*) love, on February 15. A lottery was held where men drew women's names, and the women became the men's feasting and sexual companions for the next year. (Doesn't sound terribly consensual for the women, does it?) The early Christian church didn't approve of such pagan eroticism and hijacked the festival by making February 14 the Feast Day of Saint Valentine — in effect substituting romance for eroticism. No longer would a man get a woman because he drew her name, but he would be allowed to send her a "valentine" note asking if she was interested in him.

So, what does it all mean? Given Saint Valentine's track record of opposing those who oppose love, I'd be willing to bet that if he were alive today he'd thumb his nose at the Church and perform same-sex marriages. He would also probably understand that love comes in many flavors and that not all of the flavors are to everyone's liking, but love in any flavor is still love and deserves to be honored as such.

Vanilla Halloween, Leather Halloween
Published in *Lavender* #220 (October 31, 2003)

It's Halloween. October 31 falls on a Friday this year, and that means the parties will last all weekend. This year more than most years, it's not just for kids.

I think of Halloween as Amateur Night — the one night of the year when anyone can wear anything and no one will ask questions. For some people the "anything" they wear will be a won't-everyone-be-scandalized "costume" of leather or fetishwear — which they've gone to great lengths to put together. Other people will be wearing basically the same thing, but they will have just reached into their closet and pulled it out, like they always do.

If Halloween is about scary and spooky things, be assured that for some people leather and/or BDSM fetishwear is spooky and scary. Or at least they think it is to other people, and that means that on some level it's spooky and scary to them, too. But just as we whistle when we walk past graveyards, or attend slasher movies as a way of dealing with our fears by making them seem outlandish and therefore less scary, some people do the same thing with leather. (It is only fair to note here that a drag queen could write pretty much the same thing about straight men dressing up in women's clothing on Halloween.)

So for amateurs, it's a costume. For those into leather/BDSM/fetish it isn't, of course. Or is it? You will find people in a dungeon for whom the exotic and erotic qualities of their fetishwear are turn-ons, and they only wear it in sexual situations. It seems to me that this is how the heterosexual/pansexual BDSM community has traditionally worked: A person adopts a "scene" name and may have a wardrobe of fetishwear that's never worn anywhere other than the dungeon or the bedroom—except maybe on Halloween.

Gay leather, on the other hand, doesn't seem to be so segmented. We tend to use real names rather than scene names, or else we use the same nickname everywhere. Likewise our apparel: we wear our leather anywhere it's practical, whether for protection when riding a motorcycle or just because it's cool outside. (If a jacket is called for, we might as well wear a leather one that looks good on us and makes us feel good when we wear it.) If we wear our leathers to a Halloween party, other people may look at us and think it's our costume. But we know that it's not really a costume—it's an expression of who we are.

Now, despite the differences in our approach to the whole "costume" aspect of Halloween, I would like to point out that there are many similarities between the vanilla world and the leather world. We each have many of the same impulses; it's simply that the impulses are expressed differently.

Vanilla Halloween: A chance to wear, for a change, something representing what one is not, whether that be a dominatrix outfit, female drag on a man, or even a Donald Duck costume. **Leather Halloween:** Reach into the closet, grab the leather or fetishwear, and dress to express, not hide, who we are. It's not a costume, and it's not just for Halloween.

Vanilla: Masks. **Leather:** No mask (unless it's part of a scene in a dungeon). No hiding. We've done enough of that. We'll let the vanilla folk experience for one night what it was like for us all those years when we had to hide.

Vanilla: Halloween handouts are candy for the kids (and, for fundamentalist Christians, tracts with the candy). After trick-or-treating, kids compare the loot they collected: "I got a Snickers bar!" "I got a Kit Kat!" **Leather:** Halloween handouts for everyone are flavored condoms and lube: "I got the piña colada lube—my favorite!" "I got one of those mint-flavored condoms, and I'm so bored with them! Maybe I can exchange it for one that's cola-flavored." No wonder gay men love Halloween.

Vanilla: Scary candle-lit haunted houses. **Leather:** Scary candle-lit dungeons.

Vanilla: Party decorations predominantly in black and orange. **Leather:** Party decorations predominantly in black and orange—which coincidentally, conveniently, are Harley-Davidson's colors.

Vanilla: Jack-o-lanterns with candles inside. **Leather:** Remove the candle from the jack-o-lantern and use it for wax play.

Vanilla: Party games include bobbing for apples. **Leather:** We have our party games, too. But if our heads are bobbing up and down it probably has nothing to do with apples.

Vanilla mind game: In a totally dark room, make someone stick their hands in a "bowl of eyeballs" (actually a bowl of grapes). **Leather** mind game: Tie someone up, then tell them you're running a knife blade across their back (actually the edge of a credit card).

Vanilla: Home videos of the kids in their costumes. The kids will enjoy seeing what they look like, and it will make for great memories when they get older. **Leather:** "The Making of Making Porn," a locally produced, professional-quality video of Twin Cities leathermen in (and out of) their leathers. Great documentary footage, but you probably wouldn't want to show it to children.

Vanilla: Halloween greeting: "Trick or treat!" **Leather:** Let me close with an ancient Celtic leather Halloween blessing: "May all your tricks be treats!"

Leather Carols

Published in *Lavender* #171 (December 14, 2001)

As the song says, "it's the most wonderful time of the year." What would the holidays be without Christmas carols? And what would they be without Christmas carol parodies circling the globe, riding on an e-mail sleigh and delivering mirth and joy to millions of good little girls and boys?

But although I've seen versions of Christmas carols (and rewrites of "The Night Before Christmas," too) that could be termed bawdy and/or lewd, I've never seen any leather Christmas carols. So, in the spirit of the season, I have written some and present them here for your holiday entertainment.

Master Claus is Coming to Town

Get ready to groan, get ready to sigh
Get ready to moan, I'm telling you why
Master Claus is coming to town.

With little tin cuffs, little toy clips,
Flogger-tog-togs and whippie-tip-tips,
Master Claus is coming to town.

He knows what you've been craving
And how much you can take.
He knows sometimes what's bad is good,
And he's good—for goodness sake!

So, you're gonna be black, gonna be blue
Gonna be flying when Santa is through,
Master Claus is coming to town!

I Saw Mommy Topping Santa Claus

I saw Mommy topping Santa Claus
Underneath the mistletoe last night
She took off his red suit
And said, "Gee, you sure look cute!"
And then she got him warmed up
With a flogger made of jute.

Then I saw Mommy paddle Santa Claus,
Swatting at his butt so snowy white.
Oh what a shame Dad didn't see
(He would have watched with glee)
Mommy topping Santa Claus last night!

Santa Daddy

Santa Daddy
Slip some leather under the tree
For me
Like a jacket and chaps, Santa Daddy,
And hurry down the chimney tonight.

Santa Daddy
Something that will show off my chest—
A vest!
I'd just think you're the best! Santa Daddy,
And hurry down the chimney tonight.

Think of all the fun we've had
Think of just how good I've been when I've been bad
Haven't I earned a nice return
For all that dungeon fun-time, Dad?

(Of course I have!) Santa Daddy
Forgot to mention one little thing—
A ring!
—I don't mean for my hand! Santa Daddy,
And hurry down the chimney tonight.

Jingle Bells

Jingle bells, jingle bells,
Jing-a-ling-a-ling!
Oh what fun it is to ride
In a one-horse open sling!

If you enjoyed these, try creating some of your own—it's actually not as difficult as you might think. Consider that one of the main symbols of the holiday is your basic Bear-type guy who wears big black leather boots and never goes anywhere without his toybag—and a riding crop to use on Rudolph and the rest of the reindeer. What exactly do you suppose those "reindeer games" were, anyway?

Happy Holidays, God Bless Us Every One, and To All A Good Night.

The Real Drummerboy Story
A Christmas fantasy

Published in *Lavender* #41 (December 20, 1996), reprinted in *Lavender* #119 (December 17, 1999)

Many, many years ago, in a land far away, there was a young drummerboy named Willie. Willie played his drum at the temple, where he accompanied the temple dancers. He loved drumming, and he also loved the leather harness that he wore to carry the drum. It had been a gift from his Daddy, who had made it especially for him. He loved the harness so much that sometimes he wore it even when he wasn't playing drums. His Daddy had a harness too (even though he didn't play drums at all) and most of their other friends had harnesses and other leather clothing as well.

Playing the drum at the temple didn't pay very well, but Willie didn't mind. Shortly after he had attained manhood and left his parents' house he had started living with his Daddy, an older gentleman who made a good living as a successful astrologer.

One winter night, Willie and his Daddy were lying in bed, cradled in each other's arms. Willie, feeling very contented, looked out the window at the starry sky. Suddenly he saw one star grow brighter and brighter, until it blazed with a radiance he had never seen before. As he drifted off to sleep holding his Daddy, he thought to himself that the star could have symbolized the love he and his Daddy shared.

The next day Willie had just finished playing his drum when his Daddy suddenly appeared at the temple. "Willie, take your drum and come with me," said his Daddy. "We're going on a long journey." The King had seen the same star that Willie and his Daddy had seen the night before, and had asked his Daddy's company (Weisman, Weisman & Weisman Astrological Consultants P.A.) to investigate it.

Day and night, the star continued to blaze in the sky as Willie, his Daddy and his Daddy's two partners followed it for twelve days.

Finally, it led them to a tiny stable behind an inn in an obscure village. In the stable, among the animals and the stablehands, there was a young woman, Mary, sitting on a bale of hay nursing a baby! Willie had never seen such a sight before. But what was even more incredible was that his Daddy and his Daddy's partners knelt down before the mother and child and presented them with rare and precious gifts. Willie didn't understand at all what was happening.

Willie's Daddy, seeing the look of puzzlement on his face, took him aside. He explained that he and his partners had all had a dream telling them that this child was the long-awaited Hebrew Moshiac, or Messiah, who was born to remind all people everywhere of the common humanity they share.

Willie was amazed to hear this. He understood how important this was, and he felt both honored to be in the presence of this child and ashamed that he had no gift to bring, as his Daddy had. He went over to Mary intending to apologize. But before he could say anything, Mary spoke to him. "Thank you for coming here, Willie. You honor my child with your presence. Your Daddy told me all about you." "He did?" Willie suddenly felt uneasy; many people in that time didn't approve of Daddy/boy relationships, or people who wore harnesses even when they didn't need to. Mary, who was wise beyond her years, sensed his discomfort and said, "Yes, and don't you ever worry or feel ashamed of who you are. You have every right to be part of this holy event; you are just as much a brother to this child as is any other person.

"This child was born to be brother and friend to everyone in the whole world, in each and every tribe. I know your tribe is working on brotherhood and sisterhood in your own way. You have an idea of what brotherhood and sisterhood are all about; many people in this world don't."

Willie listened, fascinated, as Mary foretold some of the events in the life of her child, Jesus. He would never condemn anyone, and in fact would associate with many classes of people whom the rest of society at the time considered untouchable. History would never record whether Jesus ever married or had children. But it would record that he had many followers, including a disciple named John who would be enigmatically referred to as "the disciple Jesus loved";

scholars would argue for centuries over the exact meaning of that phrase. And they would argue over whether or not Jesus was, in fact, Moshiac. What they wouldn't argue about was that Jesus was destined to play the most famous crucifixion scene in history.

Willie found himself lost in the wonder of Mary's predictions. Suddenly, he remembered what he had intended to tell her: "I'm sorry I have no gift to give your son." As he said this, an idea came to him: "Perhaps I can play my drum for him, like I do in the temple." Mary nodded and said, "I think that would be lovely."

As his Daddy listened with pride, Willie played his drum softly, gently and skillfully, tapping into the primal rhythms of the wind, sky, ocean, birds and animals. As he played, Mary swayed and rocked Jesus gently to the rhythm of the drum.

As they left the stable, Willie turned to his Daddy and said, "Daddy, I think we just saw something very special." "Yes," said his Daddy, "I think we did."

Chapter 15

Spiritual Life
Leather as a spiritual path

The Church of the Holy Circuit
Published in *Lavender* #290 (July 7, 2006)

Come with me now to Excalibur, "the best nightclub in Chicago." It's the Monday evening after the International Mr. Leather contest, and time for the Black & Blue Ball—the final official event of the IML weekend and one of the events on "the circuit" (as was Sunday night's post-contest "Salute" party at Chicago's famous House of Blues). This is where leathermen and circuit boys intersect.

(For the uninitiated, "the circuit" means circuit parties, a series of gay men's dance parties held in major cities around the country and the world throughout the year. Just as a distinct culture has grown up around leather runs and title contests, a similar culture has grown up around circuit parties.)

They probably haven't thought about it, but for many gay leathermen and gay men in general, this and other circuit parties serve many of the purposes that churches serve or, in many instances, formerly served. Those who worry about the future of organized religion, and who wonder where the church is headed in the twenty-first century, will find ample food for thought here. Perhaps it's not coincidental that some of the most enduring music played at circuit parties is by an artist named Madonna, and her new album is called *Confessions on a Dance Floor*.

The building that houses Excalibur was originally built in 1892 to house the Chicago Historical Society. The building's architectural style is Romanesque Revival, based on the eleventh- and twelfth-century architecture of Spain and France. The building, clad in red granite, has turrets, high-peaked and steeply sloped roofs, arched windows and even a cathedral-like rose window. It looks vaguely church-like except for the absence of crosses on the roof peaks.

Entering through an ornate, dark portico, one finds oneself in a large central entrance lobby surrounded by other rooms (side chapels?). As with all great cathedrals, the building's interior is decorated with stunning art, mostly contemporary photographs and including some interesting collage pieces. The ceilings are decoratively painted, and even the floors are ornate. Up the grand staircase from the main lobby is the main dance floor, surrounded by four levels of balconies and topped by high, steeply peaked ceilings.

The evening's DJ, Matthew Harvat, is situated in a loft over-looking the dance floor. Like the organist or music director in a church, the DJ at a circuit party is responsible for picking music that will lead to the greatest inspiration and spiritual uplift. The beat of the music inspires bliss, and the messages in the lyrics celebrate love, music, fairness, justice, brotherhood and respect for self and others. Most of the vocals are sung by soulful female voices straight out of a gospel choir.

This is what the disco music of the early 1970s, the post-Stonewall years, has become. Some of tonight's musical selections, in fact, are re-issues or remakes of classic 70s disco—notice this word—anthems.

The music, and the bliss it inspires, also are reminiscent of the idealistic, positive, hopeful and politically charged 1960s. One song exhorts listeners to "keep the faith." (Unfortunately, too often circuit-party bliss-seeking involves drugs—another way in which this scene hearkens back to the 1960s.)

The effect of the music is enhanced by a fantastic light show that uses every trick in the book. Computer-controlled lights quickly and continuously change position, color and pattern, sending light beams cascading around the room. There are also lasers, strobe lights, fog machines and a mirrored disco ball. In its time, the stained glass in twelfth-century cathedrals also served as an awe-inspiring light show.

Everyone on the dance floor is male, in leather and, according to my gaydar, gay. But within that demographic it's a diverse mix: black, white, Latino, Asian, etc. The age of crowd members ranges from the twenties to the sixties. Some are gym-buffed and some are not. But everyone is beautiful. No one seems to notice or care about ethnicity, age or physique—everyone here is equal.

The men are busy disproving the old adage that "Leathermen don't dance." The dancing is sensual and sultry. These guys know how to move and how to seduce. If dancing has always been a surrogate for sex, here it's not too far removed.

Unlike traditional churches, circuit parties do not concern themselves with ritualistically marking, celebrating and commemorating life stages—baptisms, weddings, funerals, etc. The action on the dance floor is very much centered, like Buddhism, in the here and now. In that sense it is timeless or out-of-time, if only for an evening. It is an escape from the ordinary and the mundane, although not a permanent one.

But for tonight, it will do. Tonight, this is sacred space for these men and this tribe. Tonight, Excalibur is their cathedral and the Black & Blue Ball is their proverbial Sunday morning service on, in this case, Monday night.

This is their own kind of Sabbath rites and rituals. They are dressed in their version of Sunday Best, which in this case involves lots of leather, lots of body jewelry and lots of skin. This is their version of bliss-seeking, using their bodies to reach spirit, transcendence, liberation—the kind of liberation that started with Stonewall and just keeps evolving.

"John the Baptist Wore Leather"
Group explores leather and Christianity
Published in *Lavender* #74 (March 27, 1998)

Are you looking for new places to wear your leather? Do you want to meet new people, but you don't like the bar scene? Here's an idea for you: go to church.

A Christian leather group has been meeting for about a year at All God's Children Metropolitan Community Church in Minneapolis. While the combination of leather and Christianity may sound bizarre to some, it makes perfect sense to others. Members of this group are quick to point out, for example, that the Bible is quite explicit about the fact that John the Baptist wore leather. According to Matthew 3:4, New International Version: "John's clothes were made of camel's hair, and he had a leather belt around his waist." (The Revised Standard Version calls it a "leather girdle." Whatever.) John lived and preached in the wilderness, and his food was "locusts and wild honey." Nobody back then quite knew what to make of him.

In many churches today, nobody quite knows what to make of us leatherfolk, either. The Reverend Troy Perry, a modern-day Martin Luther if ever there was one, is the founder of the Christian denomination known as the Metropolitan Community Church. He has written about the early days of his church in San Francisco (the church was started in 1968)—specifically one Sunday morning when four leathermen showed up for worship services. Murmurs went through the congregation about "those people," and Perry himself was a little unsure how to handle the situation. Were these people Hell's Angels? Were they dangerous? They certainly looked like they could be. But after the service they sought him out and spoke to him, and he was surprised and pleased to find that they were kind, gentle, intelligent people. Rev. Perry has since become a proud leatherman himself.

Since that time, Metropolitan Community Churches have sprung up in cities across the country, and many of those churches have members from the leather/SM community. The Minneapolis MCC leather group meets Wednesday evenings; they also have occasional social times on Friday or Saturday nights. The first Wednesday of every month is Leather Cleaning Night: everyone brings their leather, throws it on the table, and cleans and polishes while they talk. According to one member, "You have to clean it sometime, you might as well do it with friends."

The group is Christian but is open to all spiritual orientations; the substance of the group is what its members bring to it, and anyone wanting to explore the relationship between leather, sexuality and spirituality might find something of value here, regardless of their religious orientation (or lack thereof).

Christian BDSM
Christian? Yes. Vanilla? Not necessarily.

Published in *Lavender* #357 (January 30, 2009)

I've just been on a trip through an alternate universe. It was interesting and educational.

It all started innocently enough. An article in the *Utne Reader* (Jan.-Feb. 2009) dealt with "Sexing Up the Religious Right." According to the article, religious conservatives have realized that sexual prudery is not a concept that's going to attract the masses in today's world. So they now are busily weaving together the concepts of God, traditional marriage and fantastic sex into what they hope will be a winning package. The article makes the point, however, that some devious, deceitful and repressive things are going on underneath the surface, and warns us not to be fooled.

"Well," your humble columnist thought to himself, "I wonder if anyone is equating BDSM with Christianity?" No, of course not, I said to myself—look at all the Christian groups that for years have been trying to shut down BDSM events.

Nevertheless, I tried an experiment: I typed "Christian BDSM" into my favorite search engine. I hit the jackpot—the search engine returned over 65,000 results.

The first hit was a blog that talked about evangelical Christianity in America as a parallel "Christian Republic" existing next to, but divorced from, the secular American society created by the separation of church and state.

And, apparently, that Christian Republic has some folks who are into BDSM and other kinds of alternate sexual expression, because further down the list was christiansandbdsm.com. After a page proclaiming that the creators of the site believe in Biblical inerrancy, subsequent pages discuss "The Christian Marriage" and "The Christian Husband" before discussing "Christian D/s," Christian perspectives on Master/slave and Master/sub relationships, and "Christian BDSM," on which page the authors of the site offer the following conclusion:

"We have not found within Scriptures any condemnation of sexual behaviors or acts of B&D or S&M when practiced by a man and woman within marriage for the purposes of sexual arousal or gratification. Nor do we find these behaviors defined in Scripture as unnatural, abnormal or perverse."

Next on the hit list is sexinchrist.com and a page on "Bondage in Christ—BDSM in a Christian Marriage." The first paragraph ends with this: "A BDSM relationship between a dominant husband and submissive wife is actually the ideal of marriage set out in Ephesians 5:22-26 taken to its logical conclusion!" Ephesians 5:22 is the familiar verse, "Wives, submit to your own husbands as to the Lord."

The remainder of the page explains, Bible verse by Bible verse, how BDSM can be part of a Christian marriage. The page's authors even make the point that it can be Biblical for the husband to submit to the wife in the bedroom—as long as there is "an explicit understanding on the parts of both the husband and wife that they will adopt 'natural' roles in the rest of their daily lives. We would counsel against couples living the wife dominant/husband submissive roles '24/7', as this could lead to spiritual confusion."

Other articles at sexinchrist.com include "Anal sex and God's Will," "Oral sex and God's Will" (in which an eloquent case is made for swallowing), "Fisting and God's Will," "Masturbation—God's Great Gift To Us," "Threesomes Within a Christian Marriage," and several more. In some instances, the Bible doesn't mention the activity (and therefore doesn't prohibit it); in other instances, the Bible actually mentions an activity in a desirable way (mostly in poetic form in the *Song of Solomon*). The revisionist theology in all the articles gets high marks for creativity. I just wish the site were a little less homophobic.

According to these sites, you see, it isn't the activities themselves that are scandalous. What's scandalous is when they're done outside the bonds of holy matrimony. Even here, the "Threesome" article mentioned above twists itself into pretzels trying to make a three-way sexual encounter not be un-Biblical. If it's a man, his wife, and another man, that could be a problem, because any time you have two guys together in a sexual situation there might be homoerotic overtones. A man, his wife, and another woman, on the other hand, might be okay. This is because what the Bible says about lesbianism could be interpreted as prohibitions against women being too butch. As long as the lesbianism is the lipstick variety, it is presumed to be permissible.

A few things to note: First, unlike the examples in the *Utne Reader* article, I don't think the creators of these sites are trying to use sex to win converts to Christianity. Second, while some of the theology on these sites may be challenging, their understanding of BDSM values seems commendably orthodox. Finally, these ideas are not that new — parts of christiansandbdsm.com date from 1998.

If we as a community are trying to decriminalize BDSM and get BDSM activities removed from the list of mental illnesses in the *DSM* (*Diagnostic and Statistical Manual of Mental Disorders*), here is a whole new group of people to work with. They are obviously ready to argue with conviction that, according to the Bible, there is nothing wrong with many of the things in which they, and we, take such pleasure.

Cléo Dubois: "Secrets of Being a Good Top"
Published in *Lavender* #183 (May 31, 2002)

It is a Thursday evening at a theater in Minneapolis, and there isn't an empty seat in the house. Thunderous applause greets educator and domina* Cléo Dubois as she steps onstage to present the evening's seminar: "Secrets of Being a Good Top (and a Good Bottom, or even a Good Brat)." She is dressed in a black leather corset worn over a short black leather dress. Her legs are encased in black fishnet stockings and shiny black spike-heeled boots. She wears black leather gloves punctuated with a diamond bracelet on her wrist. There are red highlights in her black hair.

Speaking with a charming French accent, she tells us about herself. This is her first seminar in the Midwest, although she has presented seminars on both coasts for many years and is the proprietor of the "Academy of SM Arts" based in the San Francisco area. She has come to Minneapolis for the screening of her first video, *The Pain Game,* as part of the Flaming Film Festival. The video has just won an award from the Society for the Scientific Study of Sexuality. Her second video, *Tie Me Up!,* has just been released. *The Pain Game* is available at the back of the theater, but she wants to be clear that it is not about pornography and titillation; this video shows real play for

---

*Domina: A female dominant; synonyms are "domme" and "dominatrix."

the purposes of education, not simulated play for the purpose of fantasy. If it were porn, she says, it would have been a lot easier to get the movie made and distributed.

Dubois got into the San Francisco pre-AIDS gay male leather scene courtesy of a bisexual boyfriend who liked to frequent the Catacombs, the now-legendary fisting/sex club where every square inch of surface was permanently coated with Crisco. She took a liking to the action: "I was just like a kid in a candy store," she says. Dubois' mentors did more than teach her SM techniques—they showed her the psychic, mystic, ritualistic and spiritual dimensions of SM and other alternative sexualities that are now the *raison d'être* of her seminars.

In 1983, she organized what was only the second mixed SM play party in San Francisco's history. She says she's not sure she likes the word "pansexual"—"I'm more about taking the labels off altogether." She has seen the qualities, values and attitudes that are common to everyone who is willing to explore alternative sexualities, no matter what their stated sexual orientation might be.

Enough talk. Dubois and a pre-arranged volunteer from the audience stage a scene that is breathtaking both literally and figuratively: literally, because the scene involves breathplay using a hangman's noose toy made of black velvet rope, and figuratively, because the energy connection between Dubois and the bottom is so vivid and intense.

This intense connection between a top and a bottom is what the evening's seminar is all about, and Dubois tells us that the two most important factors for attaining and maintaining it are "trust, and staying present to the moment." She talks about the importance of knowing what you want (which is negotiable), what you need (things that are definitely not negotiable, such as limits and boundaries), and knowing the difference between the two.

She describes ways of tuning in to your partner through centering and breathing techniques. She discusses ways that a top, having taken control, can flow with that control ("Have a plan, and then let go of it"). Here are a few of Dubois' other tips for tops:
- To find the rhythm of the scene: first, slow down. Then note how you feel and watch your body language. You'll know if and when you can speed up again.

- Stay connected with your bottom through touch, verbalization and eye contact. Use all of these to reinforce your playspace and the magic you're creating there.
- Dubois has often seen this in public dungeons: "It's just you and the whip—the bottom doesn't even enter into the equation. Or with tit clamps, it's just you and the breast, not the person attached to the breast. *Get* and *stay* connected to your partner!"
- A good top knows the importance of nurturing a bottom after a scene. But tops need nurturing, too, especially when the play has been intense. Get the nurturing you need, and take time to process the scene.

In addition to this workshop on Thursday night and screening her video on Friday, Dubois rounded out her visit to Minneapolis by presenting a play piercing workshop on Saturday.

Dubois offers "personalized instruction and private coaching in the SM arts for adventurous couples and individuals." To find out more, or to order her videos, visit her website.

Using Flesh to Reach Spirit
Published in *Lavender* #188 (August 9, 2002)

Cléo Dubois, the subject of this column several issues ago, is coming back to the Twin Cities, and this time she's bringing her husband with her—Fakir Musafar, noted shaman and founder of the "modern primitive" movement. Together they will present a workshop/class/ritual, "Spirit + Flesh: Exploring Ecstatic Body Rites." *Spirit + Flesh* is also the title of Musafar's new book, which he will be autographing at the seminar.

What the heck is an "ecstatic body rite," you ask? Are you pierced or tattooed? Have you experienced BDSM play? Those qualify as ecstatic body rites. Musafar is one of the people responsible for the current popularity of piercing and other body modification techniques, and it is his belief that the body is a wonderful tool for getting in touch with spirit. His belief and experience is that intense physical sensation can be the gateway to transcendence, altered states of consciousness, visions, healing and transformation.

Cultures throughout history and around the world have agreed with this philosophy. Because they resonate powerfully with basic human needs and urges, the kinds of extreme physical practices that much of western culture has outlawed as "primitive" or "barbaric" existed among prehistoric peoples and continue to exist in other cultures today.

For example, most if not all of the native tribes of the North American plains practiced rituals incorporating piercing and other forms of self-torture as rites of initiation and vision quest; the most famous of these is probably the Sun Dance and its variants. As part of the "Okeepa" ceremony of the Mandan tribe, young men went through fasting and self-torture to demonstrate commitment and sacrifice to the gods and the tribe, as well as to gain spiritual power, insight and vision.

The torture involved having slits cut in the skin of the back, chest and legs. Wooden skewers were then inserted in the slits and rawhide thongs were tied to the skewers. Buffalo-skull weights were attached to the leg thongs, and then the thongs attached to the back and chest were thrown over the rafters of the ceremonial lodge and the men were hoisted and kept hanging until they lost consciousness. The next day this hoisting was repeated outdoors.

The Sun Dance modified this slightly in that the thongs were attached to a center sun-pole. The men were thus symbolically imprisoned. In order to free themselves they danced around the pole until, many hours later, the skewers tore through their skin. The torture represented death, and the emancipation represented resurrection, renewal and rebirth.

For the young men these experiences were demonstrations of fortitude and bravery, but they also induced powerful visions that were later told to the tribe's equivalent of priests. (Any similarities to Jesus hanging for hours, nailed to a cross, crying out to God, dying, being pierced in the side with a spear, and subsequently resurrecting are just coincidence—aren't they?) The U.S. outlawed the Sun Dance in 1904.

Nobody in Malaysia has outlawed the Hindu festival of Thaipusam, though, which is currently celebrated by about a million people every year. It's a procession up 276 temple steps, and many of the faithful turn themselves into walking floats by carrying frameworks weighing up to 50 pounds and decorated with flowers, colored paper, tinsel, fruits and peacock feathers. The frames are attached to the celebrants with hooks through the skin of the chest, face and back. Others simply pierce their cheeks and tongues with long skewers before making the journey. Because the revelers are in a trance there is reportedly no pain, little blood and no scarring.

Of course the use of such extreme physical practices to reach spiritual enlightenment is regarded by much of western culture as "primitive" or "barbaric," but it all depends on your point of view. Consider that our modern, civilized culture makes no extreme demands on our young men's bodies; we only expect them to sacrifice their foreskins to gods named "Health" and "Cleanliness," and the sacrifice is performed, often without anesthesia, while they are still infants because they are then too young to feel anything, right?*

But, as my colleague Ms. Dafydd† says, I digress. For fifty years Fakir Musafar has been on a journey of discovering these ancient body rites, and adapting and introducing them to Western culture. Along the way, he has fascinated some people and shocked others. A visit to his website shows some of the extreme lengths to which he has taken his spirit quest. In one photo a corset reduces his waist to nineteen inches; in another he has twin swords piercing his chest; in a third he is hanging in midair, suspended by two hooks through the chest piercings (see "Okeepa," above).

The workshop by Musafar and Dubois should be an interesting and intense evening, assuming one isn't too squeamish.

The Feng Shui of Leather
Published in *Lavender* #217 (September 19, 2003)

Sometimes it can be interesting to look with different eyes at something with which we're familiar. It can be startling to see what's different, and even more startling to see what's the same. For instance, what happens when we apply the ancient Chinese metaphysical wisdom of feng shui to leather? No, I'm not going to suggest hanging

---

*Wrong. After spending years denying that infants could feel pain, in the mid-1980s the medical community finally started to experiment with the use of anesthesia in connection with infant circumcision. The ideal balance between safety and effectiveness has not yet been found, so research continues.

† See "Lint Life," page 251.

crystals from your nipple rings and putting a wind chime on your Harley. Suspend your disbelief and let's explore.

Classic feng shui has been practiced for millennia. It deals with understanding chi, the "life-force energy" that results from the interaction of yin and yang, the two universal forces seen as equal but opposite components of one unified whole. The metaphysical principles underlying feng shui are also the underpinnings of other disciplines including macrobiotics (which has been called "feng shui for food") and the *I Ching* or *Book of Changes*,* the world's oldest oracle (the "changes" referred to are the constantly changing interaction of yin and yang). Acupuncture and acupressure are attempts to understand and control the flow of chi in the body, while feng shui attempts to understand and control the flow of chi in the environment.

The yin/yang symbol depicts a relationship that is always changing, shifting back and forth between the two energies. In the symbol yin is represented by black and yang is represented by white. But the largest part of each half of the symbol, where the black or white color is at its fullest, has in it a spot of the opposite color. This symbolizes the fact that the moment each force is at its fullest is also the start of that force's decay (and the corresponding upswing of the opposite force). Comfortable chi is achieved when yin and yang are balanced and the swings between them are not too extreme.

Besides black, other yin attributes include low, soft, dark, wet, resting and female. Other yang attributes in addition to white include high, hard, bright, dry, active and male. You get the idea.

Now let's introduce another level of feng shui: the five elements of Chinese metaphysics. The constantly changing interaction of yin and yang gives rise to five phases, or elements, of chi, composed of different proportions of yin and yang: Fire, Earth, Metal, Water and Wood. Again, comfortable chi is achieved when the five elements are in balance; discomfort arises when one or more of the elements are either too strong or too weak.

So how does this all relate to leather? Start by taking almost any article of leather apparel: vest, chaps, boots, whatever. First consider

---

*A good introduction to the *I Ching* is a book called *The* I Ching *Made Easy: Be Your Own Psychic Advisor Using the World's Oldest Oracle* by Roderic Sorrell and Amy Max Sorrell (San Francisco: HarperSanFrancisco, 1994).

the material of which the article is made: leather. Animals (including humans) belong to the fire element, as does leather, being an animal product. Fire is the most yang, or male, of the five elements. So the classic leatherman, seen through the lens of feng shui, is a male clothed in an extremely male garment.

But now consider the color of that garment. Typically it's black, the most yin (or female) of all colors. This at first might seem like a contradiction, but remember that feng shui is all about balance— we balance the strong yang of the leather with the equally strong yin of the color black. This might say something about gay leather-men's reputation for being comfortable with both our masculine and feminine sides.

Imagine, on the other hand, if our leather was white. Remember Elvis Presley—he famously wore a white leather outfit onstage in Las Vegas. If our leathers were white, the typical leather bar would look like a convention of Elvis impersonators. The extreme yang of white added to the extreme yang of leather would be overwhelming.

Now let us consider another classic piece of a leatherman's apparel: dark-blue Levis.® Plants and plant products, including the cotton from which Levis are made, fall under the Wood element. Wood is also yang, and therefore masculine, although not as strongly mascu-line as Fire. The counterbalancing color is dark blue, which is not as strongly yin as black. Again, we have balance.

Consider the hankie code, where left means top and right means bottom. Whoever formulated that code in the early days of leather may or may not have been aware that in feng shui left is yang (male, traditionally top) and right is yin (female, traditionally bottom).

Feng shui also has interesting things to tell us about dungeon design. Dungeons are generally intimate spaces (yin); feng shui tells us that high ceilings would be counterproductive, as would white walls (both are too yang). But the yin of the dark and intimate dungeon must be balanced by at least some yang in the form of the fire element (proper illumination)—otherwise the dungeon's occupants might trip and get hurt (and not in a good way).

Also, since dungeons are places where people need to feel safe in order to be able to relax and let their inhibitions down, exposed beams or rafters are not good—feng shui maintains that exposed ceiling beams or other heavy objects hanging overhead cause people to feel uneasy. So if your dungeon is in the basement with exposed floor joists overhead, feng shui says you might improve the dungeon's chi by putting in some kind of ceiling—or at least painting the exposed joists and floorboards black so they're less noticeable.

Certainly leatherfolk should be able to appreciate the wisdom of feng shui and its concepts of balancing ever-shifting energies—because that is, after all, a major part of what good sex or a good BDSM scene is all about.

The following column was inspired by The Great Divorce *by C.S. Lewis. After reading the column when it was originally printed, a friend dubbed me "C.S. Lenius."*

The Man in the Uniform
with apologies to C.S. Lewis
Published in *Lavender* #197 (December 13, 2002)

I didn't remember how I had gotten there, but I found myself in the waiting area of a large and very grand transportation terminal of some sort. I was sitting on a bench that was surprisingly comfortable, waiting for—I knew not what. I was dressed in my best leathers—boots, pants, shirt, vest and jacket, with my hat on the bench by my side—and, unusual for me, all the leather had been polished and shined to a fare-thee-well.

The crowd in the terminal was a random mix of people, but no one else who was waiting was wearing any leather at all—and I gradually became aware that the leather I was wearing was a source of amusement for some of my fellow travelers and a source of consternation for others. I overheard a man sitting across from me whisper somewhat too loudly to the woman next to him, "How did somebody like him get on this flight?" From the expression on my face he must have realized that I had overheard him; this caused him first to glare at me and then to quickly look away. Another man, a few seats away, also overheard him but didn't bother whispering as he said to the woman sitting next to him, "Yeah, when did they start letting perverts into heaven?" She laughed and replied, "If they let people like that in, are we really sure we want to be there?"

I'm not sure which was more startling: the dawning of the realization that I was dead, or the fact that even here in the afterlife I was
an object of disapproval and derision because I happened to be
wearing leather.

As I was pondering this state of affairs, a man in a uniform walked
up to the man who hadn't bothered to whisper and asked, "Is there a
problem here, sir?" The man pointed at me and said belligerently,
"Yeah, there's a problem—that guy over there! I'm not going to
spend eternity with someone of his ilk!"

The man in the uniform smiled patiently and asked, "What ilk
would that be, sir?"

At this point the man who had whispered joined the fray, but he
was no longer whispering: "You know very well what he's talking
about! First, he's obviously queer, and second, he's one of those queers
who think it's fun to beat each other up! And he's probably into all
kinds of other immoral, weird, disgusting, filthy, vile—"

The man in the uniform interrupted him by asking, "If you can
tell just by looking at him that he's such an evil person, how do you
think he got on the same flight as you?" The woman who was with
the other man said, "That's what we mean—we think there must
have been some kind of mistake!"

The man in the uniform, realizing that he was dealing with
more than one passenger with an objection, started addressing them
all as he said, "There has been no mistake. I take it you all consider
yourself Christians, am I correct?" Many heads nodded. "I thought
so. Would you have the same objection if a follower of, say, Buddhism
were sitting in your midst?" No one responded. "Is it right that someone should not be allowed on this flight just because you object to
him? You realize, I'm sure, that there are many people in the world
who hate people like you, who are convinced that all Christians are
evil. They hate the Christian infidels so much that they believe they
will achieve spiritual glory by killing them. If they objected to your
presence on this flight, would that mean you should not be allowed
to go?"

By this time I was wondering if I should just get up and leave,
but suddenly the man in the uniform looked directly at me. It was
almost as if he knew what I was thinking, and somehow his look

communicated to me the message that I should stay, that everything would be all right. He continued speaking to the crowd: "Everyone who is waiting here has traveled their own path to get here. Some of you trod an easy path, while others of you had a more difficult journey. Yet all the paths have led in the end to the same destination. Although the spiritual path this man trod was different from yours, it was no less valid and no less effective for teaching him the things he needed to learn in his lifetime."

I was surprised that the man in the uniform knew so much about me, and about my life. But he seemed to be explaining it perfectly, better than I could have explained it had I been called upon to defend myself.

He continued: "This man was part of a community that was and is much misunderstood in the world. The form of love they practice is often radical and not for the timid. But it most certainly is love! And if their methods are extreme, so too is the degree of love, learning, compassion, understanding and enlightenment they can achieve and experience. The disciplines he followed during his life allowed him to transcend barriers and taste a spiritual ecstasy that few others have tasted. He was ready for such ecstasy—he yearned for it—and therefore the means to achieve it were granted him.

"All that he experienced on his journey as part of that community has brought him here, one flight away from eternity. And he deserves as much as anyone here to make that flight." Then, scanning the crowd, he continued, "If anyone here is not ready to get on the flight with this man, perhaps they're not ready to make the flight at all."

The air was tense, and it seemed to me that many in the crowd had not liked what they had just heard. But the man in the uniform didn't seem to be bothered. He looked at his watch and then addressed me: "It's just about time. Are you ready?"

Before I could answer the room suddenly grew blazingly bright, and the air was filled with what sounded at first like a chorus of angels—but which turned out to be only a Bach chorale, played through the shrill speaker of my clock radio.

All I Really Need to Know About Leather/BDSM
I Learned in Kindergarten

Published in *Lavender* #141 (October 20, 2000)

The following was inspired by further reflection on a dungeon etiquette seminar for which I was a panelist. I present it here with apologies to Robert Fulghum, who wrote the original *All I Really Need To Know I Learned in Kindergarten.**

- It's not nice to hit people (unless you have their consent).
- Don't hog all the playground equipment. Take turns.
- Be polite. Learn to say "Please, Sir" and "Thank you, Ma'am."
- People will be more likely to play with you if you're dressed and groomed attractively.
- Not everyone will want to play with you. Don't take it personally. That's the way the world is.
- You don't have to play with someone if you don't want to. And you don't need to give a reason why you don't want to play with them. A polite "No" is sufficient.
- If it's not your property, keep your hands off. Don't play with other people's toys unless they offer them to you.
- Stay out of other people's games unless they invite you to participate. Nobody likes a buttinsky.
- Basic sanitation is important. When you're done playing, clean your toys and put them away. Keep the playroom clean, too, so it will be ready to go the next time you want to play.
- Curiosity is good. Don't be afraid to ask questions. It's one of the best ways to learn.
- Learning is good. It will make you a happier person and a better member of society.
- Respect the people who supervise the playground. They're not there to spoil your fun — they're just trying to keep the playground safe for everyone.
- Learn the rules first before trying to break them. You can only color outside the lines effectively once you've mastered coloring inside them.

---

*New York: Villard Books, a division of Random House, 1989.

- It's hard to play nicely with other people when you're upset or angry. Sometimes it's good to take a time-out and simmer down.
- Even the most energetic person eventually runs out of steam. When that happens, there's nothing wrong with taking a break (or even a nap).
- This is a free country. We all have the right to be ourselves, and we're all entitled to our likes and dislikes. But other people are also entitled to theirs. If we all respect each other, even those whose preferences might be different from ours, we can all get along.
- Finally: If you can't control the scissors, don't run with them. You could put someone's eye out.

Bottoming to God

Published in *Lavender* #173 (January 11, 2002)

So what were you doing in the dungeon last night? You might answer that question with a description of any number of activities, or you might answer by describing what you were feeling. But I submit that, although you might not have been consciously aware of it, whatever else you were doing you were also studying philosophy, theology and the humanities. You were experiencing and studying an allegory of the human condition and your relation to the Almighty.

What's the difference between BDSM play and life? Unlike a BDSM scene, life doesn't come with a safeword. In a safe, sane, consensual scene in the dungeon, if the action is getting a little too intense I can simply holler "YELLOW!" and it will slow down, or I can yell "RED!" and it will come to a dead halt. But life can be viewed as one long non-safeword scene. If the car is going hopelessly out of control or I've just been told the tumor is malignant, I can yell "RED!" all I want but it won't make any difference. Life often is not safe, not sane and doesn't seem to ask for our consent before dishing out pain. Life can be downright abusive sometimes.

Bob Dylan once sang a song in which he proclaimed that "it may be the devil or it may be the Lord/but you're gonna have to serve somebody." BDSM ears perk up when in the same song he sings "You may have . . . women in a cage . . . but you're gonna have to serve somebody." As human beings, we're all submissives, and we're all bottoming to—who? God? The Devil? Fate? If we're the slaves, who's the Master? And who's the DM (Dungeon Master), the person who's supposed to be watching to make sure things don't get out of control?

Many cultures down through the centuries have had a lot to say about these questions and the whole idea of submission, and sometimes the images they create are quite striking to modern BDSM eyes. Let's start with a culture that has been much in the news recently: the Islamic faith.

Flipping through *Newsweek* a few months ago I came upon a photo, taken from overhead, of a large group of Muslim men kneeling in a mosque during prayer. Every one of them was bowed down about as flat to the ground as they could get. Was there ever a more perfect image of submission? But this isn't surprising when we consider that the word "Islam" literally translates to "submission," in this case to the will of Allah (which translates to "God" and is in fact the same God around which Judeo-Christian religions are built). The word "Muslim" translates as "one who submits."

Good Lutherans everywhere confess their sins by acknowledging in unison that "we are in bondage to sin and cannot free ourselves." (I guess that would be bottoming to the devil.)

That same sentiment has led to a variety of people throughout history, including notorious monks and nuns, who have beat themselves as part of their penance or to induce mystical visions.* And let us not forget Jesus Christ and his supremely submissive (and transfigurative) crucifixion scene. A wonderful overview of masochistic submission throughout history, including examples from Christian, Buddhist and other cultures, can be found in a fascinating article (found on the Web) entitled "Masochism as a Spiritual Path." The author, Dorothy C. Hayden, LCSW, makes the point that "it has only been in the last hundred years that masochism has been seen as a perversion," and that for thousands of year prior to the twentieth century "a masochistic-spiritual connection prevailed throughout most of civilization."

---

*See "Who Put the 'M' in 'SM'?", page 63.

For an atheistic or agnostic point of view, we turn to Carl Orff's *Carmina Burana*. This popular "secular cantata" is based on thirteenth-century German poetry written by defrocked monks, vagrant students and minstrels. It opens and closes with "Fortune, Empress of the World," a song that bemoans (in Latin) the cruel vicissitudes of fortune and fate ("Like the moon you are changeable, ever waxing and waning"),* a cruelty to which everyone is subject. And it includes these lines that should ring true with BDSM players everywhere: "Now through the game/I bring my bare back/to your villainy."

BDSM is a way of safely, sanely and consensually exploring concepts of submission, dominance and power. For some of us who have been through situations where life went totally beyond our control (a few examples: rape, childhood or domestic abuse, major illness, alcoholism or other addictions), BDSM can be a way of both becoming comfortable with our powerlessness and paradoxically reclaiming our own personal power.

Because we engage in BDSM play, one of the names we have for ourselves is "players." Shakespeare famously said that "All the world's a stage, and all the men and women merely"—here's the word—"players." He said this, appropriately enough, in *As You Like It*, which could be the motto of dominants everywhere—or, in another sense, of submissives and slaves everywhere.

Perhaps we could make a word substitution and say "All the world's a dungeon, and all the men and women merely players." In that spirit, here's something to contemplate as this book comes to an end: a BDSM Prayer, a Prayer for Players.

> *Master,*
> *As I have entered this dungeon called Life,*
> *Here with all Your other submissives,*
> *Teach me the value of submission.*
> *May I strive to do as You command,*
> *Realizing that You will nothing for me*
> *that I do not will for myself.*

---

*Note the similarity to the concept of yin and yang, ever shifting and changing. See page 280.

Brand Your name on my heart,
Put Your chain around my neck,
Lock it with Your "Master"-emblazoned lock,
Put me on Your leash,
And lead me where You would have me go.

May I submit to every other Master
    You send me,
And teach me to be a wise Master to other
    submissives of whom You put me in charge.
From both may I learn much, and teach
    as much as I learn.
Help me to remember not only that there
    can be pleasure in pain
But that there is often pain hidden in pleasure.

And when my time in the dungeon is through,
Lead me,
Still with Your chain around my neck,
Out of the dungeon,
And take me home with You.

Glory be to the Master,
And to His Boy,
And to the Chain that is the Holy Spirit,
Binding me to You.
Amen.

Appendix

The Practical Leatherman's Guide to Leather

Acquiring Your Leathers
Published in *Lavender* #23 (April 12, 1996), newly expanded and updated

If you're going to hang with the leather crowd, it helps to own and wear at least some leather. This fact has launched countless shopping trips.

As any member of the Old Guard* will tell you, in olden days leather items were not simply purchased, they were earned. Nowadays, though, the leather mentorship system isn't what it used to be. Therefore, it will probably be necessary for you to purchase at least some of your leathers.

You'll find an amazing assortment of leather and leather-related merchandise out there, competing for your purchase. Leather is made into vests of all kinds, shirts, jackets, coats, jeans, chaps, shorts, jocks, hats, harnesses, boots, armbands, wristbands, belts, and the list goes on. (As I write this I am in the market for a leather necktie.†) Then there's denim and rubber and uniforms and western wear.

I've heard of people who discovered the leather scene and immediately spent an enormous amount on a complete leather wardrobe. Let me suggest that you do differently. Go slowly; savor each piece

---

*See glossary and page 129.

† Since purchased. Thank you, NorthBound Leather.

as you acquire it. Start simply with a good vest and a good pair of boots, for instance. Wear them with a black t-shirt and blue or black jeans (which you probably already own), and you'll be perfectly comfortable in almost any leather bar or other venue you want to attend.

First, let's discuss vests—specifically, what makes a "good" vest. For starters, think "biker" (as opposed to "cowboy" or "businessman") and you'll be on the right track. It should be rugged as opposed to dressy—black leather, not brown or any other color, and not suede. The back of the vest should be leather rather than fabric. (And there shouldn't be a buckle and straps on the back for adjusting the fit. That's a formal- or business-dress vest.)

The vest should fit you properly through the shoulders and should lie properly at the back of the neck. If there's a gap between your neck and the neckline of the vest, or if the vest is so tight against the back of your neck that it pushes your head forward and ruins your posture, it doesn't fit.

Some motorcycle vests close with snaps or buttons on the front. If so, the body of the vest should be neither so tight you can't close it nor so loose that you're swimming in it when it's closed.

A bar vest has no fasteners and doesn't close in front. It's intended to be worn open, the better to show off the wearer's chest. The rule of thumb for fit is that the front edges of the vest should graze your nipples. You won't find bar vests at mass-market leather stores like Wilson's or Tannery West.

Now let's discuss footwear. Again, think rugged as opposed to dressy. And, again, think black. Military-style boots, construction boots, cowboy boots, motorcycle boots, even hiking boots can work. Wingtips, even black ones, won't quite cut it. Whatever you do, don't wear white tennis shoes—nothing works faster to brand you as a "tourist."*

As you become more acquainted with leather life you'll be able to determine what other items you want to own, and you'll probably decide that certain items are not for you. You may discover you really enjoy uniforms, for instance, or you may decide that you really don't

---

*Someone who doesn't know the Scene. See pages 146 and 148.

want to own a pair of chaps because they're too much bother to put on and take off. (Yes, but if they make you look great, it might be worth reconsidering.)

After you've been at this awhile, you will develop your own personal leather style and your own assortment of leather items. To give you an idea of the kind of assortment you can assemble, here's a peek inside the author's leather closet:

Leather vests: My first vest was a motorcycle-style vest with snap closures on the front, and it's the vest on which I have most of my run pins.* My second vest was purchased at the Minnesota State Fair (!); it's more formal, it's made of very soft leather and it even has lapels.

I now have three bar vests, and they are the vests I have worn most over the years. The oldest one, my 1994 Great Lakes Mr. Drummer title vest, was created by two local leatherwomen (who are now club sisters through the Knights of Leather). My second bar vest has the colors† of the three clubs of which I am an honorary member. A large Knights of Leather patch is on the back, a smaller Minnesota Storm Patrol patch is on the left front, and an Atons of Minneapolis patch is on the right front. My third bar vest is similar to the second, except that a large Atons patch is on the back and a smaller Knights of Leather patch is on the right front.

Leather bodysuit: Here's something else you won't find at mass-market leather stores: a black leather bodysuit. This item was made by NorthBound Leather. The upper part looks like a black-leather athletic shirt that is cut away in front to frame the chest. Continuing down, the garment ends in a zippered pouch in front that tapers to a strap up the back (no butt coverage here). I bought mine at the International Mr. Leather Contest's Leather Market and wore it onstage when I competed in the International Mr. Drummer contest in 1994. Now I sometimes wear it with chaps.

---

*The leather equivalent of lapel pins, except they're usually slightly larger. And instead of being worn on lapels, they're usually worn on either a leather vest or an "overlay"—another vest, usually made of blue denim, sometimes worn over a leather vest for the purpose of holding a person's collection of club patches and run pins.

† Insignia, in this case embroidered cloth patches.

Leather jeans: I bought my first pair of leather jeans second-hand at Worn Out West, a must-shop store on Castro Street in San Francisco. Worn Out West sells new and used leather, latex, uniforms, western and other fetishwear. After trying on all the store's new pants, and finding none that fit (hell, none I could even get into—don't people have calves or thighs anymore?), I tried on this used pair of leather jeans and they fit perfectly in every respect.

I wore them happily until I could no longer button the waist. As God is my witness, I will slim down and be able to wear them again. In the meantime, however, I recently purchased a larger pair of leather jeans—from a guy who lost so much weight he could no longer wear them. I hope that's how I dispose of them, too.

Leather chaps: Before discussing the garment, let's discuss the pronunciation of the word "chaps." It's supposedly pronounced "shaps," but if you pronounce it that way most people will wonder why you're slurring your words. Just call them "chaps" and be done with it.

My chaps came from Mr. S. Leathers, another San Francisco leather-fetish emporium. They are outside-zip chaps, meaning the zippers go down the outside of the legs. There also are inside-zip chaps, in which the zippers start at the crotch and zip down the inside of the legs.

Inside-zip chaps are much more common, although I personally don't know why. True, they might look a bit cleaner because the line of the leg is not marred by the presence of the zipper. But inside-zip chaps are fussy to get into and out of. It's easy enough to fasten the waistband around your waist by buckling or snapping. But then you have two large, flat pieces of leather flapping around your legs. You must wrap one of them around one leg, mating the two parts of the zipper on the inside of your thigh and then zipping down. Then you must do the same thing for the other leg.

To remove the chaps you unzip the zipper on one leg, from boot to crotch, and unhook the zipper. That piece of leather is now flapping around and getting in the way while you unzip the other leg and unhook that zipper. Then you unbuckle the waistband and fold them up into a manageable pile.

One other thing about inside-zip chaps: if you ride a motorcycle the zipper can scratch the paint on the tank. So I'm told, anyway.

There's less fumbling with a pair of outside-zip chaps because the zippers are always attached—you just step into them like a pair of jeans, buckle or snap the waistband, and zip the sides down. To take them off, unzip the legs, unsnap the waistband, and step out of them. And there's nothing on the insides of your legs to scratch your motorcycle, either.

Shopping advice: Whether inside-zip or outside-zip, the chaps should both fit and flatter you. Baggy chaps do neither. Avoid them. (Other than their protective function when riding a motorcycle, chaps are used to accentuate three things: your legs, your crotch and your ass.)

Biker jackets and other leather outerwear: Motorcycle wear by domestic manufacturers like Schott and German manufacturers such as Hein-Gericke are available new at cycle shops. Don't overlook Harley-Davidson dealers—the quality of their cycle wear is high, and when they have a sale the markdowns can be substantial. (Harley-Davidson is where I bought my leather shirt.)

Many used-clothing stores also do a brisk business in cycle wear and other items of interest. You can find jackets, vests, cycle pants, chaps, and even boots, western wear and uniforms.

So where did I buy my leather motorcycle jackets? None of the above. My Hein-Gericke jacket (that converts into a vest) came from an estate sale, and three other leather coats—my black leather motorcycle jacket, my long black leather trench coat and my black leather pea coat—came from a little cycle shop formerly known as Dayton's but now known as Macy's.

Where will you find wonderful stuff? The possibilities are endless. Explore the offerings on the Internet, but also check out local leather shops. (It's hard to try stuff on over the Internet.) If you're attending the International Mr. Leather Contest in Chicago you'll want to check out their Leather Market. Many other leather events have vendors as well.

Wherever you are, keep your eyes and your mind open and you might be pleasantly surprised. I've made amazing finds everywhere from a street vendor in New York (leather motorcycle watch) to a designer boutique (Joseph Abboud leather tuxedo jacket) to the Minnesota State Fair (the vest mentioned above). Be on the lookout for wonderful things and you'll find they throw themselves at you and say, *"Buy me!"*

Another shopping tip: Especially when you're new to this, it helps to go shopping with someone who's more experienced in the Scene. If you have a leather mentor, invite them along. (If not, you have a perfect excuse to find one.)

Leather Care Basics*

Published in *Lavender* #121 (January 14, 2000)

Once you have acquired an article of leather, you become responsible for taking care of it. Unless you are part of the "dirty leather" crowd (folks for whom dirt, distress and dilapidation are part of leather's charm—and there are such folks), you occasionally will want to clean and polish your leathers. Especially if you've made a substantial investment in leathers, you'll want to give them proper care so they last as long as possible. In fact, I think the perfect way to spend long, cold winter nights is to clean and condition all my leathers until they sparkle and polish my boots until they gleam.

Did I really say that? I'm sorry, I must be having a Martha Stewart attack. The truth is, I don't count leather cleaning and bootblacking among my areas of strength. So when a Leather Life reader wrote to ask me how best to maintain his leather gear, I did what columnists do: I consulted my panel of experts. I came up with some good information—including a novel way to take the drudgery out of leather maintenance chores.

There are many leather care products available and many contradictory schools of thought on which ones to use or avoid. The reader who asked this question happens to work at a public library, where he found a book by Kelly J. Thibault called *Leather and Latex Care: How to Keep Your Leather and Latex Looking Great.*† (Comment: The fact that a public library system owns this book is evidence that, once in a while at least, our tax dollars are used effectively.) Thibault recommends plain old saddle soap for cleaning leather, and 70%

---

*Since this was the first column of 2000, the original title was "New Millennium, Clean Leather."

† Los Angeles: Daedalus Publishing Company, 1996.

rubbing (isopropyl) alcohol for disinfecting it if necessary. Read the book for the complete procedure.

Saddle soap has its detractors. The makers of Lexol, one of the most widely available families of leather care products, accuse saddle soap of being too alkaline and actually de-tanning leather over time. But among my experts Lexol was not universally admired, either. Let's ask our panel, one by one, for their leather cleaning tips and preferences.

Here's a common minimalist viewpoint expressed by an interior designer (you've seen him on HGTV) who knows leather both from a garment and an upholstery standpoint. His care recommendations are the same for both: "If it's good quality leather you shouldn't need anything more than a damp cloth. If it's not good quality leather, shame on you for buying it in the first place."

The next viewpoint is from my former cleaning boy. He has used a product called The Tannery on my leather sofa and chair, and he likes it for leather auto upholstery as well. But he doesn't like it for apparel, and he's not a fan of Lexol either. He doesn't like the smell, and he doesn't like what he considers its overly strong nature. His product of choice, for boots and apparel as well, is Huberd's Boot Grease. In his opinion, "The smell is incredible!"

Advice from a leather-store manager begins with the fact that most of the leather used in apparel for the leather community is cowhide (specifically from steers). But you may also see pigskin, lamb, deerskin, and even kangaroo hide. Such variety, plus historical and regional variations in tanning methods, make it hard to establish absolute rules in leather care.

But there is one absolute: It makes sense to keep your leathers clean to begin with—if you keep them out of the dirt, you won't have to clean them as often. Another way to keep your leather in shape: Wear it. The more you wear your leather, the better it gets.

Store your leathers properly. Use a sturdy hanger (or put several hangers together if necessary), especially for heavy items like chaps and jackets. Items should hang without creases. It's best to store thinner, lighter items like leather tank tops by folding them and placing them on a shelf or in a drawer; to avoid creases, don't place them at the bottom of a stack with heavier items on top of them. And don't store any kind of leather in a plastic bag—let it breathe.

For simple cleaning, use a damp cloth or terry towel. Lightly buff the leather dry with terrycloth. If an item is dusty, wipe the dust off with a dry cloth or terry towel (a wet cloth will only make the problem worse by creating mud).

For scrapes on black leather, buff the area with terrycloth to remove dirt and grit, then use a good black leather polish to hide the scratches (wax polishes are better than liquid polishes). To finish, buff with a buffing brush or cotton towel.

If you wear your leather to a smoky bar, and the smell follows you home, airing out smoky leathers will get rid of the worst of the smoke odor. Another leather-store owner notes that leather can become smoky just from hanging in her store.* She uses both Lexol cleaner and Lexol conditioner to remove the smoke film and restore the leather smell. "I just wipe it on with a paper towel," she says, "and all the dirt that comes off is unreal. And you don't need to use very much, so it lasts forever."

A last resort is to send dirty or smoky leather to a specialized leather cleaning company. If you do, the garment will come back in a plastic bag; remove it from the plastic bag and let it air for up to a week to get rid of the dry-cleaning smell. (Incidentally, here's leather care advice from one specialized leather cleaning company: If it needs more than a damp cloth, send it to us.)

What about Dryel, a do-it-yourself dry-cleaning product? I don't know anyone who has been brave enough yet to try it on leather. Another product, Febreze, is a spray that claims to remove smoke odors from fabrics; the leather-store manager above has used it on cloth auto upholstery but hasn't tried it on leather yet.

Here's leather care advice from an employee at The Leather Man Inc. in New York: Don't overdo it. Don't over-clean. "Good leather doesn't need a lot of care. Conditioners are okay, but if you over-clean it you'll strip out a lot of the essential oils." Never dry-clean leathers—the employee at The Leather Man was hesitant to recommend even specialized leather cleaning processes. For black leather he recommends a product called Black Dubbin, which comes in a

---

*Obviously, this column was originally published before the state of Minnesota placed limits on smoking in public places.

tin (like boot polish). When applied with a dry cloth, it covers up scratches, conditions, waterproofs, and keeps the leather supple. He also likes Pecard Leather Dressing, which is clear and helps restore essential oils. And he likes Lexol. For salt stains on the inside of pants and harnesses, clean with lukewarm water and a mild hand soap. Let dry (slowly, away from heat sources), then apply a leather conditioner to soften.

Todd Nelson of Seattle, Wash. is International Bootblack 1996 and Seattle Mr. Leather 1992. Nelson likes Lexol conditioner because he finds it easy to work with. He uses it for both garment leather and boots. After using Lexol for cleaning and conditioning garment-leather items like chaps, pants, jackets and vests, he applies a very small amount of a product called Wesco Bee Oil. He simply pours it into the cup of his hand and works it into the leather. Nelson says it "snaps up the sheen and makes it shiny black." He doesn't use Bee Oil on boots or harnesses.

Here's one way Nelson suggests to make doing your leathers fun and sensual instead of drudgery: Make a scene out of it! Wear your leather while someone else applies the Bee Oil, or apply it to someone else's leathers while they're wearing them. According to Nelson, it can be very erotic and very tactile—especially on chaps or pants, but it can also be nice with a jacket or vest. Who knew leather care could be so much fun?

Now, About Those Boots ...

Nelson has led workshops on bootblacking. Here's what he says is the biggest mistake people make on their boots, especially military boots: "Never, never, *never* use the spray-on instant shine lacquer. It creates a shell that looks shiny and pretty the first couple of times you spray it on, and then it cracks. Once that happens and it doesn't look pretty anymore, there's not much you can do to rescue the boot."

Another big mistake: "People don't read the instructions on a product. They try to clean suede, buck, colored or exotic leather with products not meant for these kinds of leathers and wind up ruining it. Suede cleaner is delicate enough to clean almost any kind of leather without staining—but you still must use care on colored, especially light-colored, leathers."

Closer to home, here's some bootshine advice from a bootblack: "You don't want winter salt to linger on your boots, so clean them with saddle soap and then put some kind of leather care on them. It's also important to shine your boots often because the wax and polish helps protect against the elements. If the boot leather dries and cracks, use a conditioner to soften the leather or the cracks will get worse." (He likes Lexol). "Clean the boots before you polish them using saddle soap to get the dirt off, then polish them with a paste wax and buff them with a brush."

So what are the leather-care preferences of your humble columnist? Personally, I lean heavily toward the nothing-more-than-a-damp-cloth school of thought. And since there are members of our community who actually seem to enjoy polishing boots, I am happy to let them polish mine. I must admit, however, that I have one leather jacket that's perpetually smoky and probably needs more than a good airing. And while I don't like leather that's so "conditioned" it feels oily, there is something to be said for leather that's polished and shiny.

Now if I can just find someone to help me apply that Bee Oil....

Acknowledgments

I am very grateful to have had assistance from many helpful and supportive people during the preparation of this book.

Copyediting of the manuscript was expertly handled by Jan Miller, who made some excellent suggestions concerning things that needed to be changed or clarified. My partner Bill Schlichting did further copyediting when he looked at the book's page proofs.

Andrew Bertke is my very capable webmaster (www.lifeleather-pursuit.com—visit it, won't you?) and also took the author photo on the back of the book.

Larry Callahan photographed the leather background that wraps around the cover of the book, and never did a photographer make leather look more luscious. Thanks also to Angel Rodriguez, photo stylist extraordinaire, who helped make the leather look luscious, and to George Roedler, of G3 Photography, who created some artistic author photos.

In publishing this book I am following the trail blazed by Robert Dante with his book, *Let's Get Cracking!" The How-To Book of Bullwhip Skills.* I am grateful to him and to Mary Anderson for their guidance, encouragement and support.

Other authors who have shared their experiences with me and offered good writing and publishing advice are Robert Ridinger, Lawrence Schimel, Raymond Luczak, Andy Mangels and SoulDancer.

Thanks to Graydancer and to Catherine Pietsch for assistance in planning promotional strategies for this book.

The Queer Voices GLBT Reading Series, a joint presentation of Intermedia Arts and Hamline University, has enabled me to connect with and learn from other queer writers from throughout the upper midwest. My sincere thanks to John Medeiros and Andrea Jenkins, co-curators of the series. Thanks also to Julie Bates at Intermedia Arts, who helped me develop and clarify my plans for this book's publication.

For support, encouragement, positive criticism, and asking the right questions in a mind-expanding way, my thanks to John Pendal and David Harris, Sassy Tongue and Claudia Pauline.

My deepest thanks to my dear partner, Bill Schlichting, for his critical thinking skills and for editorial and moral support. Thanks also to my former partner and forever family member Ken Binder, who appears in this book, and his current partner, Steve Roth.

This book would not exist in its current form if I hadn't been able to select from a fifteen-year supply of Leather Life columns. For that, a big thank-you goes to *Lavender* Magazine: Steve Rocheford, publisher; George Holdgrafer, long-time editorial associate; and J.D. Laufman, the guy who offered me the column in the first place; plus all the editors, art directors, and other magazine staff who for all these years have put out issue after issue of a magazine in which I have been proud to have my column appear.

Thanks to all the many people, whether in the leather/BDSM/fetish community or not, who have been included in the column over the years, and thanks to the community that has given me so much to write about—that has given me so much, period.

Finally, thanks to you, the person reading this page. I can write all I want, but if no one reads what I write, I haven't managed to communicate anything. So I said it at the end of this book's introduction, but I will say it again at the end of the book: Thanks for reading.

Glossary

aunties: Archaic term for older homosexual men who mentored younger homosexual men in the ways of gay society and culture.

barebacking: Fucking without a condom.

BDSM: A four-letter acronym that stands for six words. BD stands for "bondage and discipline"; DS stands for "dominance and submission"; and SM stands for "sadism and masochism". The BDSM community encompasses all of these interests, but not every member of the community is into all of them.

bears: Leathermen's hairy cousins. Bears are gay, they are male, they are hairy and they are unapologetic about it. They also may be on the husky side, but not necessarily. There is a high degree of cross-over between the bear community and the leather community, resulting in some men referring to themselves as "leather bears."

boi: This term (always with a lowercase "b") has different meanings in different communities. For this book's purposes it means a biological female who thinks and acts as a leatherboy except, in one boi's words, "without the boy parts."

bottom: A person playing the passive role during a sexual or BDSM encounter. Also used as a verb, as in "bottoming to someone."

chicken hawk: A derogatory term for an older man who pursues "chicken," a derogatory term for younger men. Notice that in this scenario no one, regardless of age, escapes derogation.

colors: Club insignia, either banners or embroidered cloth patches.

dom: A male dominant.

domina: (uncommon) A female dominant; more commonly used synonyms are "domme" and "dominatrix."

drag: In the GLBT community, males impersonating females are known as "drag queens" and females impersonating males are "drag kings." Aficionados of drag are often thought of as the GLBT community's royalty.

501s: Levi's® 501® button-fly jeans, the most iconic jeans in leather circles.

flagging: Displaying colored hankies or bandanas in the rear pocket of one's jeans as a way of signaling the kind of sexual action in which one is interested. The bandana colors displayed are chosen according to the "hankie code."

GDI: "God-Damned Independent"—someone who has no interest in joining a leather club (although they may be supportive of clubs and their activities).

kink/kinky: Sexual practices outside what is generally considered usual. Formerly a derogatory term that is being reclaimed by the leather/BDSM community in much the same way "queer" is being reclaimed by some members of the GLBT community.

leather: Predominantly a gay male (and to a lesser extent lesbian) term that names one fetish but that can stand for many more. A member of the gay male leather community may wear motorcycle leathers (think of Marlon Brando and James Dean, or even The Fonz) and/or be attracted to men wearing motorcycle leathers. But denim, uniforms (military, police, fire, etc.), rubber clothing, boots or cowboy and western wear also are seen at gay male leather bars. Although leather and BDSM are seen by many as two parts of one whole, it should be noted that not everyone who self-identifies with the "leather community" is into BDSM. It also should be noted that if someone is not into BDSM they are not looked down upon by those who are, and vice versa.

Madame: A female Master. "Mistress" is the more commonly used term.

masochism: Obtaining sexual pleasure from receiving pain or punishment, either physical or psychological.

Master: An person who has an extremely dominant role over another person, who is called their "slave." Please keep in mind that the term "Master" can include all genders.

Mistress: A female Master. Many in the community are not fond of this term because of its overtones of adultery.

munch: a term coming from the pansexual community for a social, non-play gathering of people sharing an interest in BDSM, fetish and other alternative sexualities. Usually held at a restaurant, which means food and drinks can be ordered if desired.

New Guard: A subcommunity that rejects much of the hierarchical community organization, and some other traditions, that leather culture inherited from its military beginnings.

Old Guard: A subcommunity that values, and tries to preserve, the community hierarchy and other traditions that leather culture inherited from its military beginnings.

pansexuality: In a pansexual BDSM context, pansexuality means that "anyone can play with anyone else" without being limited by gender or sexual preference.

play: People outside the leather/BDSM community would say that "play" is a BDSM synonym for "having sex," but the community's use of the word goes far beyond that simple concept. Nonsexual play may involve many different activities, but it will not include oral, anal or vaginal intercourse—if it did, it would be sexual play. Some people use non-sexual BDSM play as foreplay; for other people, BDSM play is satisfying enough that sex afterward would be anticlimactic.

play party: A party held for the purpose of BDSM and other erotic play, either sexual or nonsexual.

Prince Albert: A ring through a piercing in the head of a penis.

pro domme: Professional dominatrix. The male form of this term is "pro dom."

run: A term that originated among motorcycle clubs and referred to a club's motorcycle riding and camping trip. Now the term has broadened to include any (usually annual) weekend social event presented by a leather club and attended by members of other clubs.

run pin: The leather equivalent of lapel pins, except they're usually slightly larger. And instead of being worn on lapels, they're worn on either a leather vest or an "overlay"—another vest, usually made of blue denim, sometimes worn over a leather vest for the purpose of holding a person's collection of club patches and run pins.

sadism: Obtaining sexual pleasure from inflicting pain or punishment on others or from watching it be inflicted.

sadomasochism: The joint practices of sadism and masochism.

scarfing: Breathplay, an attempt to attain a sexual high by constricting one's air supply.

Scene (with a capital "S"): Another word for the community that has evolved around leather, BDSM and fetish. The word "scene" without a capital "S" refers to an erotic encounter, often incorporating elements of BDSM, playfulness and/or fantasy. In other words, "the Scene" is on the level of the whole community, while "a scene" is on the level of the individuals involved.

slave: One who submits to a Master.

submissive/sub: One who submits to a dom or domme.

switch: 1) A person who alternates between playing the active and passive roles in sexual or BDSM encounters. The verb form, "to switch," means to change from top to bottom or vice versa. 2) A flexible rod, often a twig or branch, used for flagellation.

tearoom: A public men's restroom having a reputation, in certain circles, as a place to have sex with other men.

Tom of Finland: pseudonym for Touko Laaksonen, a pioneering erotic artist.

top: A person playing the active role during a sexual or BDSM encounter. Also used a verb, as in "topping someone."

tourist: Someone in a leather environment who is an obvious outsider.

tranny: Shorthand for "transgender." Not meant in a disparaging way.

vanilla: The opposite of kinky. When used by someone who is kinky it may or may not be a derogatory term.

vexillology: the study of flags. Not usually thought of as kinky.

Bibliography

Archibald, Timothy. *Sex Machines: Photographs and Interviews.* A Daniel 13/Process Original. Port Townsend, Wash.: Process Media, Inc., 2005.

Berlinger, Cain. *Black Men in Leather.* Tempe, Arizona: Third Millennium Publishing. 2nd edition, 2006.

Borhek, Mary. *My Son Eric.* New York: The Pilgrim Press, 1979.

Bornstein, Kate. *My Gender Workbook.* New York: Routledge, 1997.

Comden, Betty. *Off Stage.* New York: Simon & Schuster, 1995.

Covey, Stephen. *The Seven Habits of Highly Effective People.* New York: Free Press (imprint of Simon & Schuster). 15th anniversary edition, 2004.

Dante, Robert. *"Let's Get Cracking!" The How-To Book of Bullwhip Skills.* CreateSpace, 2008.

Davolt, Robert. *Painfully Obvious: An Irreverent & Unauthorized Manual for Leather/SM.* Los Angeles: Daedalus Publishing Company, 2003.

Fulghum, Robert. *All I Really Need To Know I Learned in Kindergarten.* New York: Villard Books, a division of Random House, 1989.

Kasl, Charlotte. *If the Buddha Dated: A Handbook for Finding Love on a Spiritual Path.* New York: Penguin, 1999.

Letellier, Patrick and David Island. *Men Who Beat The Men Who Love Them.* New York: Harrington Park Press, 1991.

Lobel, Kerry, ed. *Naming the Violence—Speaking Out About Lesbian Battering.* Seattle: Seal Press, 1986.

Putnam, Dr. Robert with Lewis M. Feldstein. *Better Together: Restoring the American Community.* New York: Simon & Schuster, 2003.

Putnam, Dr. Robert. *Bowling Alone: The Collapse and Revival of American Community.* New York: Simon & Schuster, 2000.

Silverstein, Dr. Charles and Felice Picano. *The New Joy of Gay Sex.* New York: Harper Perennial, 1993.

Sorrell, Roderic and Amy Max Sorrell. *The* I Ching *Made Easy: Be Your Own Psychic Advisor Using the World's Oldest Oracle.* San Francisco: HarperSanFrancisco, 1994.

Thibault, Kelly J. *Leather and Latex Care: How to Keep Your Leather and Latex Looking Great.* Los Angeles: Daedalus Publishing Company, 1996.

Index

Viagra, 223
Vietnam War, 20, 71, 129, 191
violet wands, 219, 245
von Sacher-Masoch, Leopold, 63
Wallace, Wally, 65
Warner, Mark, 7
Washington Post, 232
watersports, 142
wax play, 47, 48, 264 (see also hot wax)
Webb, Cristo, 44-50
Weber, Stephen, 170, 171
westernwear, 22
Wet International, 17, 18, 177
whips, 41-44, 61, 63, 246, 250, 307
  cracker/lash/popper
  (at end of whip), 43

white knot for (marriage) equality, 198
Wild One, The, 20, 23
Wild, Wild West, The, 22
Wizard of Oz, The, 50
Woodhull Freedom Foundation, 232
Women, The, 182
World War I, 20
World War II, 18, 21, 23, 24, 55, 56,
  60, 129, 136
Worn Out West, 294, 295
Wright, Susan, 120
YKINOK (Your Kink Is Not OK), 102, 188
YKIOK/MKIOK (Your Kink Is OK/My
  Kink Is OK), 103

About the Author

Author and columnist Steve Lenius came out as a gay man in 1974 and became involved in the Twin Cities leather community in 1993. For fifteen years his Leather Life column has appeared in *Lavender,* Minnesota's GLBT magazine. His writings also have appeared in *The Leather Journal, Skin Two* (a fetish magazine published in London, UK), the *2008 Yearbook* of the BDSM Creative Collective (Minneapolis/ St. Paul), *Leather Tribe Leather Nation* (a yearbook published by *The Leather Journal*), *The Petal and the Thorn* (newsletter of Black Rose Society, Washington, D.C.), *International Leatherman* and *Roundup* (magazines for the GLBT leather and country/western/rodeo communities published by Brush Creek Media), *The Journal of Bisexuality* (published by Haworth Press), *The Gayly Oklahoman* (a GLBT newspaper based in Oklahoma City), *XL (Lavender Magazine's Adult Xtra)* and *Gaze* Magazine (Minneapolis/St. Paul's forerunner to *Lavender*). His Leather Life columns also have appeared on Leatherpage.com. He wrote the Introduction to *Painfully Obvious: An Irreverent & Unauthorized Manual for Leather/SM* by Robert Davolt (published by Daedalus Publishing, Los Angeles). His writing was recognized with a President's Award from Pantheon of Leather in 2003, and he was a co-winner in the category of "Best Leather Commentary on Current Events" in the True Tales Leather Journalism Awards in 2005.

Lenius is an honorary member of the Knights of Leather, Minnesota Storm Patrol and the Atons of Minneapolis. As Great Lakes Mr.

Drummer, he competed in the International Mr. Drummer contest in San Francisco in 1994. Over the years he has judged many leather title contests, including International Mr. Leather in Chicago in 2002.

For many years Lenius has helped organize Minnesota's annual Leather Pride celebration, and he was Chief Instigator for the award-winning Leather Leadership Conference XI in Minneapolis in 2007. A graphic designer and typographer working in the fields of advertising, marketing communications and commercial publishing for over thirty-five years, he has designed logos, buttons, t-shirts and collectible dog tags for many GLBT Pride and Leather Pride celebrations.

Lenius does occasional public speaking as a representative of the leather/BDSM community. He is committed to promoting safer sex and is a member of the Community Advisory Board of Pride Alive, the Queer Men's initiative of the Minnesota AIDS Project. Other interests include encouraging safe/sane/consensual BDSM play, exploring leather and gay spirituality, and working with gay male victims of domestic abuse.

The son of a minister of the Moravian Church in America, Lenius had a thoroughly idyllic midwestern boyhood. He was born in Fargo, North Dakota, and grew up in central Wisconsin, southern Illinois and the Minneapolis/St. Paul area. Currently he lives with his partner, Bill, in a first-ring suburb of Minneapolis.

Writing is in his genes—his mother, Mary Borhek, is the noted author of two books, *My Son Eric* (about her process of coming to terms with having a gay son) and *Coming Out To Parents*.

Colophon

This book has been designed and produced by the author.

The manuscript was written and edited using Pages, part of Apple's iWork suite. The book was typeset, and the pages and cover art were assembled, using QuarkXpress 8.

Fonts used are Adobe Garamond for body copy and Univers Condensed for heads and subheads. Univers Ultra Condensed has been used for the title spread.

The word clouds on pages vi, 12 and 54 were created using Wordle (www.wordle.net). Fonts used are League Gothic, Goudy Bookletter 1911 and Enamel Brush.